# Procreation and Population in Historical Social Science

# Procreation and Population in Historical Social Science

Daniela Danna

ANTHEM PRESS

Anthem Press
An imprint of Wimbledon Publishing Company
*www.anthempress.com*

This edition first published in UK and USA 2021
by ANTHEM PRESS
75–76 Blackfriars Road, London SE1 8HA, UK
or PO Box 9779, London SW19 7ZG, UK
and
244 Madison Ave #116, New York, NY 10016, USA



*British Library Cataloguing-in-Publication Data*
A catalogue record for this book is available from the British Library.

Library of Congress Control Number: 2021942256

ISBN-13: 978-1-78527-716-0 (Hbk)
ISBN-10: 1-78527-716-2 (Hbk)

Cover image: Flemish kermis/Wikimedia Commons/Public Domain

This title is also available as an e-book.

The more human beings, the more surplus value is in principle possible. It is no accident that the so-called population law of capitalism is considered to be nothing less than the "general law of capitalist accumulation" (Marx).

It is this law that turns women into child-bearing machines and is responsible for the so-called population explosion.

—Claudia von Werlhof (1984, 143–44)

Both the growth in population and the threats to life on the planet in general are caused by the use of technology solely for the pursuit of capital accumulation on a world scale.

—Peter Grimes (1999, 38–39)

More energy has allowed humans to do more work,
including that of producing more wealth and more humans.

—Hall and Klitgaard (2018, 212)

# CONTENTS

# TABLES

# ACKNOWLEDGMENTS

I thank the Beatrice Bain Research Group at the University of California, Berkeley, for having hosted me as a visiting scholar in 2011, when I started to once again deal with the fundamental topic of population, the subject of my thesis in Political Science at the University of Studies of Milan, in 1991: "John Caldwell's Theory on Demographic Transition and the Case of Denmark." I also thank the DAAD (German Academic Exchange Service) for the research grant that allowed me to access the collections of the Staatsbibliothek in Berlin. I thank the staff of the Enrica Collotti Pischel Library of the State University of Milan, of the British Library of London and of the Amilcar Cabral Center of Bologna, as well as all those who contributed to the dissemination of knowledge via the World Wide Web and peer-to-peer networking.

Thanks also to Michela Zucca and two anonymous reviewers who kindly and generously read and commented on my work. This book is based on *Il peso dei numeri. Teorie e dinamiche della popolazione* (Asterios 2019), with consistent changes and updates. The translation and revision have been made by Vera Unfähig and Freda Weitzer, whom I thank warmly, and myself.

# INTRODUCTION

Population is a subject that everybody knows a bit about, and procreation supposedly so. The problem with the "common sense" knowledge about population facts and dynamics is like the one with "common sense" in economics: it is not common sense at all, but the trickling down of liberal (and increasingly, neoliberal) theories and ideologies from high schools, colleges, universities, and therefore media and politics. And they serve a purpose: the *Weltanschauung* that these ideologies promote is the political economy that serves to sustain and advance the ruling class, the owners of the means of production through their control of transnational companies' stock, in this social system called capitalism or, as Immanuel Wallerstein started to theorize following the suggestions of Fernand Braudel, in the capitalist world-economy.

Everybody knows that the problem with the poor and with poor nations is that they multiply themselves. Everybody knows that the greater the numbers of the human species, the more we devour Earth's and Nature's resources. Everybody knows that China has decreased its population through the draconian measure of the one-child policy and that in the mid-nineteenth century the Irish suffered a horrendous famine because they were simply too many of them. Everybody knows that there has been a "demographic transition," replicated or on its way in every country. Everybody knows that reproduction and procreation are synonymous, though the word "reproduction" started to be used only in the eighteenth century, modeling procreation on the industrial "production" process, which by the way is where the masters of artificial reproduction techniques (clinics, researchers, biologists, gynecologists, and also pharmaceutical companies and politicians funding research), including gene editing, would like to bring all human procreation. Everybody knows that sex is natural, and that the instinct to procreate is part of our animal nature, perhaps justifying the dominance of the husband over the wife, as mandated by the irate God of Genesis. The notion that procreative sex is natural is increasingly questioned, but also from postmodernist viewpoints that deny even its reality (and the general concept of "reality") attributing the sexual difference entirely to language and culture.

This book deals with bringing down these ideological veils that hide what I consider a more realistic view of the history of population, and tries to open the "black box" of procreation that academics researching and writing about human numbers generally leave aside. Population dynamics at the macro level are rooted in micro level decisions on procreation that, when researched, can shed light on the reasons why population grows or stays constant (when it declines it is because of the appearance of adverse social or environmental conditions). It is a book about theories as well, as we do not have all the data needed on the past to affirm the validity of their propositions once and for all. There are no gravity laws in this book but, this is my hope, the reopening of the old and an opening of new intellectual paths that will be trodden by the next generation of researchers, increasingly devoted to historical and biophysical social science.

# Chapter 1

# POPULATION, PROCREATION AND MODES OF PRODUCTION

"Population" in the Italian Treccani encyclopedia is the "the group of people of a given locality, considered as a whole and in numerical extension." From the biological standpoint, it refers to a "group of individuals of a given species occupying a defined geographical area, and isolated at various levels from similar groups of the same species." The term originates from the late Latin *population -onis* which in turn comes from *popŭlus*, or "people," and indicates the process of populating a territory. "Population" therefore underlines the dynamics of the concept of people and its expansion over time. According to Peter Turchin (2003, 3), population dynamics studies how and why a population varies in space and time. In addition to its increase or decrease, of course, stability may also be reached.

Fernand Braudel reflected on this essential component of human history, and titled part of his work "Weight of numbers." Indeed, he began his trilogy *Civilization and Capitalism: 15th–18th Centuries* (1960) with the consideration of population in its biological aspects, describing various human facets that are intrinsically biological: births, nutrition, diseases, life spans and deaths: the elements that compose "material life" as opposed to the market and capitalism. Like all living species, human beings exist in the physical interaction of energy and matter with the environment. Since the mastery of fire hundreds of thousands of years ago, this interaction comes about through techniques and technologies[1] to obtain what is necessary for the species, and is part of the network of relationships between living beings and inanimate matter that we call ecology. Population dynamics is based on three components: births, that is, procreation, migrations and deaths. The process of procreation ensures continuity between generations and the maintenance of humanity on planet Earth. Historians and other social scientists generally do not consider it. It was the Annales school, to which Braudel belonged, that began the historical

1 There are many definitions of technology and it is not clear—that is, it is not universally accepted among researchers—what is the difference between technology and technique.

reconstructions of the European past describing how the essential needs of human life were met daily: nutrition, access to water, shelter from cold or excessive heat, possibility for rest and protection from pathogens. These are not platitudes to be taken for granted, but the fundamental basis on which human life can develop to make history.

Braudel believed that how primary needs are met in a particular society must be the first concern of social scientists. There are requisites on procreation, too. Adequate and quality food keeps the body healthy and helps in the defense against microbial infections (at least from some pathogens), while reaching a certain proportion of fat in the body mass allows women to become pregnant and give birth to new human beings who will bring continuity to historical structures. This process, triggered by the encounter of the male and female seeds in the woman's body,[2] is called procreation, a term to be preferred to reproduction, which denotes repetition (Filippini 2020, 2021). The term "social reproduction" indeed describes what contributes to the processes that ensure the self-perpetuation of a social structure.

The new human beings are always different from those they came from, due to the sexualization of the human species. Sexual dimorphism (the distinction between male and female organisms in the same species)[3] has the purpose of mixing the genes of the parent organisms in the progeny, obtaining a new and unique result in terms of DNA. This process enables variability in the species and is necessary for its adaptation to the environment, which is always slowly changing.

Population dynamics, meaning population numbers and trends that are propelled by social and natural forces, is the result at the macrohistorical level of the acts of procreation at the microhistorical level. Charles Tilly suggested replacing the "micro" and "macro" levels of mainstream economics and

2 Only since 1978 it can happen also outside the female body with in vitro fertilization (IVF): extracorporeal fertilization with transfer of the embryo into the uterus of the future mother. IVF is derived from livestock breeding and is useful in many cases of infertility, while it can be used for having kids without intercourse and for selecting seeds and embryos (Testart 2014; Escudero 2016). See ACOG (2005) for the health problems it generates in newborns. The decrease in fertility, counteracted with medicalized reproduction techniques (which are expedients but not therapies), is also caused by the spread of artificial substances (produced with synthetic chemistry) that disturb the natural functioning of bodies (Commoner 1977) and of electromagnetic fields that disrupt cellular respiration (Pall 2013).

3 Intersexuality does not constitute a third sex but is a term used to refer to individuals born with chromosomes different than the male XY and the female XX. There are only two sexes, as there are only two gametes: spermatozoon and ovum. This definition is biological, not social, while we refer to social norms for each sex's behavior as "gender" (Danna 2020b).

sociology with the terms "microhistorical" and "macrohistorical."[4] Jack Goldstone denied the independence between the micro and macro levels, too: "All *social* behavior involves *both* individual actions *and* socially generated resources language, symbols or institutional arrangements" (Goldstone 1991, 46; italics in original) therefore it makes no sense to declare, as other social scientists do, that the micro and macro levels, and also the meso level, should be examined separately according to their relevance to the issue under study. The levels are manifold, not just two or three, and the problems of structure, order, conflict and power are repeated on many different scales. Goldstone proposed a quasi-fractal concept of society, articulated in multiple levels, in which the dynamics (e.g., of power) are similar on different scales. In Nature, fractal structures repeat themselves identically at different levels, such as a coastline with inlets and promontories, within which alternation is continuously repeated on a smaller scale, but in society there is no exact correspondence of dynamics between the different levels. There can be national, regional, provincial and local levels in organizations where structures and dynamics are similar, with effects on a different scale, but there is no continuity.[5]

If Wallerstein spoke somehow abstractly of the unpredictable changes in a world-system's crisis by applying the concept of bifurcation derived from contemporary physics, Goldstone applied the concept of fractality to human societies in a more concrete sense. If the structure is rigid, conflicts on a large scale are detonated even by small actions, just as an earthquake explodes the accumulated energy from plate tectonics suddenly released after an infinitesimal shift (or today also after fracking).

Social processes become comprehensible if the sequences are analyzed correctly in order to reconstruct the forces involved. However, identifying similar sequences of events in different historical contexts is not the same as looking for general laws independent from the historical context, said Goldstone, who shared Wallerstein's refusal of ahistorical social laws. Goldstone compared the identification of these sequences with the activity of a geologist who discovers similar fossils in similar layers of rocks in different

---

4 See also the discussion in Lee (2012), starting from Braudel ([1958] 2012).

5 More generally, Goldstone notes that many antinomies that divide social scientists are false problems, since there cannot be an absolute prevalence of the conflict on the consensual order (or vice versa) or of ideal factors on the material factors or the micro on the macro, while change and continuity are not in absolute opposition. These opposite terms should be seen as extreme points of a staircase with many steps. The object of investigation of Goldstone—the crisis and the collapse of state structures (see Chapter 5)—has a fractal character as it involves (or rather, overwhelms) every level of social organization.

places, while Wallerstein drew a parallel with astronomy, where time is as important as in history. The geologist will speculate that a common process has occurred in both places and will attempt to carefully reconstruct the fossil formation process. However, this remains a process, not a "law" in the same sense in which one speaks of the immutable physical laws. Forces that obey laws also act in social relationships, and the initial conditions are never the same, so the historical sequences are understandable as the result of uniform processes, although unique in their results.

Nevertheless, for the purpose of simplification, in this work I will apply a simple polarization between the microhistorical level at which the subjects of procreation act and the macrohistorical level of the whole society, or rather of a world-system (Wallerstein 2000).

## 1.1 The Microhistorical Level

At the microhistorical level we look for the motivations behind procreative decisions. The concept of "decision" and not "event" applies to the acceptance of the new life, regardless of intention to conceive. The term "decision" signifies choice, as intent must intervene. Even in cases of an unplanned pregnancy, there must be a subsequent acceptance of the event with the raising of the child, since unwanted pregnancies can result in (legal or illegal) abortions, abandonment, active or "passive" infanticides, in which the newborn is neglected.[6]

In calling procreation a decision, I do not mean to claim that procreation is a completely rational act, but it is certainly influenced by individual and family situations and by social imperatives, since the survival and well-being of the bigger social group depend on it and its control. Rarely can a woman or couple alone meet the needs of their offspring without involving others. An important field of investigation should therefore focus on how the procreative imperative of the social system is transmitted to the subjects of procreation, for example, through religion.

In demographic historical literature, the microhistorical level is the least explored aspect, because sexual activity and the generative engagement of women are scarcely examined. Nevertheless, procreation is also determined by culture and by power structures. Procreative decisions also depend on the culture's view of children and their value as workers, which often leads to society regarding physically fit women of childbearing age as just child "producers." Anthropologist James Reed (1983, ix) questions the notion that procreation should be a natural instinct, or even universally desirable:

6 See Carr-Saunders (1922) for a review of these practices.

> Anthropologists studying human reproduction in premodern cultures have found that the desire for children is not an innate human drive but an acquired motive, which must be reinforced by social rewards and punishments sufficient to overcome the wish to avoid the pain of childbirth and the burdens of parenthood. (Reed 1983, ix)[7]

First, there is no equality in procreation, but a clear preeminence of female commitment. This obviously has both advantages and disadvantages for the female sex: the preeminent position of fecund women in giving life makes their existence precious for the social group, but it also exposes them to family and social imperatives to procreate or to *not* procreate, and this affects their bodies and their freedom. In order to reproduce, the female body has to reach a certain proportion of body fat, without which the menstrual cycle ceases. A woman's energy must be sufficient for that great biological effort which constitutes the only true production that the human species, like all animals, is able to actually make, using energy to reorganize matter (mostly organic) into a living form. Production[8] is in fact a word that we apply to the assemblages and transformations we are able to perform starting from preexisting organic and inorganic materials, or to the transformation of one form of energy into work or into another form. All this is achieved without creating new matter or energy, which animals can only manipulate. This explains why ecology scholars consider the common use of "production" to be erroneous and reserve the term to describe the activities of plants, producing new organic matter, or biomass, starting from the elements present in the air, earth or sea, combined with solar energy or—in the few chemotropic plant species—using the energy of chemical transformations (Odum 1966). Photosynthesis is indeed also just a transformation, but it builds up all biomass that animals live on, therefore its importance.

Procreation is certainly a reworking of materials that are assembled according to DNA patterns, too, but the resulting life is precisely the only living contribution that the human species can make to the cosmos. For the rest, in terms of biomass, we can only favor some species at the expense of others (which we do with alacrity: it is estimated that 95 percent of the weight of mammals on Earth is totaled by humans, pets and livestock[9]). But "giving

7 Some contemporary texts deal with the refusal of motherhood, such as Leonardi and Vigliani (2009) and Diehl (2014). Donath (2016) discusses regret of becoming a mother.

8 Etymologically, the word "production" derives from *productio -onis* which in Latin means "elongation, prolongation" (Treccani Encyclopedia).

9 Meat is a luxury as the pastures necessary for the life (when they are not confined in CAFOs) and feeding of cattle can be used directly for human consumption, with a calorie yield that has been calculated to be about 10 times greater.

life" is entirely the work of women, with the male contribution being only the sperm that the egg captures and merges with.

It is precisely from the different biological roles in the procreation of sexed animal species that the definition of the sexual difference between males and females derives. The organism called "male" produces a seed consisting mostly of DNA that detaches itself from the male body with the aim of uniting with the female seed. The organism called "female" produces a seed where the DNA is surrounded by nutrients. In mammals like us, nourishment of the embryo and fetus is also provided by the maternal organism in a more or less long prenatal phase, and then with milk at birth. This is the first nourishment, the only one in the months before the new organism becomes autonomous with weaning, and in the human species there are additional years of dependence of other kinds.

According to Claudia von Werlhof, the awareness of males' inability to generate stimulated the "alchemical project" of patriarchy which has replaced cooperation with Nature for the good of the community with "the 'Gnostic' utopia of a 'male creation' that is supposed to be higher, better, and more divine than the natural or female, matriarchal one" (von Werlhof 2012, 175). More and more contemporary practices aim to achieve this project: emblematic is the research on the artificial womb. It also includes ideologies like transhumanism, which advocates the evolution of the human race by means of science and technology, and our hybridization with their products.

Like all other activities carried out by women, procreation is underestimated and taken for granted in the patriarchal culture we live in.[10] It is a culture that emphasizes the superiority of the male and considers the female as subordinate. On the contrary, there are excellent reasons to consider the female principle as primary: for example, the common female characteristics of every sexualized embryo, including the human one. The male is a derivation from the female, a differentiation that happens during the fetal stage of development and is initiated by testosterone.[11]

Studies on prehistory indicate that in that period there was a prevalence of symbols and images of the female, to represent her preeminence. In this matrifocal phase, the maternal principle was culturally prevalent (Levy 1963, Gimbutas 1990; van der Meer 2013; Zucca 2015). This phase is also called

---

10 See considerations on the feminine principle devalued in our society in the volume edited by Barrett (2016) and in the description of the evolution of our species by Elaine Morgan (1972).

11 See the introduction of Monica Sjöö and Barbara Mor to *The Great Cosmic Mother*, Harper & Collins, 1975, reprinted as "The First Sex: In the Beginning We Were All Created Female," in Barrett (2016, 5–17).

"matriarchal," but the term does not imply the reverse of patriarchy, that is, a female domination over men (Bachofen called this hypothetic female domination "Amazonian culture").

With the progress of industrialization and urbanization and especially of medicine, there has been a progressive appropriation of the management of pregnancy and childbirth by medical professionals, who are predominantly male. They have put their exclusive, monopolized knowledge—source of economic and social power—in place of the knowledge of women, which was passed from woman to woman, being based on the actual experiences of females (Duden 1994).[12] It is true that doctors today apply scientific research for the purpose of safety and can diminish life-threatening problems that may occur, but this efficacy is relatively recent. When women about to give birth in the eighteenth century began to be hospitalized, childbirth in this institution was much more dangerous, due largely to the conditions of poor hygiene in which doctors worked and to the concentration of bacteria in hospitals, which led to the fatal "puerperal fevers," that is, infections transmitted by the doctors themselves as they did not respect elementary rules of hygiene.

Perinatal and maternal mortality have steadily decreased from the late nineteenth century to date: for example, in Italy infant mortality under the age of 5 is currently four per thousand. The price paid for the current safety of hospitals is inattention to the human factor, to the extent that (to mention only the final step of the entire gestational experience) few women are satisfied with an "industrialized" birth in the hospital (Wagner 2001; Bestetti et al. 2005; Cipolletta and Sperotto 2012). And low satisfaction is only part of it. Women feel bullied, unempowered, coerced, made to feel afraid, abandoned by nurses and doctors during the labor process and so on. They miss out on getting to feel what is arguably the most empowering experience of a woman's life: giving birth in the position she chooses, in the presence of people she chooses, not under the influence of any drugs and thus able to experience the flood of hormones that occurs following a vaginal birth.

Men's appropriation of the work and reproductive abilities of women in the patriarchal phase of society, in which we still live, has meant that—still speaking in very general terms of this *trés longue durée*—their concerns have never been so serious as to prevent unwanted pregnancies *before* having to resort to abortions and infanticides. Another method of fighting unwanted

12 The Association of American Midwives, pushed by transactivists, now speaks of "people giving birth," who in addition to women are the FtM trans who maintain their female organs that enable them to procreate. However, this does not make them "men who give birth," because subjectivity cannot cancel biology: whoever can give birth is, at least in the parts that matter, a woman.

pregnancies, again at the expense of women, is undernutrition of females of reproductive age, based on food prescriptions differentiated by sex. For example, the consumption of meat is reserved for men, or considered a luxury and not a necessity for pregnant women, thus exposing these women to more frequent spontaneous abortions. This mistreatment of female bodies and newborns happens ultimately to keep the population in balance with resources. Nancy Scheper-Hughes (1992) performed a harrowing ethnography among poor families of Northeast Brazil that detailed their ways of bringing about and justifying the premature death of some children who appeared weaker and who "did not want to live." Scheper-Hughes protested against Reagan's policy of funding only organizations that opposed legal abortion: the abstraction of having children, she wrote, seems detached from the reality of raising them, but the result of the preservation of the fetuses was the sentencing of children to death by starvation.

As the biological costs of procreation are borne entirely by the female organism, when sexual activity is defined mostly in terms of coitus, which does not lead with certainty to female orgasm as it does with the male one, excess births are inevitable. This situation is a symptom and a consequence of the fact that women have less social power than men—which is much more important than the availability of effective contraceptives. The limitation of births was however practiced even before the pill was marketed. This is shown, for example, by the ethnography of Jane Schneider and Peter Schneider (1992) of a Sicilian town in the 1970s, where in the previous 20 years there had been a reduction of the birth rate obtained exclusively through interrupted coitus, a reduction that evidently also suited the men. Although this was probably until quite recently the most commonly used birth control method, it does not mean that fertility control relied solely on this method. Since ancient times, condoms made with calf or lamb casings or with the swim bladder of some fish were used. They were very expensive, due to the specialized work required to manufacture them. There were also chemical abortion methods: the administration of poisons such as mercury, phosphorus, arsenic and also saffron and parsley in large quantities. The most used method was a decoction of fresh juniper buds or the *oleum juniper* also obtained from this plant. There have been written references to its abortive effects since 1500: doctors considered juniper a dangerous plant for pregnant women, and Linnaeus wrote that it was used by girls who wanted to be "whores in secret."

The onset of the pill as a means of controlling female fertility was hailed as the "divorce between sex and procreation" (e.g., "From a moral point of view, with the limitation of births, a dissociation came about between sexuality and procreation," Reinhard et al. 1971, 462), forgetting that this divorce is already implicit in the existence of the clitoris, the female organ exclusively devoted to pleasure. Though even in ancient times women put cloth, leaves, sponges or honey in the vagina to block semen, if we really want to identify a historical turning point linked to contraception it can be dated to the invention of the pessary (diaphragm) in 1838 and then its diffusion during the nineteenth century. Like the pill, this device is controlled by females.

The "divorce between sex and procreation" is also implicit in *male* sexual activity, which can lead to biological-only paternity, that is, to the biological father being completely unknown to his offspring after separation from the woman who was made pregnant. In addition, male sexual activity has in various ways (e.g., with marital duties) been imposed on women, who, unlike men, do not necessarily experience pleasure in conceiving: these are the most frequent cases of divorce between sex—subjectively experienced by women—and procreation.

Indeed, research on sexuality, both with methods of direct observation on large numbers (Masters and Johnson 1972) and with the collection of sexual experiences subjectively described by women, also in large numbers (Hite 1997), shows poor satisfaction for women from coitus, during which only one-third reaches orgasm. This poor satisfaction is not due (only) to poor communication and mutual listening skills of the partners, especially of the one with more social power, nor to the differences in arousal pace, but is rooted in biology: only the outermost third of the vagina is densely innervated.[13]

Stress caused by the risk of unwanted pregnancies is common and can ruin female pleasure in coitus. Although contraceptives are available today, male partners, who socially hold a position of power even in sexual contexts, do not always agree to their use in intercourse, while this remains their favorite sexual practice.[14] The very definition of "sex," "sexual act" and "sexual activity" historically and currently refers to this practice: they are all synonymous with coitus, reflecting the male point of view (Frye 1988). It might be apparent that the link between sex and coitus should be adequate from an evolutionary point of view, but human sexuality is much more diverse. And because of the risk of unwanted pregnancies (which lead to abandonment and infanticide in cases in which abortion is impossible, bloody and extreme remedies that fall on women and newborns), sex and coitus cannot be equated—at least not for women. Nevertheless, it must not be taken for granted that women always want to have few or no children. Limiting pregnancies because it is beneficial to women

13 On women's health and sexuality, see the classic *Our Bodies, Ourselves* by the Boston Women's Health Book Collective, original ed. 1970 and still updated.

14 In the biggest research on the sexuality of Italians (Barbagli et al. (2010), the question of preferences in sexual practices has not even been asked. Sex is identified with coitus without any problematization: *quod erat demonstrandum*.

concerns individual health, whereas children can be a source of pleasure, and from a social point of view they can be a future source of help for the mother, a sort of insurance against the impossibility of obtaining sustenance in illness or old age, as we will see more clearly later on.

A review of the plurimillennial history of patriarchy indicates that procreative capacity has been more of a curse than a blessing for women, since restrictions on rights and physical and social mobility have generally been enacted to control the use of the female reproductive system, primarily by making virginity an imperative. Among the various aspects of cultural conditioning on all that we call sexuality, there is the fact that the social prestige linked to sexual practice is opposite in the two sexes: in patriarchy the "Casanova" is socially appreciated, praised and envied by other men, while the whore stigma, bringing about social infamy, hangs over women (Moran 2017).[15] The stigma can befall a woman for precisely the same acts that make a man more virile, or for having transgressed other rules on female behavior, even with actions that have no sexual connotation. Depending on the context, some of these consist of leaving home unaccompanied, going to public places, talking to men who are not relatives and so on.[16] With the sexual control of respectable women, the category of prostitute/public woman is necessary to the belief that a virile male requires coitus even if it takes the use of a woman as an object, offering money in exchange for undesired sexual access.

This gender disparity (i.e., different social roles) in the meaning of sexual practices is generally found in the *trés longue durée* that began with the establishment of patriarchy. It is assumed that the domination of men over women began precisely with their desire to control procreation—and therefore female sexuality—to be sure that the offspring of a husband was truly generated from his seed. Practically all sex outside of marriage has been forbidden for "respectable women" by the religious commandments of Christianity (as of all the great religions—see Thomlinson 1965, 367), social rules and regulations. This has been a constant theme throughout history until recent times—apart from numerous small non-state societies.

Women acquired social power during the protest movements, which Immanuel Wallerstein calls the 1968 world revolution. In the years around 1968, young people rebelled against the bourgeois society by founding new leftist movements. In addition to these sociopolitical rebellions there was the

15 In this autobiographical essay, a prostitution survivor analyzes in depth the dynamics between the so-called clients and the women they consider whores.

16 In illustrating the dynamics at the microhistorical level, and also further in the book, I am forced to generalize and mention only a few historical or contemporary examples without a claim to exhaustiveness.

sexual revolution, which made the culture of sexuality less monolithic and taboo. Women and girls formed the feminist movement (neo-feminism or second-wave feminism) while they accessed waged work, dissolving an ancestral dependence on the family institution.

Along with the decrease in male control over women thanks to women's earning power (with the family ceasing to be an economic unit of production), male power also decreased in relation to procreation in a truly global movement. Göran Therborn (2004), in his monumental history of the family, documents how the axes of authority between the sexes and generations in families have shifted in the twentieth century around the world.[17] The *pater familias*'s loss of power over his wife and children is still ongoing. Women frequently decide to have children on their own, although the custody laws in many countries have recently given fathers more rights and power, should the couple separate (Danna 2020b). An aspect of proletarianization (i.e., to be forced to work under an employer having to exchange one's time for money) is access to the labor market for women. They have thus been able to enter the public sphere, previously reserved for men, apart from exceptions in the dominant classes such as female-led monarchies. Male dominance in the public sphere has nevertheless continued. Female proletarianization is certainly one of the factors contributing to the global decrease in the number of children per woman (Mason 1987), though there is certainly some dissatisfaction and frustration for the women who cannot become mothers without risking their jobs or careers.

If feminine preeminence is not recognized, the dynamics of procreative processes are obscured instead of becoming clearer. Indeed, they are the result of power conflicts within families over the costs and benefits of procreation and their distribution among family members, as discussed especially by feminist authors (such as Mies et al. 1988; Mies 1999; Folbre 2009). Shere Hite (1997) illustrates the reasons for accepting pregnancies that she considers spurious because they do not respond primarily to the desire for a maternal relationship, calling them justifications and not independent choices. A woman can get pregnant for many conscious or unconscious reasons: to cling to or possess her male partner, to hold a marriage together, to prove that she is not sterile (which is often believed to be a sin), to please her family, to appease a man who insists on having children of his own, to produce something made by herself or to have an extension of her ego. Other reasons Hite lists can also be constructive: wanting to relive her childhood as a parent, proving to her parents or to herself that she can do better than they, or out of curiosity.

---

17 Even Therborn, however, only passingly mentions population dynamics, adhering to the theory of demographic transition (see Chapter 4).

Nancy Folbre (1990) calls parenthood one of the last craftmanships in a world made similar to a machine by capitalism.

There is no naturalness in procreation, nor can expansive population dynamics be considered the *primum mobile*[18] of social analysis, as demographers write, especially in their textbooks (e.g., Dyson 2010; for a critical position, see, among others, Burch 2003).[19] John Stuart Mill ([1869] 2017, 15–16) underlined this lack of naturalness in "women's Nature," as his contemporaries called it:

> The general opinion of men is supposed to be that a woman's natural vocation is that of a wife and mother. I say "is supposed to be" because judging from the present constitution of society one might think that their opinion was the exact opposite. Perhaps this is what they think: The natural vocation of women is of all things the most in conflict with their nature: if […] any other job or pastime is open to them that has any chance of appearing desirable to them, there won't be enough of them who will be willing to be wives and mothers, i.e. to accept the condition that is said to be natural to them. If this really is what men in general believe, they should say so out loud. I would like to hear somebody openly expressing the doctrine (it is already implied in much that is written on the subject): "Society needs women to marry and produce children. They won't do so unless they are compelled. Therefore it is necessary to compel them." The merits of the case would then be clearly defined. It would be exactly the same as the case of the slave-holders of South Carolina and Louisiana: "It is necessary that cotton and sugar should be grown. White men cannot produce them. Negroes will not, for any wages that we choose to give. Therefore, they must be compelled."

Population growth can instead be driven by power, or rather by society's different powers (for a schematization, see Mann 1986) wanting to appropriate workforce and/or resources by means of it. The subjects of procreation can be at different levels from that of the individuals who materially make it, that is, the woman together with those who support her:

> James Lee and Wang Feng's pathbreaking new work on the Chinese demographic system emphasizes the role of extended kin groups, acting through lineage organizations or through the household heads

18 The first motionless motor that gives impetus to the universe, according to Aristotle.

19 Cordell (1993, 2) instead takes for granted that demographers today accept the different "demographic regimes" based on a mode of production, according to the suggestion of Gregory and Piché.

of joint co-resident families. Such groups were essential for enforcing restraints on procreation within marriage, arranging the adoptions that compensated for such restraint, and providing reasonable guarantees of old-age security and ritual continuity in cases where a given conjugal unit failed to produce a male biological heir. More generally, it has been argued that social arrangements in which bonds between married brothers remain strong provide a form of insurance that reduces the need to hedge risk by having more children to call upon. (Pomeranz 2004, 369)[20]

The subjects of procreation can therefore be women, couples, households, extended families, rural communities or even the owning class, such as the feudal lords whom the servants had to ask for permission to marry. All subjects of procreation should be understood as intentional agents (obviously in general, not in every single case without exception) and not only in the central areas of the world-system (see Chapter 2) but everywhere. Throughout history, the subjects of procreation decisions were mostly male household heads, both in extended and nuclear families. As said, until fairly recently, exclusive male appropriation of offspring was also legitimized by state laws, even in the event of divorce.

The organization of procreation by "niches" was very widespread in rural areas, in both Europe and Asia (Anderson 1988, 70; Bengtsson and Saito 2000): in an agricultural village, the production units, that is the farms, were fixed and therefore only some of the children could succeed parents and get married. It was the advent of the possibility of being paid for their work that allowed couples without land but "with two wheels to spin" to marry and therefore have children (Anderson 1988, 73 – see Section 6.3). Similarly, paid labor allowed young Kikuyu people to marry without having to ask the elderly for permission, as marriage was previously related to the availability of livestock (Cordell and Gregory 1987, 212).

## 1.2 The Macrohistorical Level

There are societies that pursue population equilibrium, others pursue its growth, while some end up collapsing (Tainter 1989). The most common representation of the global population trend in both scientific and popular

20 The reference is to James Lee and Wang Feng: *Malthusian Mythologies and Chinese Realities*, Cambridge, MA: Harvard University Press, 2003. In China, however, the state was also responsible for helping the population in the event of a famine, which was generally the task of the church in Europe.

literature (Chesnais 1991; Vallin 1995; Livi Bacci 2012) is the exponential curve. Demographers indicate the period around 1750 as the moment when the exponential increase of the population started, generally illustrated by a simplified curve which shows an increase that continues to this day in a practically uninterrupted way. Not even the losses of the two world wars have altered the fundamental trend other than at the local level. However, it is doubtful that a general count of population on a planetary scale would be of any significance before the expansion of capitalism and globalization; peaks and troughs happened at a minor scale, with the rise and fall of empires:

> Northern Europe may be an exception, but in most regions the premedical peak was reached long before 1800 and was followed by a considerable decline afterwards. Aztec Mexico, Byzantine Anatolia and Egypt, pre-Mongol Persia, and perhaps Sung China and Roman Italy and northern Africa are examples of such early peaks. (Bronson 1975, 68)

The years around 1750 are considered the end of the mass epidemics in Europe, after the plague waves that reduced the European population by almost a third between 1340 and 1400, and in 1630 wiped out a quarter of the population of central and northern Europe, with similar losses occurring in Asia and the Mediterranean basin. According to Thomlinson (1965, 12) and also McEvedy and Jones (1978), the increase is instead datable from 1650, whereas Helleiner (1965) sets it at the end of the Great Nordic War in 1721. This year marked the beginning of growth after serious losses due to the plague and other diseases in the early eighteenth century: the population of Gdansk was halved in 1709, Copenhagen lost one-third of its population in 1710–11 and 40,000 out of the 90,000 inhabitants of Marseille died in 1720. The periods of growth for the European population were instead the eleventh to the fourteenth and the sixteenth centuries.

The exponential curve, with its acceleration and the apparent absence of limits to its development, is a simplification that relegates demographic events prior to the eighteenth century to the rank of a rather insignificant start of an overwhelming progression.[21] The whole ideology of modernity, progress and growth lies behind this representation. The positive value given to uncontrolled expansion is implicit and also indicates the lack of a visible limit to the human species and to the commodified productions that we call GDP (gross domestic

21 Korotayev and Malkov (2012) propose instead to synthesize the relationship between population and product measured by GDP from ancient times to the present day with a hyperbola branch, which has a shape very similar to the exponential curve.

product), which is the measure of the monetary exchanges that occur in a unit of time. Modernity, progress and growth accept no limits. This progressive vision of history views population growth favorably without any concern for the moment when, having ignored the conditions of sustainability, our society (and especially the lower classes, as always) will experience the harsh reality of living on a planet with finite resources.[22]

The "plus" sign is always the best; it is what we must strive for indefinitely: this explains the graphic representation of human population as an exponential curve, because a logistic curve, growing fast in its first part and then reaching stability, would be more apt to represent population growth. Indeed, the succession of three logistic curves would be needed for human prehistory and history, with two points of discontinuity: the first around 10,000 BC, the period when sedentary agriculture started,[23] and the second around AD 1750, the beginning of industrialization. To be visually significant, this more adequate representation of the population trend would require a change of scale, a logarithmic transformation, precisely because the human numbers of the current historical period are unprecedented (see the curve in Livi Bacci (2012, 40) and Polgar (1972, 204), both cited in Deevey (1960)).

The logistic curve was designed in the first half of the nineteenth century to generally describe the natural growth of populations, not only that of humans. It is a simplification as it derives from observations in the laboratory, never in Nature: the first experiments were made by Raymond Pearl with the *Drosophila* genus of fruit flies. The reason it is a simplification is because the real curves which describe the growth trend of a particular population depend on which and how many different species use the same resources needed by that population within a complex ecosystem. However, the logistic curves are those that best describe the growth processes of individuals. Growth is fast in the first phase of life (for humans, childhood) and completely ceases with the maturity of the organism. The curve is transformed into a straight-line segment, constant up to the point of decline. For a new species, or when an established species enters a new territory, the population curve begins with low values. Its numbers increase rapidly, but only in the initial phase. Growth then slows down and stops before the carrying capacity limit of the environment

22 On the contrary, the concern goes in the opposite direction, fearing the decrease of the population. See, for example, in the *Wall Street Journal*, the article, "The U.N.'s imaginary babies" by Jonathan V. Last (5.8.2011, p. 18). On the Italian debate, see Danna (2012) and on politicians' concern for the future lack of labor force, see McIntosh (1981) and Gauthier (1996).

23 It is actually a variable point for different peoples.

(in terms of nutrients, competition with other species or predation) in which the species lives is reached.

Population size is stabilized, or rather the species begins to alternate between phases of greater and lesser numbers in response to variations in resources and intensity in predation. Animal species do not normally expand to the point of reaching the carrying capacity limit (see Section 3.2). Rather than infinite growth, animal populations tend indeed toward homeostasis, as numbers oscillate relative to available resources.[24] The various life forms, with their material and energy substrate, configure an ecosystem we can call "sustainable," or stable: the oft-repeated expression "sustainable development" is an oxymoron. Unlike the capitalist world-economy, discussed later, a sustainable ecosystem (but an ecosystem is by definition sustainable) is not destined to depletion due to its normal functioning, as a balance between plant production and animal consumption is reached and then maintained. Of course, unforeseen catastrophic events can always alter the underlying balance of an ecosystem and even destroy it, with the extinction of populations or even entire species due to the reconfiguration of the territory itself. The action of geological factors like erosion, volcanic eruptions, floods and displacements in tectonic plates can all dramatically change the species that inhabit a territory.

In the numerical consistency of the human species *Homo sapiens*, we therefore find two points of discontinuity, that divide the three logistic curves: on a logarithmic scale each can visually be only slightly greater, but on a uniform scale they would result in a different magnitude. The first point where the curve begins its second logistic trend represents the first radical change in the mode of production with the transition from hunting and gathering to permanent agriculture. It is worth noting that there are intermediate situations of itinerant agriculture, that is, sowing without subsequent tillage of the land, as with cut-and-burn techniques, and there is coexistence between these different modes of production, too. Agriculture permits much higher human densities on a given territory. The reason for the transition to it must have been either population growth or the domination of one social stratum over the others.

The phrase "hunting and gathering" is correct for the most ancient period in which the prey animals were the megafauna of the Pleistocene era, extinct in the last ice age due perhaps to immoderate human hunting. For the following epochs, the "hunting and gathering" sequence must generally be inverted, as the reversal in significance can be observed looking at the present-day gathering-hunting groups that are confined to deserts, or forested and mountainous areas in New Guinea and the Amazon. These human groups

24 Peter Turchin (1995, 25) recalls the fact that the notion of balance in biology is now supplanted by that of points of attraction.

base their survival on the collection of herbs, fruits, tubers, roots and eggs, mainly by women, children and the elderly. The collection offers daily food (including small animals caught in traps), while hunting expeditions organized by the male group (in some groups women can participate) occasionally bring an abundance of meat, which cannot be made the basis of daily nutrition because of its uncertainty. Only in very cold environments, such as the areas around the Arctic, is hunting always necessary to supply almost all the daily food needs, since vegetation is lacking.

Given that hunter-gatherers normally find enough food within a few hours of daily collecting, they are considered as enjoying a high standard of living (Sahlins 1980), provided that the group does not increase beyond the environment's carrying capacity, which can be suddenly reduced because of drought or other occurrences resulting in famines. Other reasons to prefer a sedentary mode of production can be increased comfort (e.g., in waterproof dwellings), the possibility of storing food and of accumulating possessions, better care for the sick, the young and the old. Bennet Bronson (1975, 63) affirms: "It is far from certain, in fact, that gathering is always less work than some kinds of farming."

The hunter-gatherers get what they need in about 600–700 hours of work per year while the average number of hours worked with the cut-and-burn system in the forests had been estimated at 500–650 hours per year in Sarawak, Borneo, Zambia and Ghana.[25] In Lower Volta in Ghana, it has been observed that farmers and fishermen who apply traditional techniques work for 4.1 hours a day, 174 days a year, for a total of just over 600 hours yearly. The values of this society discourage the ostentation of wealth; therefore, if one ignores opportunities to increase production, this does not diminish the person's social prestige.[26] Richard Wilkinson, who collected and presented these calculations, noted that in industrial society—and according to him only in industrial society—induced needs lead people to prefer work to free time. Marshall Sahlins (1980, 49) wrote: "Hunters and gatherers have by force of circumstances, an objectively low standard of living. But taken as their *objective*, and given their adequate means of production, all the people's material wants usually can be easily satisfied." Instead, poverty and hunger are linked to the

---

25 Colin Clark and Margaret Haxwell, *The Economics of Subsistence Agriculture*, London, 1970 (4th ed.), tab. XI, 51 (quoted by Wilkinson 1973, 93).

26 Rowens M. Lawson, "Innovation and Growth in Traditional Agriculture of the Lower Volta, Ghana," *Journal of Development Studies*, vol. 4, 1967, 143 (quoted by Wilkinson 1973, 200). Ambition is posed as a universal psychological trait by conflict theories, which reflect the characteristics of complex societies. But complex societies started from egalitarian minisystems that repress ambition and put the group as a whole before individual interest.

evolution of techniques, which lead to greater appropriation of Nature and/or to greater expropriation of human beings:

> The most primitive peoples of the world have few goods, *but they are not poor.* Poverty is not determined by small quantities of goods nor solely by the relationship between means and ends; it is above all an interpersonal relationship. (Sahlins 1980, 50; italics in original)

A Bushman from South Africa rhetorically asked, "Why should we plant, when there are so many mongongo nuts in the world?" (Lee 1975, 33), nuts that, incidentally, are gathered by women.[27]

The transition from hunting-gathering and itinerant agriculture to permanent agriculture has been attributed to an uncontrolled increase in the population, forcing people to accept the fatigue associated with new production methods in order to have enough food. If subsistence is guaranteed with little work, what need is there to do more by adopting complicated systems that require more effort and fatigue? Only in times of scarcity must people increase their work and accept lower rewards. With this premise Ester Boserup ([1965] 2005) suggests an increase in population density to explain the adoption of new and more labor-intensive techniques. Mark Cohen (1977) examines the transition to Neolithic agriculture in light of this theory, which his data confirm.[28] In fact, working hours increased and health deteriorated in the transition to agriculture: "Farmers were sicker as well as smaller" (Angel 1975; see also McNeill 2012, 12). Richard Wilkinson emphasizes that development is a response to scarcity, which is often triggered by an increase in the population, compelling changes in the techniques hitherto used to derive from the environment whatever is necessary to live on.

Anthropologist Steven Polgar instead underlined the importance of the absence of class exploitation to maintain population balance with the environment. An alternative explanation, or a complementary one, is in fact that the transition away from hunting and gathering was a consequence of the beginning of social stratification—even though egalitarian agricultural societies do exist. Polgar (1975, 22) finds it unlikely that a transition to more labor-intensive techniques can be driven by population pressure alone:

27 In the documentary film *Ghostland* (Germany 2016), other Bushmen visiting the city disapprove of what they see: "How much work for all these crazy things!"

28 Clearly, the available data and methods have changed since Cohen's time (see, e.g., Kaiser et al. 2012—likely already obsolete), which makes a synthesis such as his more difficult today.

> Population growth in the feudal stage was often forced to reach (and sometimes exceed) the limits of supporting capacity. [...] The pronatalist effects of colonialism are in some respects a continuation of the feudal situation. In contrast to the largely autonomous village, the peasant community is heavily affected by outside economic interests. To outsiders the "surplus" they can squeeze from the peasant's production is of much greater relevance than the long-term productivity of the land or the standard of living of the peasant family. Boserup (1965) has recognized that intensification of labor input leads to declining yields per man-day of work; but she attributes this self-defeating cycle to population pressure, failing to recognize that where external dominance is weak or absent, agricultural people are quite capable of keeping population from becoming too dense.

Agriculture made it possible to obtain more food by exploiting the territory more intensely, but the increased working hours to guarantee the harvests were possibly imposed by an armed group formed as a superior class: warriors, nobles or invaders. "Class" is the division into social groups on an economic basis. The class system is actually a hierarchical system, in which the product of the work of the lower classes is subject to appropriation by the upper classes. The mutual relationships of the classes are based on positions in the world of production—namely the economy. I use "economy" in its substantive meaning, as a system in which basic human needs are satisfied first, then individual and collective desires for the purpose of prestige. According to this substantive meaning, the economy is all of the work, as well as the relationships between people, that serve to satisfy the needs and desires of consumption, not just paid work and money-mediated relationships. Economy in a *substantive* sense is opposed to the *formal* conception of the economy, which restricts it to the circulation of money. Mainstream economists restrict the subject of their study to this limited and specialized sense, applying neoclassical marginalist tools. The division into classes puts the working capacity of the lower class at the service of a higher class that forces the lower class to surrender part of its product, usually in exchange for "protection." Intersecting classes there is also the issue of gender, that is, the attribution of social meanings and behavioral norms to the sexual dimorphism of the human species, functioning as another social class (Danna 2020c). These meanings and norms are aimed at justifying men's appropriation of women's work (Tabet 2014).

The second point of discontinuity in the three logistic curves, which represent the trend of the human population more faithfully than the unique exponential curve, corresponds to the transition from permanent agriculture to industrial society, through the large-scale use of fossil fuels that drive machines. Fossil fuels are currently the main energy source for humanity as a whole: in

2015 they represented 81.5 percent of all energy sources according to the International Energy Agency. Fossil fuels have replaced the energy sources prevalent in agricultural societies: human and animal work and the strength of the elements, exploited as an energy source by windmills, watermills, ships and the like. The industrial revolution has allowed the further numerical growth of the human species. From oil we can synthesize chemical fertilizers that increase crops, and fossil fuel energy allows new lands to be cultivated more quickly and with less effort through the intensified action of machines on Nature, reclaiming swamps, cutting down forests and building large-scale irrigation systems to meet the increased demand for food. The proportion of the population engaged in agricultural work has fallen from 80–90 percent in pre-industrial societies to single digits: currently in Italy only 3.75 percent of the active population works in agriculture.

General proletarianization occurs in industrial society; the working class loses its sustenance, whereby it formerly derived what it needed to live directly from the land. Failure to participate in the labor market means not having the means to satisfy one's needs through market exchanges: money. In industrial society, indeed, those who do not belong to the class that owns the means of production (the class named "bourgeoisie," an ancient word meaning "city inhabitants") have lost the autonomy deriving from the direct use of the land to obtain resources. In other words, they have been dispossessed, as occurred in England at the end of the Middle Ages when the nobles appropriated common lands with their enclosures. "Freed" peasants and their progeny were then forced to seek new jobs organized by companies or by the state, expanding the activities and strengthening the structures of these entities. The state, in turn, either organizes work or supplies benefits, as an inactive mass of needy and discontented people is a threat to the established order.

This second turning point in the population curve corresponds to an increase in workload, too. The social product increases, but requires a much greater number of working hours than in peasant society (Bowles and Edwards 1993). At the beginning of the industrial revolution, factory workers toiled 16 hours a day seven days a week. One of the major problems employers faced was how to force the workers to accept those demands, which people rightly believed were contrary to human nature. The historian Wally Seccombe (1995, 27–28) evaluated changes in the quality of life in the industrial age in these terms:

> In addition to these objective measures of labour-power's consumption, the cultural dimension of proletarian deterioration merits consideration. Factory workers in particular felt that they had lost independence by relinquishing control over their own time. Labourers had always worked hard over long hours; but in an earlier era they could interrupt their

> work for a drink or a chat with a neighbour, and leave when their task was done. Now, in capitalist industries, "the greater hardship was the awful regularity of time-keeping."[29]

It is useful to remember that capital is whatever asset (money, machinery, land) intended for production with the use of human labor (which Marx called variable capital) to obtain a profit. Profit equates to a larger amount of money than was needed to start production, also counting the value of the machines and of the land and/or the buildings where the production is located (i.e., the cost of rent). In order to function, capital needs a class of people who are forced to derive sustenance from the sale of their work, as they do not own the means of production. Capital therefore is not a thing but a relationship: machines can only be operated if there are people willing to work on them in exchange for money. Marx ([1867] 1992, 932–33) wrote in *Capital*:

> First of all, Wakefield[30] discovered that, in the colonies, property in money, means of subsistence, machines and other means of production does not as yet stamp a man as a capitalist if the essential complement to these things is missing: the wage-labourer, the other man, who is compelled to sell himself of his own free will. He discovered that capital is not a thing, but a social relation between persons which is mediated through things.[31] A Mr Peel, he complains, took with him from England to the Swan River district of Western Australia means of subsistence and of production to the amount of £50,000. This Mr Peel even had the foresight to bring besides, 3,000 persons of the working class, men, women and children. Once he arrived at his destination, "Mr Peel was left without a servant to make his bed or fetch him water from the river."[32] Unhappy Mr Peel, who provided for everything except the export of English relations of production to Swan River!

---

29 Quote from Dorothy Marshall: *Industrial England 1776-1851*, London, 1973, 99.

30 Edward Gibbon Wakefield, British politician, promoter of immigration incentives, aimed at increasing the workforce, and he is also the author of *England and America. A Comparison of the Social and Political State of Both Nations*, New York, Harper, 1834.

31 Original note (quote from Karl Marx: "Lohnarbeit und Kapital," *Neue Rheinische Zeitung*, n. 266, April 7, 1849): "A negro is a negro. In certain relations he becomes a slave. A mule is a machine for spinning cotton. Only in certain relations does it become capital. Outside these circumstances, it is no more capital than gold is intrinsically money, or sugar is the price of sugar. […] Capital is a social relation of production. It is a historical relation of production" (English translation, *Karl Marx and Frederick Engels, Selected Works*, Vol. 1, 159–60).

32 Original note: E. G. Wakefield, *England and America*, Vol. 2, ~ 33.

Workers did not easily submit to the factory discipline their masters ordered of them, particularly in the New World where the population was not "circumscribed," that is, people could move to new cultivable lands. As Samuel Bowles and Richard Edwards (1993, 110) underline, when the first factories opened their doors in the early twentieth century in America, employers were worried about not finding enough workers. They asked themselves: who will want a job in the workshops? It wasn't just a matter of wages, which were actually quite good. It was rather a question of status: most adult males considered going to work for someone else as humiliating and perhaps even as "anti-American." Those who did go to work for others, in the language of the time, were called servants, whether they worked in homes, factories or in the mines of others.

At the beginning of industrialization, yearly hours worked peaked at 5,000, then went down to 3,000–3,500 thanks to the bargaining power of workers' unions. Nowadays, 40 hours a week is considered normal with a few weeks of vacation, that is, less than 1,800–1,900 hours of work per year. Today, in the United States, people work more: 40 hours a week for 50 weeks, that is, 2,000 hours a year. If, with the aid of fossil fuel energy, productivity per employee has significantly increased in agriculture as in industry, the "freed" time has not translated into *otium* at all—except for the upper classes, who have always enjoyed it. The Latin concept of *otium* is indeed aristocratic and includes all the uses of time freed from duties, which instead constitute the *negotium*, the etymology of which is *nec-otium*,[33] the opposite of *otium*, which was therefore the initial (aristocratic) condition: the *otium* time could be devoted to politics, the arts, pleasures, idleness or activities outside the sphere of production.

Many have denounced a decrease in the quality of life in the transition to industrial society. Wilkinson, for example, sees development primarily as the appearance of lower-quality goods and services to replace those that have become scarce—though it is undeniable that lower–quality goods have been put at the disposal of more people:

> Looking at economic development in its ecological setting effectively removes the idea of progress from the central position it has occupied in our view of the process. Instead of regarding development as a matter of "progress" towards a "better life" motivated by an incurable dissatisfaction with our present lot, we see that it is a process of solving a succession of problems which from time to time threaten the productive system and the sufficiency of our subsistence. (Wilkinson 1978, 105)

33 *Negozio* means "shop" in current Italian, or "business" in outmoded language.

For the English social epidemiologist, development is the way to solve new problems that have arisen by interacting with the environment: "A rising GDP might just as well be taken as evidence of the increasing needs and problems which make higher consumption necessary" (Wilkinson 1973, 195). Wilkinson does not deny that technological change can lead to improvements in living standards, but he doubts that this is the underlying impetus for development or its manifest goal. In industrialization, each task is specialized with the division of labor, thus becoming monotonous and disorientating. The social purpose of work is no longer evident, often because it does not exist. Furthermore, through specialization, the experience of work is not shared, distancing people from each other: social forces push toward individualism.

In class systems, the unit of reference is no longer the whole group and the inequalities are not corrected with redistribution. One could starve alongside wealthy families, who do not need to limit their fertility. In addition, the upper classes often impose their own vision of abortion and infanticide—practices abhorred by those who are not forced to adopt them. These practices, according to Wilkinson, are no longer considered necessary evils, but absolute evils and are often made punishable, something that for abortion is not only unacceptable but also useless and cruel to women—unlike infanticide, because once pregnancy is completed, the newborn might be raised by others. Wilkinson did not fail to note that the multiplication of the poor is a benefit to the ruling classes, which can profit from a bigger workforce.

## 1.3 Industrial Society in Perspective

On the "day of life" that humanity experienced on Earth since the origin of *Homo sapiens* dating back to at least 200,000 years, the mode of production of hunting and gathering occupies 22 hours and 40 minutes. The industrial revolution came about only after 23 hours, 47 minutes and a few seconds. Another incisive metaphor that can make us realize the exceptional feature of the current situation is the photo album of the last 100,000 years. The images that would illustrate the living conditions of the Stone Age would constitute nine-tenths of the collection. If it were made up of a thousand pages, it would look like this: endless pages filled with hunting and gathering scenes, with the first change of scenery showing the breeding of animals and the cultivation of plants only after page 900. Cities would appear around page 950, and only

> a little after page 950 you would find images of the construction of the great pyramids of Egypt, and later still you would begin to see the first picture of individuals whose names you would recognize: Moses

> on page 967, Aristotle on page 976, Cleopatra on page 979, Jesus on page 980, Muhammad on page 986. (Nolan and Lenski 2004, 3)

Only in the last three pages of the volume would the inventions that pertain to our daily existence in industrial society appear: first the steam engine, followed by the internal combustion engine, then the airplane and finally the computer.

Gerhard Lenski (2005, 27), to whom we owe the metaphor of the photo album, illustrated the estimated trends of the world population and of the consumption of energy other than food, which grow in parallel. The first turning point was the use of fire (Chazan 2017), which increased the calories available to each person over the 2,000 kcal of food necessary per day. Another turning point was the domestication of animals, which took place 10,000 years ago, and allowed the average energy consumption per capita to be raised to around 10,000 kcal per day. Today the consumption of energy per capita is about 50,000 kcal per day and is equivalent to each human being having at his or her disposal the average output of 24 people. The mean for a US citizen is 60–80 servants, mostly made of fossil fuels.

The use of fossil fuels has greatly increased the resources available and has stimulated or simply made possible a new phase of population growth, still ongoing. This is also a period of increasing inequality—even if not always within nations, certainly among them—due to the functioning of the capitalist world-economy, which I will discuss in the next chapter. An average figure is therefore not very significant. Some human groups still live in a way in which the resources they use have time to renew themselves, while others use the lion's share of fossil fuel energy:

> The advanced capitalist countries, the "North," comprise 18.8 percent of the world's population, but have been responsible for 72.7 percent of $CO_2$ emissions since 1850—not to mention the inequalities within nations. At the beginning of the twenty-first century, the poorest 45 percent of the human population was responsible for 7 percent of emissions, while the richest 7 percent produced 50 percent. A single average American citizen—always without considering class divisions within nations—emitted more $CO_2$ than 500 citizens of Ethiopia, Chad, Afghanistan, Mali, Cambodia or Burundi. (Malm and Hornborg 2014, 64)[34]

---

34 Data from J. T. Roberts and B. C. Parks: *A Climate of Injustice: Global Inequality, North-South Politics, and Climate Policy*, Cambridge, MIT Press, 2007, 64.

## 1.4 Sources on Population

Before concluding this introductory chapter with an outline of the data collected by the United Nations (UN) on worldwide population, I will describe the main sources that can be used by those wishing to quantitatively examine population dynamics in history, while the qualitative sources on procreation are quite varied. An original synthesis of quantitative and qualitative historical sources to reconstruct and compare community life in the East and in the West is the Eurasia Project on Population and Family History coordinated by Tommy Bengtsson and Osamu Saito. Three volumes of this work have been published to date.

The ability to gather information about one's population is a privilege of the richest and most organized countries. Large spending is necessary to have people and resources to control and record what is happening in a territory, and this happened for the primary purpose of taxation. The word "statistics" was first used in the mercantilist era (from the mid-fifteenth to the eighteenth century) with the establishment of what we call modern states. "Statistics" indeed derives from "state," and means the set of data collected primarily with state resources and for government purposes. In the past, they were the documents produced by political or religious authorities, such as censuses (which generally only included adult men), population registers and parish registers. Historical demography and economic history are the disciplines that use these archival sources to provide concise overviews. Little remains of population records before the eighteenth century.[35] Exceptions include the Florentine land register, documents on the population of the thirteenth-century Venetian Republic and the Sicilian *Riveli di Beni e Anime*, 15 censuses carried out from 1505 to 1831 on the island of Sicily, rich and prosperous in the modern age (Beloch 1994; Del Panta et al. 1996).

Governments have performed censuses since ancient times. Around 3,000 BC, the pharaohs of ancient Egypt organized them in order to collect taxes, and later for military purposes. Some incomplete lists of inhabitants have been found in Egypt. In Mesopotamia, tablets with cuneiform writing dating back to 2,800 BC list people to be taxed and their goods. The Bible's Book of Numbers, as it is aptly named, narrates the divine request for Moses to count the population of Israel that could go to war in 1491 BC. The Indian book *Arthasastra* of the third century BC contains an inventory of the resources of India, including men. It contained the order to record births and deaths and

35 Ancient sources are systematically described by Reinhard et al. (1971). Another fundamental text is *Population in history* (Glass and Eversley 1965).

to provide a list of the dwellings and the occupations of residents, but these documents are lost.

The cities of ancient Greece, including Athens, kept records for tax and military purposes. "Census," however, derives from the Latin *census*, performed regularly every five years throughout the Roman Empire. It officially recorded the age of citizens, the composition of their families, their wealth and the number of their slaves, births and deaths. The most ancient total is handed down from Roman times: "The fundamental datum is that provided by the *Res gestae* of Augustus according to the inscription of Amcira. The datum of 4,063,000 citizens in the year 28 BC was considered sufficiently reliable to be adopted by historians" (Reinhard et al. 1971, 58). In China, censuses were performed more than two millennia ago, but all records before the eighteenth century are lost. Confucius wrote: "For a government the two most important things are the people and food supplies."[36] Censuses were held every six years from 1721 onward. In Japan too, censuses were carried out in ancient times, such as that of the seventh century AD, which recorded a total number of about five million inhabitants. In the middle of that century the first registers of civil status were compiled and used for redistribution of lands. They were also used by the tax authorities in the drafting and in the assignment of the corvee. The oldest register compiled by the clergy dates back to AD 720. Available Japanese data show population fluctuations similar to those in China (Reinhard et al. 1971, 199), which in turn oscillated in line with those of the European continent. In Southern Asia, however, the cycles were very different (Hall and Turchin 2007) and perhaps corresponded with changes in climate, which are consistent along lines of latitude (Diamond 1998; Dull et al. 2010).

In Denmark, the first population counts were made in 1645 in small areas on the islands east of Storebælt (Sjælland, Lolland-Falster and smaller islands) recording only the population above the age of 16.[37] In 1660, the entire population subject to capitation was counted to calculate the appropriate amount of taxes. There are reports of other local censuses, the results of which have not been preserved, while the first national survey was carried out on August 15, 1769. Censuses were held in the Habsburg Empire in 1695, in Prussia, Mecklenburg and Bavaria during the eighteenth century, in Spain in 1717 and so on. The oldest European sources are ecclesiastical. The Church, another power that anchored itself to written records in order to better manage its subordinates, kept the parish registers of baptisms, marriages and

36 Quoted without mentioning the source by Reinhard et al. (1971, 189).
37 Data about Danish social history is taken from Danna (1991) and related bibliography.

burials. This practice was established at different times in different areas. The earliest reference to this is in a draft by the bishop of Nantes written in 1406. From 1450 onward this custom was regular in Spain. Over time, states took over from churches in keeping the population registers and established their own registry offices. The first registration of the national population, regardless of religious belief, was made in Norway in 1685. In France, the registry was established in 1800 under Napoleon. In England, births and deaths have been recorded with their causes since 1838. In Italy, the national registry was established in 1871, while previously it existed only in some municipalities. The worldwide collection of personal data is not complete even today: it is estimated that 50 million minors in the world are not registered, both those living in war zones and those in areas not under the authority of any state.

For ancient times and other places, there are estimates such as those collected by McEvedy and Jones in their *Historical Atlas of the World Population* and by August Maddison and Brian Redman Mitchell (see "References and Datasets"). John Durand (1977) evaluates the historical sources and estimates. Then there are the testimonies about the peoples subjected to European colonialism: the writings of travelers and missionaries with the assessments of their indigenous interlocutors speak of the structure and composition of families and demographic trends in a qualitative rather than quantitative sense (see Chapter 7). Subject counts were distorted by false identity statements made in an attempt to escape capitation (Axelsson and Sköld 2011).[38]

In contemporary times, quantitative research on procreation is carried out with statistically representative samples using questions regarding social norms and individual or family choices. The World Fertility Survey began in 1972 and was carried out in 42 countries until 1987. Data is available on the Office of Population Research website at Princeton University[39] (see Basu (1992) for methodological criticisms of this and other investigations as those on contraceptives use: "Knowledge, Attitude and Practice"). Italy participated in the World Fertility Survey with the 1979 fertility survey (INF-1), followed in 1983 by the Italian National Institute of Statistics (ISTAT) survey on family structures and behaviors and then by the current system of multipurpose surveys on families. The multiscope survey has been carried out annually by ISTAT since 1987 on the daily life of individuals and families, with a

---

38 See also number 1 of 2007 of *Annales de démographie historique: ADH*, dedicated to population in the colonies.

39 http://opr.princeton.edu/archive/wfs/.

**Table 1** Exponential growth of the human population after the first billion

| World population | Year | Time when 1 billion was added |
|---|---|---|
| 1 billion | 1804 | 200,000 years + |
| 2 billion | 1927 | 123 years |
| 3 billion | 1960 | 33 years |
| 4 billion | 1974 | 14 years |
| 5 billion | 1987 | 13 years |
| 6 billion | 1999 | 12 years |
| 7 billion | 2011 | 12 years |

*Source*: United Nations Population Fund.

sample of 28,000 families, whose members are all interviewed. The Fertility and Family Surveys were conducted in the 1990s in 23 states of the United Nations Economic Commission for Europe (UNECE – https://www.unece.org/pau/ffs/ffs.Html), and in this field the Italian INF-2 survey was carried out in 1995–96. Since 1984, the United States Agency for International Development (USAID) has been conducting the Demographic and Health Surveys using representative samples (http://dhsprogram.com/). These surveys occur regularly in more than 90 countries that have limited resources to devote to the collection of statistics.

Since 1950, when the United Nations Population Division (UNPD – https://esa.un.org/unpd/wpp/) began collecting and publishing the most reliable population statistics available, the number of human inhabitants on the planet has tripled. In 1950, the combined total of statistical data and national estimates placed global human population at 2,525,149. In 2015, the total number was 7,349,472 (United Nations Population Division 2015). The latter figure is quite reliable as it includes the results of censuses held in numerous countries in 2010 as well as data from the latest Demographic and Health Surveys.

In 2011, the world population reached and exceeded seven billion. The last billion is made up of humans born in the previous 12 years, and so is the penultimate billion, as seen in Table 1.

The rate of increase recorded in 1950–55, the beginning of the collection of UN statistics, was 2.18 percent. It then rose to reach the maximum of 2.93 percent per year in 1980–85 and is now decreasing. The average increase since 1750 is estimated to have been 0.74 percent per year (Coale and Watkins 1986, 1). At the beginning of this period, Europe and its emigrants to the New World showed the greatest growth, while today it is the inhabitants of poor countries who grow more.

## 1.5 Current Data

Today the world fertility rate is 2.5 children per woman. This is a constructed measure of the number of children that every living woman will have on average at the end of her reproductive life and is calculated from the specific rates for each age cohort of women living in that period. We are therefore still in a phase of demographic expansion because the replacement rate that keeps the population stable is 2.1 children per woman. The decimal compensates for perinatal mortality (more precise calculations could be made for different situations of minor or major risk in different countries or areas).

The UN states that from 1950 to present there has been a constant drop in the number of children per woman. In many developed countries this was already taking place at the beginning of the collection of population statistics, for example, in France before 1801 and in general in Europe since the mid-nineteenth century. In Italy, the total fertility rate is estimated to have decreased starting in 1850. Some African countries had a rise in the fertility rate, such as Kenya, peaking in the 1970s at eight children per woman.

According to UN estimates, the fertility rate in the period 1950–55 was 2.8 children per woman in developed countries, while in the least developed countries it was 6.1 children. In the period 1975–80, the fertility rate based on statistics from individual countries, or on their estimates, was 3.87 children per woman. It then started to drop, reaching 3.04 children per woman in the period 1990–95 and 2.56 children per woman in 2005–10. The latest figure released is 2.5 children per woman in 2019. The reduction in the fertility rate is strong, but the population continues to increase due to the large number of young women of reproductive age: this is the phenomenon called "population momentum." A breakdown of the world population by age reveals the following: 26 percent are children and adolescents up to 14 years of age; teenagers and adults aged 15 to 59 are the largest group making up 62 percent; finally, 12 percent are aged above 60 years.

The UN classifies countries into three categories according to their low, intermediate or high fertility rate. Forty-six percent of the world population lives in low-fertility countries with less than 2.1 children per woman: all of Europe, North America, 20 countries in Asia, 17 in Latin America and the Caribbean, 3 in Oceania and only 1 African country: the Mauritius Islands. The largest countries in this group are China, the United States, Brazil, Russia, Japan and Vietnam. The countries with intermediate fertility rates include 46 percent of the world population and are found in all geographic regions. Their fertility rate is still very high, between 2.1 and 5 children per woman. The largest countries in this group are India, Indonesia, Pakistan, Bangladesh, Mexico and the Philippines. The remaining 9 percent of the world population is in high-fertility countries: five or more children per woman. There are 21 countries in this group, all of which are African, except two. The largest are Nigeria, the Democratic Republic of the Congo, Tanzania, Uganda and Afghanistan.

Sixty percent of the world's population lives in Asia (4.6 billion). The second most populous continent is Africa with 17 percent (1.3 billion). Fourteen percent of the world population lives in the Americas (1.1 billion), followed by Europe with 9 percent (747 million). Oceania has only 42 million inhabitants, 0.5 percent of the world population. 19 and 18 percent of the world's population live in China and India, equaling respectively 1.4 and 1.3 billion human beings.[40] The demographic dynamics of the two countries, applying the present rates to the future, are such that in 2027 India will surpass China.[41]

Life expectancy, or average age, is quite high on all continents: 60 years in Africa, 72 in Asia, 75 in Latin America and the Caribbean, 77 in Europe and Oceania and 79 in North America, higher than ever before. This value has increased greatly on all continents from 45.5 years, which was the average life expectancy in 1950–55, to 72.5 years in 2019. Life expectancy at 65 years has risen from 11.4 to 16.2 years. Population growth has remained particularly high in the 48 countries that the United Nations groups as "minimum development countries," of which 27 are located in Africa. The annual growth of this group is 2.4 percent, a doubling of their inhabitants is expected from 2019 to 2050. In contrast, 48 countries will instead experience a population decrease, including Bosnia and Herzegovina, Bulgaria, Croatia, Japan, Latvia, Lithuania, Moldova, Romania, Serbia, Ukraine and Hungary. Europe is below the replacement rate of the population with 1.6 children per woman, though this value is expected to increase slightly.

Just as the population trends of the past are shrouded in uncertainty, the projections for the future are only indicative. The UNPD develops scenarios of high, medium and low fertility starting from current data. The UNPD simply projects the present onto the future, like all demographers who make "predictions," which are actually projections. A continuous increase in the world population is expected until the next century. Should the number of

---

40 Some texts regarding China's demographic policies are the works of Poston et al. (2006) and Susan Greenhalgh (e.g., Greenhalgh and Winckler 2005); on the beginning of demographic policies in India, see Banerji (1980); for Bangladesh, see Akhter (1995, 2005); for a summary of the policies in Asia, see Piotrow and Rimon II (1999), and for a general reflection, see May (2012).

41 Source for all these data is the UN's *2019 World Population Prospects*, in particular: https://population.un.org/wpp/Publications/Files/WPP2019_DataBooklet.pdf. The following data, in the last paragraph, are from the 2017 version.

children per woman increase by 0.5 compared to the current rate, the human population is expected to double around 2085. If instead growth slows down by 0.5 children per woman, population will reach its peak around 2045 (UNPD 2012). The mortality trend is not subject to scenarios other than the current one. In any case, the complexity underlying birth, mortality and migration trends is probably too high for even medium-term forecasts to be accurate, especially in this phase of climate change which is deeply altering the ecological balance.

# Chapter 2

# HISTORICAL SOCIAL SCIENCE

## 2.1 Historical Social Structures

Population dynamics as based on procreation are essential topics in the analysis of historical structures. This concept is central to world-systems analysis, founded by Immanuel Wallerstein: the historical structures are the world-systems, which are the main units of analysis of social science—not the states and not society, the twin concept of state. Comparative analyses that consider countries as case studies are problematic also due to the different numbers in their populations, which makes quantitative research uncertain. Is it legitimate to consider states as independent and comparable entities, as if they were different "cases" drawn from a single population? Can China and India really be considered on par with tiny city-states like Andorra or San Marino (Babones 2014)? Of course, the states are the entities that collect and provide uniform statistical data on the national territory, ready for analysis, so it is easier to use them. But how can the connections between the states and especially their stratification be ignored? For example, the transition from feudalism to capitalism, to which Wallerstein applied his new analytical tools, certainly did not happen independently in one state after another, as those who reason in terms of national histories implicitly consider, as if borders were insurmountable. Capitalism is not established by replicating its process of modernization in every new state in which industrialization has reached a certain threshold, because the dynamics of the spread of both capitalism and industry are supranational. Industrialization often (perhaps normally in non-hegemonic countries) occurs with foreign capital, its inputs are often imported and its outputs exported. Nowadays analysis that merely compares states cannot determine the mechanisms of a world-economy in which many companies are multinational giants with a turnover larger than the GDP of medium-sized states. A study by Global Justice Now (2016) shows that 69 of the 100 largest economic entities in the world are multinational corporations. In the list of the 200 largest entities the proportion rises: 153 are companies (Inman 2016).

The colonized countries, producers of raw materials used in First World industries, are by no means in a "backward" position in a hypothetical race of states toward Modernity & Progress. These countries found themselves on the losing side of the unequal exchange necessary for capitalist production and its expansion, as already claimed in the 1950s by the UN Economic Commission for Latin America chaired by Raúl Prebisch. AndréGunder Frank (1969) called this interdependence the "development of underdevelopment." For Arghiri Emmanuel (1972), unequal exchange is measured in terms of the quantity of labor incorporated in the commodities exchanged, applying the labor value theory of Ricardo and Marx. Emmanuel's concept highlights the center's appropriation of the value of labor at the expense of the periphery, because production in the periphery countries—then called "Third World" and today referred to as the South of the world or Global South—demands more manual work, while the core uses more machines per worker.[1] For Frank (1998), technology is not European, but concerns production techniques that are used (or not) according to the relationships between all areas and classes of the world system. Underdevelopment represents the dark inseparable part of the development that takes place in the dominant areas of the world, thanks to the plundered resources of other peoples and territories that were conquered and forced to produce and deliver them in unequal exchanges.[2] Generally, the losing parties culturally accept these exchanges after their subjugation by force. Power first imposes itself with violence and then strives to bring the status quo of its dominant relations into culture, aspiring to govern by consensus and with minimal use of open repression.

In his proposal from the 1970s, Immanuel Wallerstein spoke of a world-systems perspective or analysis, and not of a world-systems theory, because the theory under construction is the unidisciplinary and scientifically based historical social science. To this description I would add another adjective: *biophysical*, taking the suggestion from the authors promoting biophysical economics (Hall and Klitgaard 2018), a suggestion that has its roots in Marx's work, whose effort to understand society always included its biophysical foundations. Biophysical economics is based on the consideration of the energy and materials used in economic activity, and develops Nicholas

---

1 Brenner (1977, 31) claims that "production to obtain profit on the market" can explain the development of the productive forces through innovation, that is, the accumulation of capital on an enlarged scale. But are production and trade not two sides of the same coin, when it comes to profit realization?

2 Responding to the unequal exchange analysis, the orthodox Marxist critique (Carchedi 1991) reaffirms instead the transfer of surplus value to capitalists and not workers, even in international dynamics.

Georgescu-Roegen's (1970) approach including entropy and waste in economic analysis. This is their definition of biophysical economics:

> A rather imperfect but growing approach to economics that is based upon the recognition that wealth is fundamentally generated through exploitation of natural resources and that recognizes that economic policies are mostly about directing how energy is invested in that exploitation. (Hall and Klitgaard 2018, 272)

Elementary biophysics should be common knowledge for all social scientists, grounding our propositions about society in material realities and not in the ideal world of self-definitions, of the culture detached from behavior, of interpretations that exclude either the existence of facts or our possibility of knowing them.[3] Absolute truth is not the goal of social science; nevertheless, the provisory truth that the scientific method can discover is nonetheless truth, just with a different and more realistic adjective. The separation of social and natural sciences is also deplored by Christophe Bonneuil and Jean-Baptiste Fressoz (2016), who argue that the "earthless" human sciences produced by industrial modernity must be substituted by new human environmental sciences, beyond the division between environment and society, for example, with the concept of "socio-ecological systems" (Berkes and Folke 1998). Bonneuil and Fressoz (2016, 32) write:

> On one side, therefore, were the natural sciences with their non-human objects, their concept of objectivity and their modern certainties; on the other, humanities and social sciences became "a-natural" by conferring on 'society' a self-sufficient totality, free from natural determination (despite the observations of Marx, Sergei Podolinsky, Patrick Geddes and many others on socio-ecological metabolism).

The concept of historical structure, based on the world-systems analysis, seems to bear a contradiction in identifying history, that is, change, with structure, supposed to be stable. This is because there are structures in

3 An example is the language of "gift" to describe what happens in surrogate motherhood, that is, the handing over of a newborn being commissioned by contract to his or her mother in exchange of money. This positive, even flattering description is the common way participants in the exchange delude themselves that they have not taken part in a new market dealing in human beings in the quality of sons and daughters. Marvin Harris's (1979) distinction between *emic* and *etic* knowledge is a useful tool for social analysis: emic refers to the subjective truth, while etic is the behavior registered or reconstructed by observers who strive for objectivity (the analogy is with fonemic and fonetic).

world-systems that give them stability, but the way they function leads to crises that induce transitions from one world-system to another. Wallerstein made this consideration with the future evolution of the present world-system (i.e., the capitalist world-economy) in mind. His idea of bifurcation, like many other ideas of world-systems analysis, is also the renewal of Rosa Luxemburg's perspective seeing either socialism or barbarism coming among the destructions of capitalism.

Social laws are not universally valid but only in limited spaces and epochs, that is, within historical structures. Structures are immersed in the flow of history, and population dynamics contribute to the development of the historical trajectories of the world-systems. In each world-system, the new generations will become workers and will represent a source of political power for the social groups to which they belong. However, their size must be proportionate to the resources available to the family and society, according to the production relationships within the system itself, including the environment, technologies and energy sources that are at the society's disposal. In *The Modern World System*, Immanuel Wallerstein (1974, 198) wrote about population as a variable subject to constraints, but also as an object of maximization by power: "Numbers meant strength in war and industry. It also meant people to rule and mouths to feed. The optimal size is far from clear."

The authors who belong to the school of biophysical economics underline the relationship among energy use, GDP and population growth. A perfect correspondence among these values in the predicting sense cannot be found; however, the general idea that the multiplication of economic activity measured by the exchanges of money is based on the expansion of the use of fossil fuels, that is, on the exploitation of *past* solar energy accumulated in the soil, is certainly warranted. This enables the population to grow, detaching more and more people from working the land, as they are substituted by machines, pesticides, herbicides.

Population dynamics are the result of the interaction between world-system requirements and the choices made by its institutions (see further). As seen, population dynamics encompass births, deaths and, locally, migrations. Mortality rates of course cannot be completely determined by the social context and can be an important factor in changing class relationships, as in the so-called Fourteenth Century Crisis after the Black Death: in Western Europe, depopulation plus the outcome of the class struggle under these changed circumstances led to increased wages, while in Eastern Europe, servitude was reintroduced with the Second Serfdom.

The possibility of emigration must be included in the analysis of population dynamics since children as an investment acquire more value in poor circumstances if there are good chances of emigration. Conversely, economic crises can lead to decreases in births, as during the Great Depression that started in 1873 (Andorka 1978). Virginia Abernethy (see Section 3.6) bases her theory of fertility trends on the perception of good or bad times ahead. But procreative dynamics are the result of power conflicts within households and across classes regarding the costs and benefits of procreation and their distribution among individuals. These depend on personal and social power relationships, gender, age and cultural power, which is based on the superiority achieved in power relations in the past (Wallerstein 2004, 121). Biological disparities in physical strength have also played a role.

## 2.2 World-Systems Analysis in Brief

World-systems analysis strives to comprehend history and contemporary facts with their historical roots through a unidisciplinary historical social science. All social science is a study of the past, remarks Immanuel Wallerstein:

> The first step we must make if we wish to understand our world is radically to reject any and all distinction between history and social science, and to recognize that we are a part of a single discipline of study: the study of human societies as they have historically evolved. There are no generalizations that are not historically time-bound, because there are no systems and no structures that are unchanging. (Wallerstein 2000, 107–8)

World-systems analysis rejects the current division of the study of society into disciplines, because the division among history, sociology, economics, political science, anthropology and demography obscure the understanding of social phenomena instead of clarifying them. Phenomena always have economic, cultural, political and legal aspects that must be known and considered together.

Historical social science is unique. The disciplines that liberal ideology has divided, while promoting the theoretical and practical separation between the state, the market and civil society, must be reconnected. For liberalism, instead, the state and the phenomena considered purely political must be the object of the specialized study of political science; the market, which according to liberal theory should be free from the so-called interference by the state, is the realm of economics; civil society and its culture, considered arbitrary, is studied within sociology. This division of intellectual work instead of helping hinders the understanding of social phenomena and leads to the creation of ideologies. For example, the neoclassical analyses that still dominate economics describe a cosmology in the place of reality:

> Cosmologies tend to rationalize the shortcomings of the social order. Among the most obvious shortcomings of the current world order is its inclination to generate abysmal inequalities and ecologically disastrous patterns of consumption and resource use, and yet our mainstream discourse tends to represent these conditions merely as the deplorable but unavoidable side effects of progress. (Hornborg 2016, 3)

Instead, these conditions are intrinsic to the current social organization and to its normal functioning. It is for this reason that capitalism is not sustainable over time and sustainable development, as said, is clearly a contradiction in terms, no matter how often the magic formula is repeated. For Alf Hornborg, exponent of world-systems analysis and director of the Institute of Human Ecology of the University of Lund, ecology and economics (i.e., economic analysis as it should be) study parallel systems, but with one important difference:

> Indeed, both biomass and "technomass" represent positive feedback processes of self-organization, where the system's use of harvested resources is "rewarded" with new resources in a continuing cycle. Both are dissipative structures, requiring inputs higher than outputs and subsisting on the difference. A crucial difference is that biomass is a sustainable process whereas technomass is not. For biomass, energy resources are virtually unlimited, and entropy—in the form of heat—is sent out into space. For technomass, resources are ultimately limited, and we are left with much of the entropy in the form of pollution. For biomass, growth is a morally neutral reward granted by nature itself, whereas for technomass it is a reward resulting from human ideologies and generating unequal, global relations of exchange. (Hornborg 2001, 17)

Hornborg stresses how a correct vision of technology must necessarily include social relationships:

> When the destructive nature of our economic system is emphasized, economists will often reply by expressing with confidence in better technologies, but when technologists are asked why these have not yet been introduced, they tend to refer to faulty economics. These mystifications are founded on a conceptual dichotomy between

> "technology" and "economy," that permits us to shift back and forth between two presumably independent levels of reality, without grasping the techno-economic logic through which they are connected. New, environmentally benign technologies that are more expensive than conventional ones will automatically be the prerogative of a global minority, and thus also a means of generating an unequal distribution of the environmental quality, drawing on resources in the periphery to keep the center clean and "green." (Hornborg 2001, 17)

The unit of analysis of historical social science must therefore be the network of connections for the circulation of basic necessities for daily use (this implies the circulation of people for commerce): this is the definition of a world-system. This circulation is obtained with the appropriation of resources in peripheral parts of the world-system by the core or center (Korzeniewicz 2018). Immanuel Wallerstein began to reason and write in terms of world-systems in the 1970s in contrast to positivism and structural functionalism then dominant in sociology. Now mainstream social disciplines have changed and the search for ahistorical generalizations is no longer common, on the contrary the pursuit of every particularism is. Postmodern philosophy, now intellectually fashionable, theorizes the absolute impossibility of generalizing (Sokal and Bricmont 1999). Subjects and their interpretations of what they experience are given prime importance, however idiosyncratic they might be, while the investigation of reality and any form of quantification is despised (Harvey 1993; Garcia 2016). From the Scylla of the positivist search for the supposed iron laws of history, we moved on to the Charybdis of anti-science, which denies the importance of pursuing objectively valid propositions about social events for the purpose of knowledge, prediction and intervention. The intellectual movement of postmodernism is certainly related to the resumption of the wealthy class's power over the working class after the end of the protests of 1968, because the university did not return to educating only the elite. As Giovanni Dall'Orto (2017) writes, if today the ruling class wants to maintain legitimacy it must deny reality, for example, denying climate change caused by the greenhouse gas emissions inherent in industrialization. New generations are consequently deprived of valid analytical tools to understand society.

The political use of theory, a word of Greek origin which simply means "vision" is underlined by Nancy Folbre:

> Marxist theory aims (with occasional success) to improve the outcome of working-class collective action; feminist theory aims to improve the outcome of women's collective action. Neoclassical economic theory

> discourages such forms of collective action by downplaying their relevance and understating their probability of success. (Folbre 1994, 67)

This is currently done by postmodernism with the aim of fragmenting the subjects. The postmodernist approach even denies the possibility of understanding reality in its general characteristics, as it states that there are only points of view and no objectivity. World-systems analysis instead maintains the aspiration to construct a unified historical social science. On the other hand, if social science renounces what postmodernists label "great narratives," only obscurantism will remain: that of postmodern cultural relativism, in which everything is presumed to be a social construction, and that of religions.

The definition of a world-system in Wallerstein's version is a social structure unified by the circulation within it of food and other commodities essential to daily life: a world-system is held together by the division of labor within it. Historical systems come in three types: minisystems, world-empires and world-economies. World-systems for Wallerstein are only world-economies and world-empires, but for Christopher Chase-Dunn and Thomas Hall (1997) it does not seem justified to create a separate category of minisystems, because they do not view the presence of cities and core-periphery exchanges as essential to the definition of a world-system. Chase-Dunn and Hall have empirically sought to answer the question of whether all world-systems are structured by the relationship between a center, or core, and its periphery: in many cases have found that there wasn't. Chase-Dunn and Hall then define world-systems as belonging to more numerous types than those listed by Wallerstein. A world-system is a network between groups in which some exchanges (trade, information, marriages, even war) are necessary for the reproduction of its constituent units and influence the changes in these units. If world-economies are "held together" by exchanges in food and raw materials that establish their boundaries, other world-systems can be bound by cultural connections and still others by different types of trade, such as that of luxury goods or objects that are necessary to make alliances through marriage (Schneider 1977); other world-systems are defined by war clashes; finally others by the collection of taxes or by plunder, as it is a form of incorporation. Therefore Chase-Dunn and Hall affirm that Africa was incorporated when slaves were sold to Europeans, and not with the development of colonial agriculture, as Wallerstein believed. Charles Tilly's work is a point of reference for these two authors in that it shows the connections created by political structures in Europe's past, such as vassal relations or the collection of taxes. No matter what mechanism is used, if the actions of a political elite have repercussions on a significant portion of the population of another part of the world (e.g., a tenth of the inhabitants, say Chase-Dunn and Hall to operationalize the concept), these groups are connected in a political world-system.

André Gunder Frank was an analyst of the world system in a variant without the hyphen. For Frank, there has been for 5,000 years a single capitalist world system since its origins in antiquity: the formation of the first state in Mesopotamia (Frank and Gills 1993). Claudia von Werlhof attributes to this unique world system the name of patriarchy, a social system characterized by the progress of technology and driven by a misogynist male design to replicate life and replace it with artificial means. This is the illusion that is pushing life on the entire planet to destruction. Nature in patriarchy is considered dead matter entirely available to the alchemists-scientists involved in its presumed improvement. The techniques are considered as neutral or as a result of progress, in a design that has remained unchanged since the times of alchemy:

> The new, alchemical idea of a creation under male control, or even as an independent male "creation," is based on the negation, transformation, destruction, and "replacement" of the female creation, of nature in general, and ultimately of the human being itself. Destruction is becoming the pre-condition of "creation" or "production," and a conscious deterioration the pre-condition for a supposed "improvement"! [...] In the texts and justifications of modern progress, it is argued that all matter/life has to be appropriated, brought to the laboratory, cut into pieces, put together with other materials, and transformed into something supposedly higher, better, and more civilized. (von Werlhof 2012, 175 and 176)

The fundamental idea of patriarchy is that of a male God, creator by pure will and independent of Nature, mothers, goddesses and Earth. It is with this God that the alchemist/scientist identifies himself. For Werlhof, Western modernity is a civilization that seeks to create the utopia of a supposedly better life in a higher form, replacing ever larger parts of Nature with capital, which should improve Nature and replace life itself. The project is the construction of a new artificial world replacing the existing one, an aspiration that—as mentioned—can actually be found in transhumanism and includes research on the artificial womb (as if three-and-a-half billion women were not enough). But the magnum opus of a male creation of matter/life has never been realized nor will it ever materialize due to the complexity of living beings. Werlhof is engaged in the construction of the Critical Theory of Patriarchy:

> The Critical Theory of Patriarchy helps to leave behind the confusion, ideologies, illusions, belief systems, and propaganda about "the West"

> and the Modern World-System. It allows for a completely new insight into the real, long-term character of modern civilization at the very moment of its failure, and it is therefore necessary for all those who want to move forward to real, "deep" alternatives. (von Werlhof 2012, 177)

The basic idea for all the analysts of the world-systems school of thought is, however, that a social unit cannot be considered isolated and studied as such if it has significant exchanges with other social groups, even if it is a separate political unit.

## 2.3 Wallerstein's World-System

Returning to Wallerstein's vision, before the world-systems there were the minisystems, that is, the tribal societies. Being self-sufficient in satisfying their basic needs, they did not maintain significant interactions with other groups, though they may have participated in cultural exchanges, for example, with the circulation of luxury goods or ritual objects. Minisystems operate within limited territories using simple tools, and for Wallerstein they are practically extinct today. The ban on hunting imposed on the various tribes of Bushmen in 1990 in Namibia and in 2014 in Botswana seems to confirm his statement, though there are currently about 30,000 people still living as hunter-gatherers. And contrary to Wallerstein's idea that minisystems must necessarily integrate into the capitalist world-economy at the moment of establishing exchanges with it, there is evidence regarding, for example, the Siane of Papua New Guinea, who bought industrially produced steel axes because they reduced the amount of work necessary for subsistence activities compared to their stone axes, but this innovation did not lead the Siane to change their way of life, rather to enjoy more free time.[4]

World-empires do not have significant exchanges outside their borders, they are self-sufficient. However, they often clash with peoples across their borders in order to expand or defend themselves. The rules and ends of the economy are dictated by political power with an effectiveness that depends on its strength, but which generally manages to block the M-C-M' logic of capitalist expansion. This is the formula with which Marx has epitomized capitalist development: the money-commodity-more money circuit is symbolized as M-C-M', going from money (M) through commodities (C) to a larger amount of money (M'). Hans Christoph Binswanger (2013) called it more properly a spiral, as it implies and necessitates expansion.

4 R. F. Salisbury: *From Stone to Steel*, Melbourne, 1962.

World-economies are systems of states without unified political control. The boundaries of these states are permeable to exchanges of what is necessary to satisfy the basic needs of their populations. Only a world-economy can be capitalist like the present one, meaning that this world-system sets its primary objective in the organization of collective actions to obtain profit from capital investments. The functioning of capitalism means that the satisfaction of an increasing amount of human (social) needs, desires and whims must take place through commodities with the use of money. The expansion of the market, of M-C-M', means the progressive commodification of every thing and every relationship,[5] through a process of unceasing social change pushed by technological innovations that increase profits, and by the continuous creation of socially determined "needs" in order to sell new commodities. This transformation of everything into money recalls the alchemical principle of Werlhof's Critical Theory of Patriarchy.

The private economic initiative comes to a halt when there is little prospect of earnings, as recognized by the liberal economist John Maynard Keynes, an advocate of increasing state spending with budget deficits in order to counteract the stagnation phases of the capitalist cycle.

The pervasiveness of the M-C-M' spiral tends to override any other value or consideration, even the will to power that drives politicians, generals and heads of states. The plurality of states in a world-economy puts them in competition with each other: economic powers can choose to install their business in the political units which are most favorable to them, recently with the establishment of special economic zones (SEZ) designed to attract companies with low taxes and laws that are unfavorable to workers. This is a crucial difference between world-systems in the modern era: in world-empires blocks of new technology and economic activity could be enforced, while in the European world-economy inventors, merchants and adventurers could move their residence under the ruler most tolerant of their activities. Historian Carlo Cipolla reports an emblematic example of this conflicting relationship between economic power and political power in the Elizabethan age. British artillery manufacturers and island rulers thought differently about exporting cannons to the enemies of the kingdom:

5 For an analysis of the current transformation of filiation (and concretely of newborns) into commodities with the manipulation of the relative legal and cognitive categories (what is a mother? what makes a mother legally?), see Danna (2017a, 2017b). On the commodification of all kind of personal relationships in the United States, see Hochschild (2012).

> Foreign demand also became progressively more significant and by 1573, according to Master Hogge, most of the cannons made in England "did not remain in the kingdom." This sparked the apprehension of politicians. The English cannons were, in the words of Sir Walter Raleigh, "a jewel of great value;" the politicians argued about why the British had to put such a "jewel" in the hands of potential enemies. This view was widely shared in political circles, and in 1574, Elizabeth ended up issuing an ordinance that limited the manufacture of cannons in England to those "for exclusive use of the kingdom." From then on, the export of cannons was the subject of constant conflict between artillery manufacturers concerned about selling as many cannons as possible inside and outside, and politicians, no less eager to prohibit their export altogether. (Cipolla 1999, 24–25)

The export of cannons indeed was not totally prohibited, since permits could be obtained to sell them to friendly Protestant powers, from whence the cannons often still took the road to the Catholic states, the enemy of the British.

The current world-system has maintained its characteristics of being a world-economy since its origins in the Long Sixteenth Century, the age of explorations, when it began to expand from Europe to other core states continents. In the 500 years since then, it has never been a world-empire, that is, it has never had and does not have unitary political borders: hegemonic states have never annexed the others. The centers of political power are multiple and the states differ in the amount of power they have, depending upon where they belong: core, semiperiphery and periphery (often colonies). In the core there is a hegemonic power that enjoys the additional profit accumulated from its imperialist relations with other countries, on which it imposes its trade prices. The hegemonic power is the holder of financial, military and productive power, and defends free trade, being able to outcompete foreign firms, who, on the contrary, need protectionism in their countries in order to develop. From the Long Sixteenth Century onward, this role was initially held by Holland, then from the eighteenth century by Britain and currently by the United States since World War II.[6] For Wallerstein, the United States has been experiencing a period of economic decline since the 1970s, which will soon or late have an impact on that country's military power. The parable of the political and economic

6 For other authors such as Braudel, who together with Marx is the main inspirer of Wallerstein, in the seventeenth century the Spain/Genoa pairing was equally, if not more, important than the Dutch United Provinces—the first as a military power and the second as a financial power that supported it economically.

power of the various hegemonic states has always been concluded by phases of financial expansion, such as the current one, for the lack of satisfying profits in the production (Arrighi and Silver 2003).

The concept of hegemony has been criticized by David Wilkinson (2000), who argued that the power of the supposed hegemonic states has never been absolute. In contrast to the idea of a single hegemonic country that Wallerstein derived from Braudel, Christopher Chase-Dunn and Thomas D. Hall showed how in many historical periods there was a situation of polycentrism, for example, during the times of the English and French rival colonial empires. Chase-Dunn and Hall also find expansions and contractions of the systems to be normal. World-systems always pulsate geographically, economically and demographically. Wallerstein, on the contrary, speaks of pulsations only with regard to the capitalist world-economy and its Kondratiev long waves, or K-waves, with expansions and contractions (phase A and phase B) each lasting 50–60 years.

Hegemony can then be redefined as the leading economic position reached with monopolized or semimonopolized production and commercialization processes, permitting spending in the cultural sphere that make the country the leader in architecture, art, philosophy, intellectual life in general. The hegemonic role is therefore not one of absolute power, but of relative force. Productivity is the key to reach hegemonic power: it permits higher remuneration of workers in the core, in response to their struggles. Productivity is nothing else but the multiplication of human labor through machines, powered by sources of energy other than labor power.

The hegemonic role of the Dutch United Provinces, Britain and the United States at the head of the world-economy seems to have been based not only on their capacity to extract resources from the periphery of the world-economy, but also on their possession of large energetic bases—respectively, turf, coal and oil (prevalent from the second half of the twentieth century).

In the seventeenth century, the use of fossil fuels, the intercontinental commercial network and the exploitation of colonies ushered in a *Gouden Eeuw* (Golden Age) for the United Provinces, with the blossoming of arts and intellectual life. In the United Provinces, wood had become extremely scarce by the mid-seventeenth century, and the leading role in energy provision passed to the turf dug up from the Dutch subsoil. In just one century, until the middle eighteenth century, the usable peat diminished drastically, and new techniques to extract it were implemented only another century later (de Zeeuw 1978). With regard to the population, Giovanni Arrighi (1996, 264) reports that in the systemic cycle of accumulation in which the United Provinces were the hegemonic country, they had a demographic increase from 1.2 million inhabitants in 1550 to 1.9 million in 1650, with a subsequent small decrease in the number of inhabitants in the decline stage. Between 1500 and 1650, the Dutch territory increased per capita product, augmenting cultivated areas. Since Dutch merchants controlled the European grain trade, there was no problem feeding the additional population, who migrated from the countryside to the city or those who were employed by rural industry. Indeed, this importation of grain allowed an increase of the variety of crops grown on Dutch soil with the introduction of various fruits and vegetables. The Dutch downward demographic trend in the declining phase was however common to other European states. This diminution of inhabitants did not occur in the cycles of the other hegemonic countries, in which the increase in population was continuous (it was so almost everywhere). The population of Britain more than doubled between the 1801 census (7,750,000 inhabitants) and the 1851 census (15,300,000 inhabitants). It still continues to grow, though with declining rates: from 10–20 percent every decade during the nineteenth century to lesser rates in the twentieth century, with troughs as low as 1.5–2 percent in the 1930s, 1940s and 1990s. Statistics published by the United States show very high rates of population growth in the colonies since Columbus's arrival. In the nineteenth century, rates were still ranging from 21 to 36 percent in a decade. In the twentieth century these rates slowed down, reaching a minimum of 7 percent in the 1930s. Considering the US hegemonic period, population in 1945 was 132 million, 203 million in 1970 and 308 million in 2010. The estimate for 2020 is about 330 million.

In addition to the hegemonic country, in the core or center there is a circle of states in which the production or sale of products is largely based on monopolistic processes. The center-periphery juxtaposition does not actually designate states, but either monopolistic or competitive production processes. This juxtaposition is called by Wallerstein the axial division of work. Very consciously, entrepreneurs shy away from competition in the actual market and try to secure the much greater profits of the oligopolistic and monopolistic regimes (Braudel 1977). Joint-stock companies in the interstate system seek the most favorable conditions for themselves as regards taxation, relations with workers and freedom to pollute due to lack of environmental protection laws. The working class suffers the repercussions of these actions, as they are much less mobile. The monopolistic processes necessarily go hand in hand with the strength of states, because to maintain a monopoly it is necessary to rely on political power, and if the state is weak, production will remain subject to competition, especially from abroad. In this way the center accumulates surplus value,[7] which can be partially distributed to the working class of these

7 The terminology is still Marxian, although world-systems analysis does not need the labor theory of value, nor does it start from the formation of classes (Brenner 1977; see also Denemark and Thomas 1988).

countries. It is the control of money that ensures maximum profits: bankers and other money creators or dealers enjoy the best economic positions.

The periphery is made up of weak states or colonies, in which competitive production processes prevail. These have the characteristic of generating very low profits that practically only remunerate the work of the entrepreneur.

In the last area, the semiperiphery, there are production processes of both types. Italy was in this position for much of its history.

All states try to rise in the hierarchy that goes from the periphery to hegemony, while the hegemonic power strives to maintain supremacy. All hegemonic powers will fall with the passing of time, due largely to the growing military expenses to maintain hegemony, a cost which sooner or later becomes unsustainable.

Starting from the Long Sixteenth Century, the capitalist world-economy has incorporated ever larger areas, enveloping them ever more closely in its network of exchange of goods, migration and cultural transmission. The current world-economy comprises the entire planet. The center currently uses imports from low-labor-cost countries, including textiles, everyday food items (sugar, coffee, tea, wheat, corn, soybeans for animal feed, etc.) and energy that is consumed daily either directly in production or indirectly in the movement of people and goods to distant parts of the planet. The push for the planetary expansion of the European capitalist world-economy has reached the spatial limits of the globe, with the partial exception of the "rogue states" not fully integrated into international trade, while a few others, such as China, maintain significant barriers to the entry of foreign capital and goods. In addition to this expansion with the incorporation of external areas, which in recent times has been called globalization (according to Wallerstein, globalization had already begun with the European expansion of the Long Sixteenth Century), there are other long-term trends in the capitalist world-economy: commodification; proletarianization; increase in the power of states both by extension in a geographical sense and in greater control over the lives of citizens; increase in the size of businesses, which must either grow or disappear; replacement of labor with capital (i.e., with machines) (Hall 2000).

The labor theory of value has never been strictly necessary for world-systems analysis (Brenner 1977; Danna 2019) as it attributes the accumulation of surplus value in the countries of the center to the unequal exchange of goods derived from competitive (peripheral) production processes with goods derived from semimonopolistic (central) production processes.[8] Hornborg,

8 With currencies adjusting their values, a balanced foreign trade can be considered simply as exchanging goods.

too, considers it illusory to seek physical equivalents of value (i.e., price), as this measure is purely social. The contemporary economic theory in which value is determined by the subjective preferences expressed in terms of money, making up the demand curve, is considered valid by the Swedish anthropologist; for him the labor theory of value is surpassed, in the sense of Hegel's notion of *Aufhebung*. The question of whether labor value should be completely discarded as an explanation to the functioning of capitalism is still open. It is indeed energy that enables the so-called growth, that is the multiplication of money exchanges, which have become the basis for the material survival of more and more people (i.e., proletarianization). So the Ukrainian physician Sergei Podolinsky seems to come back in spite of Marx and Engels's dismissal of his theory, which considered energy as the factor on which prices depend (Martinez-Alier 1987). Podolinsky, striving to find physical quantities underlying economic values, considered not only human labor, as did the writers of the Communist Manifesto, but also the labor obtained from other energy sources—though it remains true that Nature receives no payment: money can circulate only among humans.

## 2.4 What Is Technology?

In capitalism new technology is introduced to save on labor costs (thus increasing the number of the unemployed, pushing wages down) or to save on other costs, reducing the number or quantity of inputs or accelerating production processes. Governments have always supported these dynamics, for example, by making certain production techniques and consumption items legal obligations (usually using safety as a justification or excuse) or by using them in the public sector, generally for the benefit of large companies. Certainly, technological innovation also enables us to perform actions that were impossible before. The first use of the steam engine at the beginning of the eighteenth century was to remove water, allowing the extraction of minerals previously unreachable below the water table. Today we know how to fly and even leave Earth's atmosphere going into outer space and coming back. We can build remote information systems and directly modify the genetic code of plants, animals and humans. Apart from these "absolute innovations," and apart from the technology developed in the field of war, in which states pay no attention to cost in producing weapons systems, materials and techniques to manage information and map territories, new technologies are adopted only when they become profitable for the owners of the means of production.

The following two examples are taken from Bowles and Edwards (1993, 222–23).[9] The first concerns the food canning industry in the nineteenth century in California, where there was a single highly specialized task: closing the tin cans to store all types of foods. The skilled workers doing this job managed to earn high wages by threatening to go on strike at the time of the harvest, as the delay in canning would cause the food to rot. James Cox invented a machine that closed the cans, and factory owners bought the machine immediately, even though it did not work very well, in order to threaten the workers: if they went on strike, the machines would take their place. Little by little, Cox's machine was perfected and used in factories, thus saving owners the wages of the specialized workers. Why was the machine cheaper? Because the matter and energy employed in its construction and then its use came from the work of people whose labor time was rewarded in a cheaper way than the specialized workers' time, in an economic calculation comprehensive of the estimated future yield of the machine.

The second example is taken from agro-industry that seeks a monopoly as all industries do. Hybrid wheat developed in the mid-twentieth century did not yield more product than already existing varieties. It just did not produce seeds that farmers could later sow: all hybrids are in fact sterile. The seed production companies adopted these varieties exclusively for this characteristic. In a capitalist system this does not constitute an evil, but is instead necessary to guarantee the profits required for the survival of a company in a competitive market. Evil and antisocial actions are thus necessary to succeed in the capitalist system (Bakan 2004). In capitalism you either earn a profit, largely to be allocated to technological innovation (indeed, the goal of the system can be defined both as a pursuit of profit and as an incessant accumulation of capital) or exit the economic game ending in bankruptcy. The result is that economic power is increasingly centralized and businesses either grow or die, that is, go bankrupt. Bowles and Edwards (1993, 223) underline that inside companies there is no freedom but dictatorship and the entire world-system we live in is a dictatorship of markets (especially financial ones) and transnational companies:

> While the markets once seemed to promise the replacement of command relations and a sort of one-sided relationship with a kind of inequality between the buyer and the seller, they have actually produced a system

9 Their original sources are Martin Brown and Peter Philips: "The Historical Origin of Job Ladders in the U.S. Canning Industry," *Cambridge Journal of Economics*, vol. 10, 1986, 129–45, and Jean-Pierre Berlan and Richard Lewontin: "The Political Economy of Hybrid Corn," *Monthly Review*, vol. 38, n. 3, 1986, 35–47.

> with precise choreography of subordinate leaders and workers, superiors and subordinates. [...] And while capitalism once promised to abolish (feudal) hierarchies and give people the freedom of voluntarily signed contracts, we now find that most people in the capitalist economic system practically spend the whole of their working existence in occupations organized hierarchically.

In industrial society the dynamics that lead to the constant replacement of human labor with machines powered by fossil fuels are not the introduction of innovations that better meet the needs of human beings and alleviate our fatigue. The goal of saving labor is to save on wages for the owners of the production means. The time gained in industrial society by employing machines is, so to speak, beneficial mainly to the unemployed instead of being redistributed by decreasing the working hours of each worker, which is impossible in capitalism because of competition among individuals. This competition was alleviated with the compromise between the capitalistic and the working classes in welfare states, assuring that people losing their jobs were no longer forced to immediately seek new employment, thanks to unemployment benefits and other social policies. This compromise started in the 1930s in Scandinavia to overcome the Great Depression. It diffused since then in various other rich countries, particularly in the 1970s, through labor union struggles and electoral victories of social democratic parties. In the United States, even the Republican president Nixon introduced important welfare measures. Now the welfare state is on its Sunset Boulevard, substituted mostly by workfare measures. It has been defeated by free trade agreements (World Trade Organization, European Union, NAFTA, etc.), which always include the free movement of capital, thereby establishing its supremacy over the working class on a global scale, as capital can move toward taxes, legal conditions and labor laws that benefit it most.

There is a more general critique of the vision of technology as embodied Progress than to point at the political and economic reasons to adopt (or not) innovations. Technology is not just the product of human ingenuity, because inventions can be applied and concretely become usable machines only if they are part of a web of *social* relationships, where the inequality in the rewards for work between the builders and the users of the machines permits their construction and application. As Alf Hornborg (2019, 40) writes,

> Although the notion of "technological progress" since the Industrial Revolution essentially reflects the capacity of human societies to harness fossilized sunlight, this capacity has for two and a half centuries been inextricably linked to global asymmetries in purchasing power, and

> ultimately also implies the capacity to appropriate, by means of the market, the products of photosynthesis from land surfaces in other parts of the world.

The social conditions within the world-system, not those within individual states, permit the adoption of technologies. The world-system is constituted by areas where work is remunerated at very different levels and connects them with transportation that is cheap in terms of both workers employed and energy used.

Many authors also stress the importance of gender relations, observing that technology is rarely introduced into production to save female labor (Ware 1988, 279). In some situations studied by Boserup (1970), the introduction of capitalist production relations initially worsened the position of women because mechanization was applied only to the tasks of males and made more laborious those relegated to females: for example, fertilizers stimulated the growth of weeds, that were eradicated by women. In the course of time, however, the traditional gender-based division of labor changed, benefiting women, too.

Only technology that is economically advantageous is adopted, that is, when it saves money for the owners of the means of production, as well as time for consumers, whose time on the labor market is more worth than the time of the workers. Hornborg (2019, 76 and 173) observes the international conditions that made the development of industry possible:

> The Industrial Revolution in England was made possible by the global flows of embodied labor and land. Industrial technology is an enhancement of the productivity of local labor through the appropriation, by means of asymmetric exchange, of commoditized human time and natural space. […] industrial technology as a local augmentation of labor productivity through net imports of resources from elsewhere. Technologies, in other words, are not just manifestations of scientific discoveries and congealed local labor, but products of asymmetric—and incontrovertibly social—global resource transfers.

Unequal ecological exchange is fundamental to the definition of industrial technology. For English factories to function and return a profit, demand for clothes must come from the whole world, with cheap—or, for some authors, underpaid—raw materials:

> The British shift to steam power was a response to the world market demand for great volumes of inexpensive cotton cloth. Much of this demand came from slave traders in West Africa and slave owners in

**Table 2** The asymmetric exchange of human time and natural space obscured by world market prices of raw cotton and cotton cloth in 1850

| Commodity | Volume for £1,000 in 1850 | Labor time embodied | Land area embodied |
|---|---|---|---|
| Raw cotton | 11.84 tons | 20.874 h | 58.6 ha |
| Cotton cloth | 3.41 tons | 14.233 h | 0.5 ha |

*Source*: Hornborg (2019, 102).

> America, and these very slaves supplied the British cotton textile industry with inexpensive raw material. The steam engine, in other words, was made possible not only by James Watt's engineering, but by the 18th-century world-system in which capital accumulation in Britain was based on African slave labor and depopulated American land. (Hornborg 2016, 17)

The demand for cotton clothes also came from the expanding white population in North America: from 300,000 in 1700 to 6 million in 1800. In 1801, America imported 60 percent of the textile production of Lancashire (Bonneuil and Fressoz 2019, 286). In books celebrating the Industrial Revolution, it is hardly mentioned where the increasing numbers of products were sold. The most lucrative commerce was with sugar, produced by slaves at subsistence cost. Until the beginning of the nineteenth century, more Africans were forced to cross the Atlantic Ocean than Europeans did.

The application of the steam engine was propelled by the establishment of inequitable world trade. Hornborg exposes the basic social inequality at the root of the adoption of technology, which is always local to the center, with an international "time-space appropriation":

> In 1850, a sale of British cotton manufactures on the world market for £1,000, and the purchase of raw cotton for the same amount, would have been tantamount to exchanging 14,233 hours of embodied British labor for 20,874 hours of Afro-American labor, and of less than a hectare of embodied British land for 58.6 hectares of American land. (Hornborg 2019, 102)

Industrial technology thus requires a specific world order:

> Industrial machines *are* social phenomena. These inorganic structures propelled by mineral fuels and substituting for human work *could not be*

> *maintained* but for a specific structure of human exchange. [...] (Thus, to tell the whole story, technological textbooks should always begin with the qualification, "If world market prices can guarantee access to sufficiently cheap forms of exergy, then..."). [...] Industrialization no longer suggests a temporal development progressively emancipating the human species from ecological constraints, but a spatially restricted emancipation that is *illusory* precisely because it is local and dependent on the exploitation of other sectors of global society. (Hornborg 2001, 107; italics in original)

The causation can also be reversed: if some workers can be forced to produce raw materials and energy at low enough prices, then technology will be widely adopted elsewhere, provided that cheap transportation is possible. As Marx observed, new techniques based on machines powered by fossil fuels are introduced in place of human work and other sources of energy in order to increase profit. This occurs not only when the machines enable actions that were previously impossible, but also when their use is economically advantageous or when they increase a nation's military potential. These two logics—increase in wealth or increase in power, both understood as *power over s*omeone and as the *power to do* something—drive the history of stratified societies.

I would add some other considerations to Hornborg's assertion that a new technology is introduced in order to directly save labor. New technologies are also introduced to save on other factors of production—which in Marxian dynamics are always ultimately based on the price of labor. Second, they are always introduced according to the assessments and forecasts of the management and ownership of the corporations. Technological change can be the introduction of new types of machinery, and will be brought about by capitalists whenever a new technology is available *and* whenever they believe that the new production method will increase profits. Nevertheless, as Hornborg writes, time saved on the one hand is time stolen on the other and made invisible by monetary exchanges. If I am able to buy a vacuum cleaner with my money, what I buy is not just an inanimate technological object but also the time of those who manufactured it and those who extracted the materials and energy required for its construction and operation. I save time in cleaning by using the product of other people's work: the time spent by Asian workers in the production line which is worth only a fraction of my labor price—if it were to cost more, there would be no vacuum cleaners. The same thing happens with machines used in production in the place of human labor.

Bowles et al. (2011, 217) define technology as the relationship between inputs and outputs in a working process. Thus, profits can be increased with technology that reduces the materials used, increases the durability of machines, reduces the amount of capital goods used per hour of work, lowering labor costs per unit of production by increasing work efficiency and intensity. Of course, profits can also be increased by paying lower wages. The definition of technology for Alf Hornborg (2019, 95) is very different from the one given by Bowles and Edwards (1993), and from all others' who consider technology as progress embodied and apply some form of technological determinism to human history:

> I restrict the definition to a system of material artifacts that locally augments the capacity of a certain social category in some respect (e.g., by reducing necessary expenditures of human time), while being contingent on the rates at which biophysical resources (including embodied labor) are exchanged on the world market [italics omitted].

Hornborg (2019, 103) does not define technology as a purely material fact because it needs social processes, in particular inequality, to be operative: "machines, like money and commodities, are global social relations of exchange masquerading as things."

A new technology is never introduced in production because it is intrinsically "more advanced" or "better" than the previous methods or just because it saves labor, but it is instead always chosen on the basis of an economic calculation, with a political intent. Historical studies confirm that even in the Industrial Revolution, the timing of the adoption of machines was propelled by the need (political rather than economic) of the owners of the means of production, or capital, to replace hostile and unreliable human labor with obedient machines. Technological innovation is used as a weapon in order to prevail in class struggles.

However, the Swedish anthropologist does not start from orthodox Marxism, but from world-systems analysis, that, as we have seen, uses the category of unequal exchange. For Hornborg (2001, 2019), the unequal exchange in a world-system, be it a capitalist or a pre-capitalist system, should not be measured in terms of value of any kind, but of physical quantities (and qualities) of matter and energy exchanged between different areas. These quantities can be uniformed in terms of calculating their ecological footprint, that is, the extent of the territory needed to produce or renew each of them.[10]

10 The extension of economics to the analysis of the physical quantities in the production system has been developed by the research group on Material Flow Analysis founded and coordinated by Marina Fischer-Kowalski at the University of Vienna, as well as by the World Resource Institute.

Swedish iron was imported by Britain in the 1760s to build machines, yearly representing around a million hectares of forest and almost 14,000 person-year equivalents of Swedish labor. Hornborg (2019, 125) comments: "Not only are the asymmetric flows of material resources culturally invisible, but concomitantly also the operation of modern technology as an apparatus for orchestrating such flows." Both Marxists and ecological economists instead consider the use of technology as being independent of social inequalities.

The ideological interpretation of history as the development of the forces of progress involving technological innovations is labeled by Hornborg as "technofetishism":

> modern technology is perceived as independent of the global resource flows that sustain it, which ultimately means that it is perceived as independent of the world economy [….] However, the illusion that technological progress is propelled primarily by ingenuity tends to persist, independent of prevailing exchange rates in the world market. This illusion […] can be referred to as technofetishism. (Hornborg 2016, 7)

Marxism is not immune from technofetishism because, in the Marxist vision, technology, like population, is limited by the relations of production of capitalist societies, whereas in the socialist future without class division technological progress will be able to unfold its power by making everyone's life better: the USSR lived in this illusion. Technology is thus considered to be independent of relations of production, and the promise of Marxism is precisely what also liberalism proposes: the advent of a cornucopian society freed from material constraints thanks to rationality and human ingenuity, no longer constrained by the logic of capital. The difference with liberalism lies in the fact that for the free-market thinkers, on the contrary, only competition in the markets can spur ingenuity and innovation.

A weak point of Hornborg's theory of technology is the fact that in oil extraction high-tech, low-labor-intensive techniques are used. This is not casual: the choice of developing infrastructures and machines fueled by oil instead of coal has been on one hand a political one, precisely in order to avoid employing numerous workers, and on the other hand a technical one, as oil power is more concentrated than that of coal (see the historical research summarized in Bonneuil and Fressoz (2019)). So there remains a doubt that the relationship between technology and inequality is only a part of the story, while a more decisive role in structuring society should be attributed simply to the availability of energy, spurred by inequality but led on paths determined by the results of class struggle, with its political and economical aspects.

## 2.5 Other Modes of Production in Capitalism

What is the relationship between the concepts of "world-system" and "mode of production"? Both concepts focus on the material aspects of social life and, according to Wallerstein (1978, 1988), they are identical. In this book I have used and will use "mode of production" closer to the Marxian concept denoting a system of social relationships and of organization of production. Marx considers the mode of production as the basis of society's organization: this is his materialism, looking first at what is indispensable to socially organized life for everybody's survival, whereas ideologies (religions and philosophies) are consequent superstructures that serve to justify what is necessary for the maintenance of life and established order. These ideologies are dismantled by his scientific analysis examining facts and reality, revealing how the capitalist production mode really functions.

Wallerstein showed how capitalism feeds on modes of production that differ from those of the proletarian industrial system, such as slavery (see also Moulier-Boutang 2002). Steven Bunker applied the concept of "mode of extraction" to the workforce to designate slave trafficking. Generally speaking, immigration of any kind is appropriation of the workforce by the receiving nation, which has not incurred the costs of reproduction and training. Slavery provided the workforce for the cotton, tea and sugarcane plantations that were indispensable for industrial production (as raw materials) and for the workforce management and energy: sugar gives cheap calories and coffee and tea sustain industrial workers in the inhuman factory rhythms.

Within the world-economy there is and has always been another radically different mode of production that is not based on money. This concerns the sphere of subsistence, the gratuitousness of which is vital to the realization of profit. Much of the work for social reproduction (the term with which Marxists designate the day-to-day re-creation of the workforce with food and rest, plus procreation and childcare[11]) is free labor, which contributes to profit because it lowers the monetary costs of the workforce for the capitalists. This is the paradox of capital. The organization of the economy based on the pursuit of profits can be profitable for the owners of the means of production only if there are economic sectors outside the monetary circuit such as free domestic work (done mostly by women) and subsistence production. In urban areas, this sphere of profitability consists mainly of transforming raw materials into what

---

11 But procreation is scarcely examined, even by political economists who purport to do it: in Bakker and Silvey (2008), perinatal death is said to be the main cause of death for women on the global scale, while in 2017 only 295,000 women died of maternal causes worldwide.

is suitable for satisfying needs, such as foods that become meals, self-produced goods and tools for the home and domestic work, including all the caregiving that is necessary to ensure the growth of new generations. As discussed earlier, this means not only pregnancy and childbirth but also the work of caring for children. If the household has access to land, in addition to everything already listed, it can also produce food and other plant or animal products for its sustenance. Those living in a household with these resources can thus accept low-paying jobs as they do not need to satisfy all their needs with market exchanges. Logically, the social reproduction of the labor force becomes more expensive for the owners of the means of production if the households are proletarian rather than semiproletarian. According to Wallerstein's definition, a semiproletarian household is one that self-sufficiently produces the equivalent of more than its monetary income, thanks to subsistence production or having sources of income other than paid work (small businesses, subleases, pensions, other transfers or annuities), even though the quantification is problematic. It is clear that what we do in subsistence production cannot be precisely measured by money at market prices, as there is no need to pay for it.

This recognition of the importance of work that orthodox Marxists generally call "unproductive," since it is not performed for a capitalist who would then realize its surplus value by selling the product, integrates world-systems analysis with feminist theory. Since the 1970s, feminists have considered unpaid domestic work as one source of profit (Dalla Costa and James 1972; Mies 1999; Federici 2014). The feminist movement criticizes men who, for private reasons even before political ones, considered the free work of their wives or female companions "unproductive" while benefitting from it. With a case study in Narsapuram, an Indian lace-producing town, sociologist Maria Mies (1999) demonstrated how the social devaluation of women's work (even if it is for the market) is functional to profit. The lace produced by the women was sold by their husbands who appropriated all the gains. The women were unpaid because their work was deemed valueless and considered simply a pastime.

For Wallerstein, the long-term trend toward proletarianization, far from representing the full realization of capitalism, is one reason for its crisis. In particular, the proletarianization of women exerts pressure on wages which must rise to meet an increasing proportion of needs, including the needs previously met by the unpaid work of wives and mothers. This makes the capital–labor clash more severe and pushes capital to migrate to the areas of the globe that have not been proletarianized, which are shrinking and will soon disappear. The latest globalization wave has now put nearly all the workforce around the world in competition, as noted by Richard Freeman (2005), who drew attention to the doubling of the workforce with China's entry into the

World Trade Organization in 2001. In fact the same happened when India opened its borders to the free market in the early 1990s. But there cannot be similar events anymore.

With the expansion of proletarianization, however, both the work of the housewife and the products she once made, ranging from meals to preserves, from clothes to consumer goods such as candles and soaps, from cleaning to caregiving, have all become commodities that companies turn out. What she produced is now available on the market at ever-lower prices, especially considering the fact that women's work has acquired a direct market value, and women's employment continues to rise, as does the money at women's disposal.

The proletarianization process undermines the foundations of the M-C-M' spiral, which is the progressive monetization of the satisfaction of needs. Proletarian workers who no longer enjoy a subsistence base have to request higher wages than the semiproletarian ones who still have this base, thereby eroding the profit margin. They would otherwise be driven to resort to illegal economic activities (and often they are). Proletarianization is not a sign of an efficient capitalist system—of course according to its criteria. What corporations seek when they move to poorer countries are semiproletarians, and their subsistence economy explains why work is cheaper there.

Will the drop in labor costs taking place in core countries today offset the rise in labor costs in the southern hemisphere, causing an oscillating movement of capital? For Wallerstein it will not. There is no going back, because the working class in the proletarianization process has become increasingly educated, organized and aware of its needs. A return to being semiproletarian is nevertheless apparent in Italy today, as the younger generation accepts low (or even no) wages, because they are able to rely on contributions to their subsistence such as being able to live in their parents' home and use the incomes or pensions of the older generation, thanks to the redistribution of various incomes that occurs within a household. The long-term trend toward proletarianization not only seems to have slowed down but also have actually been reversed by the absolute growth of the rural population in the periphery and semiperiphery countries. Urban population, on the other hand, continues to grow in relative terms, and today more than half of the inhabitants of the globe live in cities, reflecting the progressive mechanization of agriculture.

## 2.6 World-Systems and Population

To redirect population research with the categories proposed by world-systems analysis, I provide the following list of questions, some of which are pertinent on the microhistorical level, and others on the macrohistorical one. To take into account population's role in historical systems (i.e., in minisystems and in the two types of world-systems: world-empires and world-economies), the main questions in macrohistorical terms are as follows:

1. Are there specific imperatives concerning human procreation—in a given world-system or in a minisystem—that make it congruent with its historical structures? If so, what are they?
2. Are these imperatives the same for each of the three types of historical systems?
3. How are the requirements of a particular historical system transmitted to the microhistorical level at which procreation decisions are made?

It is then necessary to answer a series of questions also at the microhistorical level:

4. Why do people have children? What is their culturally determined role in the household and in society?
5. Who makes procreation decisions, that is, who is (are) the subject(s) of procreation?
6. How is the number of children decided by the subject(s) of procreation?

On the macrohistorical level, the fundamental question is whether there is an absolute tendency toward biological expansion or whether procreation is subject to self-regulation mechanisms depending on the social structure and the modes of production. In reality, both dynamics can play a role, and this does not depend on the type of historical system. There are historical systems that aim for expansion, and others that pursue stability, that is, homeostasis, which is a possibility even demographers take into account: Chris Wilson and Pauline Airey (1999) dedicated an article to the review of theories and empirical evidence on the homeostasis of ancient populations, which they called "pre-demographic transition." Albeit with great caution, they proposed homeostasis as the basis for an alternative paradigm to that of demographic transition (described in Chapter 4) (see also Hirschman 1994).

Keeping the population stable is indeed important in circumscribed situations. In Robert Carneiro's terminology (1970) this indicates a social and/or environmental circumscription, or closure: the existence of physical or social barriers to settling elsewhere. If emigration is prevented, stability of the population must inevitably be pursued. Thomas Malthus was aware of the possibility of self-regulation (see Chapter 3), and Alexander Carr-Saunders theorized in 1922 that human populations tend to limit themselves by means of cultural prescriptions to avoid unbridled and disastrous growth and achieve *optimum* balance in relation to available resources. Among these cultural prescriptions, he listed infanticide (more or less voluntary), taboos on coitus, prolonged breastfeeding and abortion.[12] Carr-Saunders believed that these practices already existed in prehistory and developed as soon as hominids reached brain mass adequate to understand the intertwining of population and resources. However, many animals act according to similar mechanisms without awareness or intention. In an appendix to *The Population Problem* (1922, 483–85), Carr-Saunders made a complete list with references to sources on 200 primitive societies that limited their population. In the 1970s, Wilkinson declared this list widely extendable using subsequent anthropological works.

Population stability seems to have been a characteristic of many minisystems, of the Middle Ages in Europe after the plague epidemics, of island populations (see Chapter 7) and of many more social systems. In minisystems based on gathering and hunting and nomadic life, infants must be transported and this is not possible if there is more than one per adult. Births, therefore, have to be suspended until the youngest child is walking independently.

If the balance with the environment is likely to break with the increase in population, the solution is the migration of the excess population to a different area, which is how the human species spread throughout the planet from Africa, where we originated. A model of geographical diffusion according to the demographic behavior of small populations equipped with simple technologies has been created by the researchers of Christopher Chase-Dunn's group at the Institute for Research on World-Systems (IROWS) at the University of California, Riverside (Fletcher et al. 2011).

As the economist Ester Boserup ([1965] 2005, 1970) has shown, population growth can also trigger a change in techniques for feeding the increased numbers, such as using greater amounts of human labor. She found that population growth leads first to an intensification of the workload, especially in agriculture, because a greater social product must be obtained for new generations and this pushes the adoption of new techniques. Boserup referred to what had happened in Africa and Asia when the techniques of the Green Revolution were introduced, and then extended her reasoning to the historical

---

12 The Caldwell demographers, father and son, launched themselves against the thesis of infanticide as a normal population regulator in many human groups. Caldwell and Caldwell's (2003) thesis is that the knowledge and implementation of fertility control systems by hunter-gatherer populations is an exaggeration resulting from few and vague statements by contemporary scholars and reinforced by an intense work of mutual citation. They consider the knowledge on the power of herbs negligible (but Linnaeus already classified parsley and juniper as an abortifacients). However, the testimonies on this practice remain innumerable; see, for example, the reconstruction of population dynamics in the village of Nakahara in eighteenth-century Japan by Eng and Smith (1976).

steps that changed production technologies: from hunting and gathering to horticulture and then to agriculture (Boserup 1981).

World-empires are subject to the same alternative as minisystems with the choice of homeostasis or migration/expansion, depending on the natural and human environment beyond their borders. Some classes aim at procreative stability, such as sharecroppers, small peasant owners and often tenants: fertility is contained so that the succession of the cultivation of the land is assured without exceeding the number of mouths that it can feed. For example, over the past centuries in the countryside regions of Portugal, the total fertility rate differed according to different inheritance laws (Livi Bacci 1971, 51). On the contrary, the issue of inheritance and land subdivision is absent where land is not privately owned.

As mentioned, if there is an excess of population with respect to the resources gathered by the techniques in use given the relationships of production, innovation could be stimulated to increase the productivity of the land. However, in world-empires the ruling classes are generally wary of new technologies (including those that can ease population pressure) for fear that existing social relationships will be subverted. For example, in 1436 the Chinese Empire decided to ban the further construction of large deep-sea vessels that could have been able to reach the New World and allow its exploration. The decision was taken after Admiral Cheng Ho made expeditions that in 1405–33 reached Zanzibar with hundreds of such warships and tens of thousands of men. Although Paul Kennedy (2006, 40–41) believes that one of the reasons for the ban was contingent on the renewed commitment on the anti-Mongolian front that absorbed all the energies of the Empire, the policy of closure to innovation in the field of navigation was maintained even after the end of this emergency. William McNeill attributes this in part to internal struggles in the bureaucracy, in part to a need for investments in defense and in part to the achievement of grain self-sufficiency, thanks to the better distribution of crops realized with the construction of the Grand Canal between the Blue River and the Yellow River, navigable year round (1982, 44).

Similar events of renunciation of new technologies are found in Japanese history. In 1636, during the Tokugawa era, the construction of ocean vessels for navigation on the high seas was also prohibited. Japan tried to keep trade with Europeans and their products under strict control and succeeded in doing so until 1853. At this time the arrival of the black ships of the American commodore Perry in front of Tokyo Bay imposed trade on the Japanese Empire, using the threat of cannons to obtain access. The country was thus incorporated into the capitalist world-economy.

These events clearly indicate the importance of the particular culture and interests of the ruling classes in choosing a homeostatic or expansionist direction. An example of decisive cultural differences is the fact that "as far as we know, the Chinese never plundered and killed—unlike the Portuguese, the Dutch and other European invaders of the Indian Ocean" (Kennedy 2006, 39). Indeed, the satellite states of the Chinese Empire were recipients of gifts and not a source of taxes.

Population expansion can bring benefits to those who dominate a world-empire. It is known that the Chinese and Roman empires were ideologically in favor of the creation of new family units. In some Greek city-states and also Rome in 131 BC, there were proposals to make marriage mandatory, with the specific purpose of founding the procreative unit—which is the social meaning of marriage. According to Marvin Harris and Eric Ross (1987), the ancient states such as India before the period of dynasties, dynastic China, the states of Southeast Asia and those of Central America and Peru were strongly pronatalist because they were constituted through conquests, and the warrior caste was maintained by the work of the lower social strata. The increasing number of available peasants and other workers could increase the surplus available to warriors if there was new land on which the additional population could settle or if a greater productivity of the fields could be obtained with the contribution of more labor.

The world-economy, wherein the fundamental push for social action has always been the incessant accumulation of capital, welcomed demographic expansion both in the center and in the periphery[13] starting with the lucid theorization of the need for a continuously increasing population in the mercantilist states of the sixteenth century. For example, in the case of Denmark, clear evidence of this ideology can be found in the *Danmark-Norges Oeconomiske Magazin* (Economic review of Denmark-Norway), which was published in the years 1757–64: "A state has no power except for its population and wealth. The bigger they are, the bigger its power."[14] Furthermore,

> There is nothing that can make a state powerful, if not the number of its population, even if a state like ours is endowed with the wisest laws that show everyone their duties and keep them within their limits. Furthermore, nothing can make a state more fragile than a modest number of inhabitants.

---

13 Demographic policies became anti-natalist in the periphery only after the war, upon the push of the center with its geopolitical worries about future unfavorable population balances.

14 Quoted in Danna (1991).

It is to this ideology that we owe the early collection of demographic data in the Kingdom of Denmark: a royal letter dated May 20, 1645 (strengthened by a second letter the following year), ordered all parish priests to keep a register of births and deaths. In the majority of cases, however, this requirement was interpreted instead as a need to record baptisms and burials, and it took decades for proper population registers to become widely diffuse.

Before the establishment of the capitalist world-economy, the picture was different:

> During the Middle Ages, as Christian Europe devolved into feudalism, rulers seldom worried about births except within their own families; attention to demography as a policy issue practically vanished. The most interesting writers on population and power were Muslim and Chinese (for example, Ibn Khaldun and Ma Duanlin) who lived in regions where empires still thrived. [...] The era lasting from roughly 1450 to 1750 in Europe thus showcased an unparalleled obsession about the connection between demography and geopolitics. And most of it consisted of a one-sided advocacy of populationism—a virtuous circle of higher birthrates, more employment, more income, more taxes, more public works, attractive opportunities for immigrants, and exploitative opportunities for emigrants. (Jackson and Howe 2008, 17–18)

Marx believed that each mode of production has its own historical laws concerning population dynamics, so that in capitalism,

> If accumulation is to be a steady and continuous process, then this absolute growth in population—although it may be decreasing in relation to the capital employed—is a necessary condition. *An increasing population* appears to be the basis of accumulation as a continuous process.[15]

Marx added that all the above remains valid on the condition that the paid wages can allow this growth, so that the additional population would have the possibility to purchase the goods necessary for its own livelihood. Of course, an implicit condition is that these commodities exist, that these goods can be produced. As biophysical economics teaches us, surplus energy must be present in order to obtain an increase in production.

15 *Theories of Surplus Value*, Marx 1861–63, [chapter 17] Ricardo's Theory of Accumulation and a Critique of it. (The Very Nature of Capital Leads to Crises) (https://www.marxists.org/archive/marx/works/1863/theories-surplus-value/ch17.htm). Italics in original.

The tendency of the capitalist system is clearly toward population expansion, though only since the eighteenth century the global population has in fact grown exponentially. Homeostatic mechanisms came about only later and as unintended consequences of the long-term proletarianization of women and the compulsory education of children, as will be discussed later. The imperative of the capitalist population growth system is translated into incentives that influence the choices of the subjects of procreation. Among the cultural means of influence, the most important for the capitalist world-economy is the reproductive imperative of Christianity (only in marriage) and the compulsory heterosexuality associated with it. These were made law by the states and imposed on the colonies where the population was not already regimented in other religions with a high degree of hierarchical organization. From the core areas to the periphery, procreation is still defined as a public issue, with restrictions on contraception and abortion that remain in many states and policies (albeit not very effective) encouraging births in core countries (Handwerker 1990; Hartmann 1995).

## 2.7 Institutions of the World-Economy and Population

In the capitalist world-economy the institutions are states, the interstate system, markets, firms, classes, status/identity groups and households. The structure of the contemporary capitalist world-economy consists of the relationships between its different areas (namely, the core or center, the semiperiphery and the periphery) and of the interactions between its various institutions. What are these various institutions' stakes in procreation and how do they try to influence the subjects of procreation?[16]

States, like world-empires, have a strong interest in both population growth and in the political stability which population growth can undermine. Just like the world-empires of the past, modern states of the capitalist world-economy (rivals in the interstate system) thrive when they have a large population from which they can extract labor, taxes and military force. The king Frederick II of Prussia made it mandatory for widowers to remarry. Elsewhere in the German

16 This research has not been on the agenda of world-systems analysts. Joan Smith and Immanuel Wallerstein (1992) coordinated a historical analysis of households belonging to different classes and regions of the world-system. Their research highlighted the strategic ways of using paid and unpaid labor (including that of children) and the adaptation of household composition to the various phases of the world-economy. However, the authors never specified if and how such an adaptation involved procreative choices.

states marriage was forbidden for those who could not maintain their family, as in Bavaria and Württenberg. The Prussian king wrote to Voltaire:

> The number of men makes the wealth of the states [...] I consider [men] to be the same as a herd of deer in the park of a great lord: their only task is to populate and fill it.[17]

Since the mid-fifteenth century, at the beginning of the capitalist world-economy, states encouraged population growth under the influence of mercantilism. Nation-states did the same starting from Napoleon's organization of the army, which was massively enlarged by the draft. The Church, starting with the message of Genesis "be fruitful and multiply," espoused above all by Saint Augustine in the fifth to the sixth centuries, pursued and persecuted those who sought to obstruct births. Silvia Federici and Leopoldina Fortunati (1984; Federici 2004) consider the witch-hunts as an attack of the nascent bourgeoisie becoming pronatalist (but also of the other ruling classes: aristocracy and clergy) on the ancient knowledge of women regarding birth control. Elderly women were persecuted since they were the custodians of knowledge on how to regulate births and deaths. This knowledge had to be suppressed to achieve the economic, political and religious goals of increasing the population. Regarding the Council of Trent, which in the early sixteenth century established Catholic orthodoxy in contrast with Protestantism, Michela Zucca (2010, 155) wrote:

> The change and destruction of a horizon of values and a popular and peasant culture that had persisted for millennia was marked with the prohibition of parties and Carnival, and with the emphasis on sexual sin, the delimitation of marriage as the only area of possible love, and procreation as the only legitimate result of sexuality (and the definitive prohibition of any type of divorce).

Political authorities anyway tried to encourage procreation, including through economic incentives. In France, for example, the Edict of Colbert of 1666 granted a pension to fathers of 12 living children, whereas those who reached 10 children, as well as young people who married below 25 years of age, were exempted from the payment of the *taille*. Unmarried men, on the other hand, had to pay extra taxes from the age of 20 onward.

At the same time, states generally restricted, or at least did not encourage, the growth of the "inner enemy," the racialized members of the working class who were descendants of slaves or immigrants. This was practiced in

17 Quoted in Reinhard et al. (1971, 325).

the United States in the 1960s and 1970s (Littlewood 1977). States started to assume a part of the costs of reproduction and procreation because of the need for healthy men to draft into the army for defense or to fulfill ambitions of military conquest. However, welfare measures were rooted in the class struggles of the post–World War II economic boom of *Le Trentes Glorieuses*—the Glorious Thirties from 1945 to 1975. Workers won public support for social reproduction in the form of services for children and education organized by the state. The socialization of the social costs of reproduction then lost ground due to neoliberal policies that pushed for the privatization of all that was once included in public services. This privatization is ongoing, though welfare provisions are sometimes substituted by cash transfers (Teeple 1995, Harvey 2007). While the core states with low birth rates introduced incentives (monetary or in the form of services) to encourage procreation, population control policies were adopted by periphery nations mainly in response to economic incentives from core countries. This conformed to the rationale that per capita income would increase if the population remained constant or decreased, as suggested by Coale and Hoover (1958) and popularized by Ehrlich (1968). This is a fallacious deduction because each quantity calculated per capita is a synthesis that hides individual variability, mathematically manipulated specifically to obtain the per capita value. It follows that this value cannot retroactively affect the whole that determined it.

As for the other institutions of the capitalist world-economy, corporations (be they monopolistic or competitive) can reap profit from a large population both as workers and as consumers (if they have cash or credit), benefitting from high unemployment, which is the "relative surplus population" that reduces the cost of labor as analyzed by Marx (see Section 3.3). While corporations benefit from the lower wages associated with crowded labor markets, they refuse to make any contribution to the costs of social reproduction if they are not forced to do so by law. In their hiring policies, they usually discriminate against women because they are or could become mothers. Some states, driven by the struggles of male and female workers to extend citizenship rights, have forced corporations to bear part of the costs of procreation, for example, by protecting women from discriminatory layoffs. In Italy, protection had been obtained by enforcing the registration of layoffs on a progressively numbered register in order to avoid the (illegal) practice of forcing women, as soon as they are hired, to sign a resignation letter without a date—a measure introduced by the second Prodi government and immediately repealed by the fourth Berlusconi government. Few corporations offer childcare or other types of support for employed parents, and when they do, it is in response to tax incentives or with the aim to retain skilled workers by offering them benefits.

Cooperation and internal cohesion prevail in egalitarian minisystems, while in stratified societies—both world-empires and world-economies—status or identity groups based on nation, race, ethnic group, religion, sex and sexual orientation—benefit from their own multiplication, as they gain political power over opposing groups. Dorothy Stein so reflected on the reasons for the imperative "be fruitful and multiply" common to the peoples of the Book (those who consider the Bible sacred), Confucianism and many other doctrines and religions:

> Each religious movement is also a political movement, and given that births are the main form of religious recruitment, it is not surprising that the ruling wings of world religions, those whose concerns cover the tiniest details of human behavior, come together in encouraging the number of families with both social and doctrinal means. (Stein 1995, 34)

Status or identity groups also try to put limits on other groups that are antagonistic to them, in order to obtain the political power given by an organized mass—as those who are not organized rarely acquire power. All of this is also true for the sexes. In patriarchal history, there was often a preference for male children, which also translated into "excessive" female mortality. The phenomenon of missing daughters is not a contemporary Asian anomaly which arose in republican China as a consequence of the one-child policy issued in 1979 (and canceled in 2013 without raising the birth rate very much) and in many parts of India to avoid dowry expenses for the weddings of daughters. The practice is part of the ancient customs of these and many other peoples, justified by beliefs of various kinds. Selection by sex occurs with the differentiated feeding of boys and girls from birth. It is often believed that breast milk is not good for daughters, who are then weaned early placing them at greater risk of malnutrition and undernutrition, with potentially fatal health consequences. Selective female infanticide was the choice of many male-dominated families and societies. Harris and Ross (1987) considered it one of the factors that controlled the population, whether consciously or unconsciously, because to stop population growth limiting females is more effective than limiting males. Harris and Ross also hypothesized that misogyny derives from this method to control the population, with the simplified association between a positive vision of women and population growth, on the one hand, and a negative vision of fertility and its bearers, on the other. Also homosexuality is tolerated and sometimes even institutionalized as a rite of passage toward adulthood because it helps to control population growth; otherwise it is not only discouraged but repressed and persecuted.

The prevalence of males in the population existed also in Europe: from the mid-thirteenth century until the Black Death in England there were four men for every three women. The imbalance disappeared after the plague, which killed more men than women, but the disproportion was subsequently restored.[18] As for Sweden, the medical historian Sheila Johansson[19] believed that the evident disproportion between the sexes at the beginning of industrialization was due to the relative value of male and female labor. While in agriculture the work of the two sexes had equal value, with the expansion of markets, urbanization and industrialization, male children were preferred because their work had become more profitable. Excessive female mortality was also evident in colonial America. Indentured child labor was common on farms: children were indentured to pay off family debts or in exchange for a sum of money. This was an obvious incentive to prefer male children since the proportion sent to work was 10 boys to 1 girl. "Excess" female mortality disappeared in the nineteenth century, when for the first time the labor demand in cities was predominantly for females. In general, not only in North America, cities of the 19th century were inhabited mostly by women (de Vries 1984). Compulsory education also canceled the social advantages of having male children, because they could no longer be earmarked for paid work outside the home.

Population dynamics are also the result of power relations between the sexes. Procreation biologically costs nothing for males, although it could bring disadvantages such as sharing the domestic unit and the wife's attention with a new family member (Federici et al. 1988). There may also be socially established disadvantages such as the taboo on sexual relations during lactation.

In our society the social exemption for fathers from the work of raising children has long endured. The many letters Marie Stopes received from women requesting help to stop pregnancies show the women's dissatisfaction at the beginning of the twentieth century, aptly called "the women's century":

> I am busy here for ten people and I never leave the house [...] yet he can hang his jacket and hat and then leave when he likes. So a house full of

---

18 See Josiah Cox Russell, *British Medieval Population*, Albuquerque: New Mexico, 1948, 149, quoted by Wilkinson (1978, 73).

19 Sheila Ryan Johansson, "Deferred Infanticide: Excess Female Mortality during Childhood," in Glenn Hausfater and Sarah Blaffer Hrdy (eds), *Infanticide: Comparative and Evolutionary Perspectives*, New York: Aldine, 1984, 463–85, quoted by Harris and Ross (1987).

> children makes no difference to him [...] who then takes on the hassle and effort if not the woman for the sake of her children?[20]

Today, the lower birth rate of Southern European countries compared to those of Northern Europe is attributed to men's refusal to share domestic work, which is culturally absent from the male gender role, and performed by women as part of the female one.

Putting aside psychological factors such as the joy of having a son or daughter, and her or his reciprocated love, from a material point of view, the subjects of procreation in the household encounter the dilemma expressed by Wallerstein (Section 2.1). On the one hand, an additional child increases the political power of the household;[21] on the other hand, it requires a commitment in terms of time and work as well as resources, even if the additional child can constitute a medium-term "investment" in societies where lower-class children are put to work at a tender age.

Indeed, the social and economic role of children differs in the various classes, but demographers generally disregard class analysis, believing that "Children work because people make children, rather than the reverse, that people make children because children work."[22] This interpretation defends the naturalization of procreation, without explaining what is undoubtedly a cultural fact: children can become a resource to be used, but children's work must be allowed by customs and labor laws (where they exist). In one of his important works, *Determinants of Fertility in Advanced Societies* (1978), Rudolf Andorka shows the irrelevance of psychology in accounting for the differences in birth rates between social groups (explained for him by culture).

Due to the growing complexity of machines and, above all, to the growing complexity of the administration of corporations and states, workers must now have more education than was formerly required. Education prolongs the period of apprenticeship to enter the productive world and prevents proletarian households from employing their children in factories at an early age.

The general pronatalist climate of speeches and actions of politicians, above all, in the countries of the center, particularly those with lower birth

---

20 Letter to Maria Stopes quoted by Seccombe (1993, 362) and published in *Mother England. A Contemporary History*, edited by Maria Stopes, London, Bale and Danielson, 1930, 144–45 (2nd ed.).

21 Although often the advantage is only with the birth of a boy, especially where the social rule requiring the payment of a dowry by the bride's family is in force.

22 Dyson, Tim, "Child Labor and Fertility: An Overview, an Assessment and an Alternative Framework," in Ramesh Kanbargi (ed.), *Child Labor in the Indian Sub-Continent: Dimensions and Implications*, London, Sage 1991, 81—quoted by Wilson and Airey (1999, 126).

rates, stems from the competition between states in the interstate system. The debates about pensions is shaped by neoliberalism, seeing the reduction in birth rates as a cause for concern. As Giovanni Mazzetti wrote (2013, 164n14): "contemporary professors argue that pensions should be taken out to return to generating many children, and consider procreation as a modern form of investment superior to others."[23]

The pronatalist message is still present today in the teachings of the great religions, supporting the capitalist imperative of unlimited population growth. But the Christian Church has not always been pronatalist: in its early stages it spread the conviction that the world was full and one had only to wait for the Messiah, without sinning nor procreating. It was when Christianity became the official religion of the Roman Empire, whose declining population worried the authorities, that it took on a decidedly pronatalist position.

Wallerstein (1998) predicted a final crisis of the world-economy and its transition to another system because of the exhaustion of its long-term asymptotic trends: the depletion of low-cost labor due to the shrinking numbers of semiproletarian families; the continuous improvement of the political organization of the working class, also increasing labor costs; the increase in taxes for businesses due to growing public expenses for infrastructures, welfare, environmental protection; and finally the reaching of environmental limits, with growing costs of renewable and nonrenewable materials and energy, and an intensification of peoples' struggles for health and against the externalizations of corporations that pollute the environment. Another asymptotic trend could be added in terms of population dynamics: the exhaustion of the continuous growth that characterized the last two–three centuries. On the next descending arc of the population parable, which is set in a non-remote future (see Section 1.5), one of the conditions for capital accumulation—the growth of the labor force—will no longer be satisfied. As the Marxian analysis foresaw, the system could compensate with the extension of working hours or with an increase in the retirement age (or with the abolition of pensions *tout court*, which, as seen, had already been theorized as a remedy for raising the birth rate). However, there is no guarantee that the expansion of the labor force necessary for the accumulation and growth of capital can be restored. On the side of consumption (necessary to keep the M-C-M' spiral going), a contraction because of the less numerous new generations is foreseeable—all

23 The reference is to Vincenzo Galasso, Roberta Gatti and Paola Profeta, *Investing for the Old Age: Pensions, Children and Savings*, paper presented in Milan, August 30, 2008. See also Paul Demeny (1987), linking pensions to reproductive behavior.

other things being equal. The end of "population accumulation" will also make the capital accumulation mechanism uncertain.

But the most important trend underlying the world-economy's future are the diminishing energy returns on energy investments (EROI or EROEI), also expressed as diminishing net energy (the first is a proportion, the second a subtraction). A lesser EROI means also that the price of energy is destined to go up (King and Hall 2011), as more energy must be spent in order to have new energy at our disposal, making machines less convenient for all uses. According to Smil (2008) EROI peaked at 200 as oil and coal deposits began to be used, and it is currently calculated at less than 10 for both oil and natural gas.[24] All renewable energy has an EROI less than 10 at the consumer level.[25] A solar-based society cannot sustain current population numbers and economic output levels. Degrowth, both of population and of the economy, is presaged by the decline of this measure. This is our future. The return to the pre-industrial era will not happen because of the exhaustion of fossil fuels, but because of diminishing EROI: as the energy return on energy investment approaches 1:1, it will not make energetic sense to use more energy than the amount that can be reaped. It should not make economic or political sense either, though also energy quality is important, and there are documented cases of deliberate wasting of energetic potential in order to convert solid fuels into liquid ones, for example, in war.

24 The calculations are complicated and disputed and not precise. Here I am using the summary of Hall (2017).

25 These are values presented in Hall and Klitgaard (2018). Ugo Bardi reports greater estimates, notably for hydropower and wind power (personal communication), but also for photovoltaic power (see: https://ugobardi.blogspot.com/2016/06/ma-qual-e-il-vero-eroei-dellenergia.html and quoted bibliography).

# Chapter 3

# THE PRINCIPLE OF POPULATION VERSUS THE LAW OF CAPITALIST ACCUMULATION

## 3.1 Malthus's Message

At the end of the eighteenth century, Thomas Robert Malthus began the debate on the existence of a universally valid population principle or law. This was one of his contributions to the construction of the liberal (i.e., free market) economic theory. In the first edition of *An Essay on the Principle of Population* (1798), he highlighted the irreconcilable contrast between the arithmetic proportions of the growth of crops and the geometric growth of human beings, a famous statement that nevertheless is overly simplified. The historical starting point of the debate was the fact that the Europeans colonizing North America at Malthus's time doubled their numbers every 25 years. Although such dynamics cannot be found in many other times and places, Malthus's observation correctly underlined that resources are limited and are therefore not commensurate with the generative capacity of our species. This principle inspired both Darwin and Wallace to formulate the principle of natural selection. Beyond his mistaken representation, Malthus defined the principle of population as "the constant propensity of all living beings to multiply beyond what the available means of subsistence allow" (Malthus 1965, 3). In biology this is called r-selection strategy and it is typical of small organisms. Bigger species, in which procreation is more costly, developed a K-selection strategy that invests more in fewer offspring.

The Malthusian principle therefore advances the idea of a natural propulsion of the population to multiply if resources allow it, and also beyond that. Widely dubbed as "Malthusian," the theory that the human population has a natural propulsion to grow until it reaches ecological limits, in particular that of food production, actually greatly simplifies Malthus's idea, as he also noted that "the population does invariably increase when the means of subsistence increases, unless this is prevented by some very powerful and evident constraints," referred to as "moral restriction, vice and misery."[1]

Following Adam Smith and David Ricardo, Malthus developed his reflections on population trends in the economic law of diminishing returns. The law of diminishing returns states that the yields of a field can be improved with more work or capital (e.g., the purchase of fertilizers, deeper plowing by means of larger and heavier plows and irrigation), but any additional input of one of these "factors of production" (as they are called by free-market theorists) will give an additional yield that is lower and lower. To feed the extra population, marginal lands need to be cultivated, but their yields will not increase in proportion to the land. The resources available for human life and its growth are thus limited, this is the correct message of the law of diminishing returns. For Malthus, the right proportion between the inhabitants of a territory and the resources they need is normally maintained by "positive checks," that is famines, wars and epidemics. However, he proposed that a population should achieve balance through conscious social planning that lowered the birth rate through "preventive checks," or "moral restraints": basically increasing age at marriage, the foundation of the procreative unit.[2] In the 1803 edition of his work, Malthus claimed that in Europe preventive checks prevail over positive checks, as opposed to trends of the past or of uncivilized areas.[3]

In the *Principles of Political Economy* (1821, 203) he also affirmed that the tendency of populations to grow has a social cause: "What is mainly necessary to a rapid increase of population is a great and continued demand for labor," which historically led to the lowering of the age for marriage. He therefore did consider the importance of social mechanisms. But the autonomous propulsion of the population to multiply is still attributed to him and widely used in demography (e.g., Dyson 2010; Weeks 2012), while on these grounds economists have built the unified growth theory (Galor 2011), and other scientists have developed the structural-demographic theory (Goldstone 1991; Turchin and Nefedov 2009).

The population principle that Malthus formulated is, more properly, the limitation of the number of human beings that can live, obtained either by consciously restricting procreation or by allowing the increase of hunger, war and disease. The principle of population opposed the mercantilist policies that

1 Quote by Thomlinson (1965, 40) from the conclusion of the third chapter of the sixth edition of *An Essay on the Principle of Population* (1826).

2 Indeed, it is very incongruous that the proponents of the contraceptive means persecuted by churches and states between the nineteenth and twentieth century were called "neo-Malthusians." Malthus was an Anglican pastor, far from making this practical suggestion.

3 On page 315 of the second edition of the *Essay*, quoted by Smith (2002, 105).

were at the time hegemonic. As seen, mercantilists advised rulers to stimulate continuous population growth as a source of prosperity and power for the state. In accordance with the mercantilists, the triumphant bourgeoisie of the French Revolution gave population a fundamental importance which, as Michel Foucault noted, translated into the protection of human life which he called biopower. Biopower strives to appropriate the creation and maintenance of life, for example, by treating the bodies of pregnant women as the property of the state and of other powerful groups. When in the mid-eighteenth century doctors discovered the immunological potential of breast milk, they enforced breastfeeding on women:

> It was the concern to increase the population—a population that had to be healthy and robust—that determined the new interest of doctors, moralists and rulers in breastfeeding and, more generally, in the methods of early childhood care. Consequently, in the numerous brochures and treatises published in the second half of the 18th century, the duty to breastfeed was presented as a duty towards society, the state and the *Patria* ["fatherland," the homeland] (a word that was then beginning to be used) that needed healthy citizens. (Lombardi 2008, 175)

The supreme act of bourgeois power according to Foucault was no longer the destruction of human life as with the monarchical power of previous centuries, but its proliferation—although other authors have noted that, among the instruments of the ruling class, the "necropower" has undoubtedly remained.

## 3.2 A Biological Mechanism?

Another powerful message launched by Malthus was that the excessive procreation of the lower classes is the main cause of their misery. With a certain ferocity, Malthus proposed the abolition of the Poor Law, ensuing from his principle of population, as in this perspective helping the poor could only serve to guarantee their multiplication. The Poor Law from the sixteenth century ensured meager aid to those who could not find work or were unable to work. This law regarding the poor of the Elizabethan period was not motivated by the sentiment of charity, but was intended to discourage vagrancy, since the poor had the right to assistance restricted to the parish where they officially resided. With liberal political hegemony, the law was repealed in 1834 and an obligation to enter a workhouse was instituted in its place, that is, forced labor and segregation were introduced in exchange for assistance.

The following sentence, the crudest version of Malthus's thought, appeared only in the first edition of the *Essay*, published anonymously, and was expunged from the following editions:

> A man who is born into a world already possessed, if he cannot get subsistence from his parents on whom he has a just demand, and if the society do not want his labour, has no claim of right to the smallest portion of food, and, in fact, has no business to be where he is. At nature's mighty feast there is no vacant cover for him. She tells him to be gone, and will quickly execute her own orders, if he does not work upon the compassion of some of her guests.[4]

This message has given rise to simplified interpretations of history which considered the "overpopulation" of an area as the cause of the mortality crises that took place there, without addressing class and power analysis. The debate on the Great Irish Famine of 1845–52 is paradigmatic. The destruction of potato crops by the downy mildew mushroom resulted in one million deaths out of eight million inhabitants of the island and pushed another million to emigrate. Many scholars have considered famine as the catastrophic and inevitable outcome of an excessive birth rate of the island's poor: "breaking all the demographic constraints, Ireland went rapidly towards the catastrophe, thus providing a belated, though tragic demonstration of the theories of Malthus" (Reinhard et al. 1971, 431). Other authors have instead highlighted how the absolute availability of food on the island had not diminished to the point of starving the population. The cause of the deaths was the food market. English landowners continued to export wheat from Ireland while the populace was starving due to the destruction of the potatoes they grew for sustenance. In Ireland, the introduction of potatoes in family plots made it possible to feed larger families, whose members worked the land for wheat destined for England. Pastures for cattle were converted into wheat fields to satisfy the demand of the English working class. In the same text quoted above, Reinhard et al. (1971, 303) attribute the increase in the Irish population to English landowners' demand for work in their Irish wheat fields:

> The root cause of all these changes was the possibility for owners to sell their grain to England. In this way, the industrial revolution and the discovery of America contributed to the increase of the population in

4 The passage appears only in the second edition: Malthus ([1803] 1992, 249). On its omission from subsequent editions, see Foster (1998).

an area that in itself was certainly not industrialized or in the process of becoming so.

They also wrote that no preventive demographic checks, like a delayed age for marriage, were there, precisely for reasons of organization of production:

> This fact is undoubtedly connected to the beastly exploitation of the Irish peasants at the hands of English landlords. They wanted to increase their rents and move to intensive agriculture and extend the plowing. The owners indeed pushed the splitting of the estates, especially since now, thanks to the potato, even a small lot was able to ensure the existence of a family. (Reinhard et al. 1971, 431)

The population principle is rooted in a vision of Nature as ruthlessly cruel. Instincts lead to uncontrolled procreation, which is then tragically limited by the intervention of the Four Horsemen of the Apocalypse. This view is not shared by biologists, who speak of self-regulation of the population, which mostly controls procreation according to its density. The first observation of self-regulation through density is a 1933 article by A. J. Nicholson (Turchin 1995, 19). Later, Vero Copner Wynne-Edwards (1962) showed how animal populations tend toward stabilization through group selection.[5] The existence of group selection was initially rejected by other scientists, but today it is recognized as part of natural selection, which acts at several levels, not only on the single specimen. Since it is true that every population has the biological potential to grow exponentially beyond the limits of its resources, the best strategy to avoid catastrophic changes in a group if the environment is stable is precisely by limiting its numbers. In a state of ecological equilibrium, it is indeed normal for each species to thrive, because its interactions with the others remain sustainable until the continuous changes in the inorganic environment reconfigure the territory and its resources. Wynne-Edwards (1962, 8–9) wrote:

> Where we can still find nature undisturbed by human interference [...] there is generally no indication whatever that the habitat is run down or destructively overtaxed. On the contrary the whole trend of ecological evolution seems to be in the very opposite direction, leading towards

5 See his text for more precise bibliographical references to observations and experiments on individual species. Wynne-Edwards is no longer mentioned in Cappuccino and Price (1995), who however report many other examples of populations' self-regulating through density.

the highest state of productivity that can possibly be built up within the limitations set by the inorganic environment.

Even insects, such as the flour beetle and grain weevil, or other relatively simple organisms, such as the Barbados minnows, have shown birth-limiting behaviors, such as laying fewer eggs, eating them and eliminating young individuals to adjust to the amount of resources available to the group. Experiments or observations on mice, rats, rabbits and other mammals have demonstrated the existence of population control mechanisms such as the interruption of oestrus or mating, or the reabsorption of embryos into the female womb.[6] Infanticide is also practiced by many species: birds break eggs, kill chicks or leave the nest. In one experiment, nesting stalls were doubled: the result was that more couples spawned, but the number of offspring per couple decreased, and far fewer hatched a second brood compared to when they had fewer stalls.

Wynne-Edwards thus demonstrated that competition within a single species does not occur directly for food, which would be detrimental to the group and its cohesion, but instead for the territory or sites to reproduce in. In wolf packs, only the alpha male and female mate and procreate. Birds regulate the size of their territories according to the resources they offer. Swallows return to the same nests every year and only reproduce there. In the territories of many other species, some birds are debarred, thereby allowing only a few couples to procreate. Sea birds and those that feed on insects in flight can hardly delimit a territory, so they live and reproduce in colonies, from which "extra" individuals are expelled and consequently cannot reproduce: this is their way of regulating their numbers.

Deliberate starvation of some individuals never occurs as the typical constraint on population. This is not the normal mechanism for regulating the relationship between population and resources. Starvation would mean that the expansion of a species has come too close to the level of overexploitation of the resources on which it depends. To maintain the ecological balance, the population (contrary to what Malthus wrote) needs to settle at a level lower than that at which its dietary needs would actually approach the limit of resources needed for its survival. For Wynne-Edwards, animals regulate themselves in this way and only starve in particular periods of transition or because of exceptional reduction to their food sources. It has not been proven that the whole natural world bases self-regulation on density, but many species certainly do so.

---

6 The sources are several scientific contributions quoted by Wilkinson (1973, 24–26).

Marshall Sahlins (1980, chapter 2) collected anthropological data that showed the validity of this mechanism for human beings as well, hence he also denied Malthus's principle of population for our species, and destroyed the image of Nature as cruel. Richard Wilkinson noted that Malthus lived in a specific period of transition, when hunger, disease and war kept the population in check. Malthus therefore thought that what he observed was a mechanism valid in all circumstances, for the whole human species, while this happens only in times of crises. Among other things, Malthus himself (1798, 40) gave evidence that the native peoples of North America were not in poor physical condition at all in spite of what he called their uncivilized state; on the contrary, they enjoyed excellent health. He believed, however, that this applied only to warriors in the prime of life, and not to women and children, whom he supposed to share the same degradation as the working class in civilized states. It was also Malthus (1798, 40) who reported the interesting observation that when a Native American family settled near European settlements, women had more children—even five or six more than in their villages—whereas in the "savage state" this rarely happened: only one or two children normally became adults.

## 3.3 Population, Work and Technology in Marx

Malthus's biggest opponent was Karl Marx, who clearly rejected his law of population as a universal claim, affirming that population dynamics are governed instead by specific historical laws. Essentially, the writings of Marx and Engels against Malthus (collected in Meek 1971) reveal and attack his role as defender of the status quo in which the bourgeoisie dominates. "The most open declaration of war of the bourgeoisie upon the proletariat is Malthus's Law of Population and the New Poor Law framed in accordance with it," wrote Engels in *The Conditions of the Working Class in England in 1844* (1845).[7] While Malthus and his followers believed that overpopulation perpetuated poverty, Marx and the Marxists identified the bourgeois social order as the main barrier to human and economic development, precisely because of its division into classes, based on the private ownership of the means of production (Bebel 1910; Baran 1975). If Malthus and the Malthusians considered the multiplication of the poor as irrational, Marx and other radical thinkers believed that it was the only investment the dispossessed classes could make. This was also indicated by their use of the concept of proletariat. In

7 Friedrich Engels, *The Conditions of the Working Class in England in 1844*, 1845 (Panther Edition 1969), (http: //www.marxists.org/archive/marx/works/1845/condition-working-class /ch13.htm).

ancient Rome, the term indicated the *nullatenenti* ("those who own nothing") who contributed to the greatness of the *Res Publica* only with their offspring, since they had no way of paying taxes.[8]

Marx did not investigate the law of population in its totality but only as it relates to the functioning of the capitalist economy, forging the concept of "relative surplus population"—even though he was aware of the fact that to increase surplus value, capitalists could either increase the working hours or employ more workforce. In this second case, the accumulation of capital requires the expansion of the population, that is, of the proletariat. In the manuscripts titled *Grundrisse: Foundations of the Critique of Political Economy*, Marx wrote:

> The more working days capital can enter into exchange with at once, during which exchanges are objectified for living labour, the greater its realization at once. It can leap over the natural limit formed by one individual's living, working day, at a given stage in the development of the forces of production (and it does not in itself change anything that this stage is changing) only by positing another working day alongside the first at the same time—by the spatial addition of more simultaneous working days, e.g., I can drive the surplus labour of A no higher than 3 hours; but if I add the days of B, C, D etc, then it becomes 12 hours. In place of a surplus time of 3, I have created one of 12. This is why capital solicits the increase of population.[9]

Profit, meaning surplus in the form of money, comes from all the unpaid labor that workers provide in addition to the hours of work necessary to produce what is required to satisfy their needs (i.e., its cash equivalent), to which their salary is limited due to competition among workers for jobs. Marx used the labor theory of value of the classic economist Ricardo to measure the surplus value which the class owning the means of production appropriates from the proletarian class by remunerating the workers only with subsistence wages. In Marx's vision, the subsistence wage does not correspond to the absolute minimum necessary for survival, but takes into account the social needs considered indispensable in each epoch. Indeed, if capitalism is based on the unlimited expansion of production, someone will have to buy and consume the goods produced. If at the beginning of its product cycle a commodity represents a luxury, then it will gradually spread among ordinary people. Subsistence

---

8 Daly (1971, 25) however states that this meaning was lost in the nineteenth century.

9 Karl Marx, *Grundrisse* (Penguin Books, in association with *New Left Review*, 1973), 325, (https://www.marxists.org/archive/marx/works/download/pdf/grundrisse.pdf).

wages can therefore rise, but only up to the level at which they begin to disturb the accumulation of capital. On the contrary, Engels and Lassalle spoke of an "iron law of wages," which leads to the leveling down of any wage increase due to the multiplication of the proletariat: this represented a Malthusian dynamic under another name. For Malthus, indeed, any possible increase in the working class's standard of living would be canceled by the subsequent increase in their numbers. As Malthus, Engels and Lassalle thought that the increase in wages would be absorbed by the needs of larger new generations, pinning down the working classes at the level of pure subsistence—understood in this case as the satisfaction of only basic biological needs.

In *The German Ideology*, Marx and Engels considered the relation between population and technology to be paramount. Population growth is the cause that leads to technological change, and this began from the time humankind started to produce its own means of subsistence. This same scheme would be subsequently detailed and completed with empirical evidence collected in poor countries by the (non-Marxist) economist Ester Boserup. She wrote that the problem of feeding a larger population pushed to find innovative solutions in agriculture—innovations that in turn demanded more labor.[10] However, this dynamic is not absolute: on the contrary, McCann (1995) found intensification of agriculture without population growth in contemporary Ethiopia, and John Heath and Hans Binswanger (1996, 67) wrote:

> We argue that the Boserup effects are far from automatic. We view them as the outcome of investment decisions by farmers. In order to come about, the investments require a positive incentive regime, and access by farmers to soil and water resources and to markets. If these conditions are denied by adverse policy regimes, impoverished peasants are forced to mine the land resources, rather than augment them.

While Malthus saw a zero-sum game in the relationship between population and resources, Marx contested this naturalization of class dynamics: it was the investment and overconsumption of the bourgeoisie that took resources away from the proletariat, who had created them with their work. However, for Marx, the less it costs to raise a new future worker, the more the "production of workers" would increase. A boost to population comes from economic development that causes commodity prices to decrease as the use of capital increases.

10 Boserup also noted that the population of African cities was often fed with low-priced imports from industrialized countries.

Marx predicted population growth (and the turning point caused by the increase in the cost of raising children) by postulating an almost Malthusian mechanism valid only for the proletariat: a decrease in the price of the subsistence items encourages procreation in working-class families. The multiplication of the proletariat benefits capital, which puts them to work during its expansion phases:

> The increase in population increases the productive force of labour, since it makes possible a greater division and combination of labour etc. The increase of population is a *natural force* of labour, for which nothing is paid. From this standpoint, we use the term *natural force* to refer to the *social force.* All *natural forces of social labour* are themselves historical products.[11]

The natural aspect is the fact that procreation occurs without remuneration and therefore adds free workforce to the existing group of workers. The labor force is chained to capital, which multiplies with its "enlarged reproduction," forcing the laboring population to increase, as Marx wrote in *Capital* ([1867] 1992, 763–64):

> The reproduction of labour-power which must incessantly be re-incorporated into capital as its means of valorization, which cannot get free of capital and whose enslavement to capital is only concealed by the variety of individual capitalists to whom it sells itself, forms, in fact, a factor in the reproduction of capital itself. Accumulation of capital is therefore multiplication of the proletariat.[12]

---

11 Karl Marx, *Grundrisse* (Penguin Books in association with *New Left Review* 1973, 345), in https://www.marxists.org/archive/marx/works/1857/grundrisse/ch07.htm. Italics in original.

12 Original note (from Karl Marx, "Wage Labour and Capital"): "'If the masses are all oppressed equally, the more proletarians a country has, the richer it will be' (Colins, *L 'Economie politique. Source des revolutions et des utopies pretendues socialistes*, Paris, 1857, vol. 3, p. 331). 'Proletarian' must be understood to mean, economically speaking, nothing other than 'wage-labourer', the man who produces and valorizes 'capital', and is thrown onto the street as soon as he becomes superfluous to the need for valorization possessed by 'Monsieur Capital', as Pecqueur calls this person. 'The sickly proletarian of the primitive forest' is a pretty Roscherian fancy. The primitive forester is the owner of the primitive forest and uses it as his property, meeting as few obstacles to this as an orang-utang. He is not, therefore, a proletarian. This would only be the case if the primitive forest exploited him, instead of being exploited by him. As far as his health is concerned, such a man would well bear comparison, not only with the modem proletarian, but also with the syphilitic and scrofulous 'quality'. However, Herr Wilhelm Roscher no doubt means his native heath of Lineburg when he talks about a 'primitive forest'."

Marx also described the importance of the mass of workers as consumers for the individual capitalist: "The greater their number—the number of the industrial population—and the mass of money at their disposal, the greater the sphere of exchange for capital. We have seen that it is the tendency of capital to increase the industrial population as much as possible."[13]

In the manuscripts of 1862–63 later entitled *Theories of Surplus Value* on which he based *Capital*, Marx wrote about expanded reproduction and listed the various possibilities of finding the additional labor force needed, without directly affirming that the greater demand for labor is the basis for population increase. Once the surplus value has been set aside for the acquisition of new variable capital, that is, labor force, the previously unproductive workers must be dragged into the capitalist system, or else women, children and/or poor people who do not work will have to start doing so. Otherwise, as a logical last resort, the population has to grow. Marx stressed the need for adequate wages to support large families if this growth is to be sustained (see Section 2.5)—but wages only represent the *possibility* of finding one's subsistence through the market. It is not only a matter of price: of course, this is possible if food and all the other items necessary for survival of the extra population can be obtained—which has happened since the beginning of the industrial era with increased energy consumption for production and transport.

In *Capital*, Marx furthermore explained in detail the concept and dynamics of "relative surplus population," also called "industrial reserve army," whose work is rendered superfluous by technological unemployment.[14] The surplus population grows in periods of capital expansion, during which machines supplant workers so that capitalists save on the cost of human labor. Marx ([1867] 1992, 782) wrote that the acceleration of technical progress in production, that is, the increasing use of machines instead of human work, causes

> an apparently absolute increase in the working population, an increase which always moves more rapidly than that of the variable capital or the means of employment. But in fact it is capitalist accumulation itself that constantly produces, and produces indeed in direct relation with its own energy and extent, a relatively redundant working population, i.e. a population which is superfluous to capital's average requirements for its own valorization, and is therefore a surplus population.

---

13 Karl Marx, *Grundrisse* (Penguin Books in association with *New Left Review* 1973, 345), in https://www.marxists.org/archive/marx/works/download/pdf/grundrisse.pdf.

14 Chapter 23 "The general law of capitalist accumulation" (especially sections 3 and 4 on relative overpopulation) and chapter 25 "The modern theory of colonization."

In contrast to Malthus, Marx declared that the true "law of population" is the one that establishes that workers produce those means which, in a new production cycle, will make them superfluous:

> We can now understand the foolishness of the economic wisdom which preaches to the workers that they should adapt their numbers to the valorization requirements of capital. The mechanism of capitalist production and accumulation itself constantly effects this adjustment. The first word of this adaptation is the creation of a relative surplus population, or industrial reserve army. Its last word is the misery of constantly expanding strata of the active army of labour, and the dead weight of pauperism. (Marx [1867] 1992, 782)

This mass of unemployed workers will exert pressure on wages to keep them close to the subsistence level:

> The working population therefore produces both the accumulation of capital and the means by which it is itself made relatively superfluous; and it does this to an extent which is always increasing. This is a law of population peculiar to the capitalist mode of production; and in fact every particular historical mode of production has its own special laws of population, which are historically valid within that particular sphere. An abstract law of population exists only for plants and animals, and even then only in the absence of any historical intervention by man. (Marx [1867] 1992, 783–84)

For Marx, relative surplus population is one of the conditions necessary for the existence of the capitalist mode of production. In other words, capitalism cannot solve the problem of unemployment because unemployment benefits the ruling class, as it has the effect of keeping wages low—as well as motivating the employed to work harder for fear of being replaced. It is also a matter of capital outlay calculation:

> It is the absolute interest of every capitalist to extort a given quantity of labour out of a smaller rather than a greater number of workers, if the cost is about the same. In the latter case, the outlay of constant capital increases in proportion to the mass of labour set in motion; in the former that increase is much smaller. The more extended the scale of production, the more decisive is this motive. (Marx [1867] 1992, 788)

For Marx, Malthus's mistake is to look at the absolute increase of the population. Although Marx does not deny that this happens, it is the movement of capital that leads to a relative surplus population and its miserable conditions in unemployment, and also keeps the working population in misery:

> Capitalist production can by no means content itself with the quantity of disposable labour-power which the natural increase of population[15] yields. It requires for its unrestricted activity an industrial reserve army which is independent of these natural limits. (Marx [1867] 1992, 788)

Nevertheless, in *Capital* we also find hints at explaining population with labor demand. Workers get married early and have larger families as their lives are wasted early, but also for the monetary premium in their "production of children":

> Hence, rapid replacement of one generation of workers by another (this law does not hold for the other classes of the population). This social requirement is met by early marriages, which are a necessary consequence of the conditions in which workers in large-scale industry live, and by the premium that the exploitation of the workers' children sets on their production. (Marx [1867] 1992, 795)

The German philosopher also noted the following:

> In fact, not only the number of births and deaths, but the absolute size of families, stands in inverse proportion to the level of wages, and therefore to the amount of the means of subsistence at the disposal of different categories of worker. This law of capitalist society would sound absurd to savages, or even to civilized colonists. It calls to mind the boundless reproduction of animals individually weak and constantly hunted down. (Marx [1867] 1992, 796–97)

On a macrohistorical level, in investigating the push for the expansion of the M-C-M' spiral, Marx showed how the bourgeoisie's work had resulted in the expansion of markets, with an ever-increasing demand for a larger workforce to produce more and more goods.

---

15 The expression "natural increase" of population occurs in *Capital* only two times.

### 3.4 The Work of Boys and Girls

Friedrich Engels and August Bebel emphasized the importance of child labor for the survival of families with no other sources of income. Socialist and communist militants became increasingly aware much earlier than social scientists that in capitalism a large number of children was the consequence of poverty, since their families needed their earnings. This was later formalized by the English economist Sydney Coontz in his demand-for-labor theory (Chapter 6). In *The Conditions of the Working Class in England in 1844* (1845), Engels described in detail how capitalism imposed high fertility on working-class families, where child labor was necessary, whereas the ruling class reproduced less. In the "dark Satanic mills" of the Industrial Revolution, child labor was mostly favored as it was cheap.

In *The Origin of the Family, Private Property and the State* (1884), Engels elaborated on the theory of matriarchy presented in *Das Mutterrecht* (The mother's right/maternal law 1861) by the anthropologist and law historian Johann Jakob Bachofen. Patriarchy—male power over female sexual and generative faculties—essentially equates to the division of the population into classes with the institution of private property:

> The overthrow of mother-right was the world historical defeat of the female sex. The man took command also in the home; the woman was degraded and reduced to servitude. She became a slave to his lust and a mere instrument for the making of children. This degraded position of the woman conspicuous especially among the Greeks of the heroic and still more of the classical age, has gradually been palliated and glozed over, and sometimes clothed in a milder form, and in no sense has it been abolished. (Engels [1884] 1942)

August Bebel, leader of the German Social Democratic Party, wrote in *Woman and Socialism* (1879):

> On the other hand, the capitalist mode of production pushes for the production of children. Cheap "hands," in the form of children are necessary for its factories and workshops. Among proletarians, bringing children into the world becomes a sort of calculation, as they earn their own bread. The proletarian employed in the domestic industry is even forced to have many children, because they help him to be competitive. This is certainly an abominable system: it increases the pauperization of the worker and his dependence on the employer. (Bebel 1910)

With the widespread diffusion of *Woman and Socialism*, Bebel influenced the socialist movement in setting among its first objectives the equality between the sexes and the emancipation of women, which socialist countries achieved in law. In China, after the Maoist revolution, a severe ban on the crippling of girls' feet eradicated a millennial-old custom. This deformation, perceived as an esthetic modification, represented the brutal implementation of the rule prohibiting women from leaving the house, and was even considered sexy (Daly 1979). Women could not go out of their home even in the lower classes, something to which Jack Goldstone (1996) attributed the failure of China to have the first industrial revolution because of the lack of cheap labor, an explanation not denied by Kenneth Pomeranz.

Bebel backed Laing's thesis (approved by Marx) that desperate poverty led to large families, and he predicted a time when social justice and women's empowerment would lead to smaller families (Eversley 1959, 159). The recognition of the exploitation of the reproductive capability of women in *The Woman and Socialism* occurred at a time when wives still had no right over their children and would lose them in case of divorce because fathers were inevitably entrusted with their custody.

However, Bebel also said that socialism would be able to preserve the balance between livelihoods and population, which will be able to freely multiply, and this became orthodoxy in later debates. Engels[16] criticized Karl Kautsky when, in his book on population *The Influence of Population Increase on the Progress of Society* (1880), he observed that improvements in the conditions of the working class were accompanied by the counterproductive growth of its size and that this should be countered with contraception. In his following book, *Growth and Development in Nature and in Society* (1921), Kautsky stopped recommending birth control and wrote instead that procreation was the duty of women: "public opinion and individuals' consciences will make women's duties clear."[17] Only Eduard Bernstein, who was not an orthodox Marxist, expressed favor for a birth strike, calling it "a revolutionary weapon" (Eversley 1959, 159) as anarchists did.

In France, the socialist feminist Nelly Roussel and the founder of the Ligue de la régéneration humaine (League for the human regeneration, 1896) Paul Robin campaigned against births so that the children of the proletariat would not become cannon fodder or capitalism's industrial reserve

16 Letter dated February 1, 1881 (http: // www. marxists.org/archive/marx/works/1881/letters/81 02 01.htm).

17 Quoted in Petersen (1988, 84). The original titles of the two works are *Der Einfluss der Volksvermehrung auf den Fortschritt der Gesellschaft* and *Vermehrung und Entwicklung in Natur und Gesellschaft*.

army.[18] The trial of Annie Besant and Charles Bradlaught in England in 1877, which ended with the condemnation of their books describing birth control methods, testified to the fact that states certainly considered birth control information as a threat to public order.[19] Besant and Bradlaught, after being condemned, responded with the foundation of the Malthusian League.

## 3.5 The Role of the Population in Marxism

Among others, Rosa Luxemburg, Paul Sweezy and Robert Brenner gave population a role in their theories. For Rosa Luxemburg, under the pressure of the capitalist mode of production, the peasant economy and the "primitive forms of production" in non-European countries are destroyed. All these economic forms, based on subsistence work, are dragged into commodification and into the M-C-M' spiral. Expansion in external areas is vital to capitalism because without it, in order to expand as M-C-M' requires, a large increase in population would be necessary. In *The Accumulation of Capital* (1913) she argued that the "natural increase" of the working class (a Malthusian view) was too slow and insufficient to support the expansion of capital, and that only with the incorporation of new areas could the number of producers and consumers needed by the system be reached (Luxemburg 2012, 475). These areas outside the system were to be incorporated in order to obtain new profits from those to whom the surplus products were to be sold—goods that the working class that produced them could not afford to buy due to their low wages. This, in short, is called the Consumption Theory. In her reply to those who had rejected *The Accumulation of Capital*, titled "What the Emulators of Marxist Theory Have Done: A Counter-Critique" (in Luxemburg 2012), the Polish communist addressed in detail the question of population, but continued to use the concept of its "natural increase."

In accordance with Luxemburg's line of thought, Paul Sweezy (1956, 224) also concluded: "Looking back over the last four centuries, we must recognize that the population factor has been extremely favorable to rapid and uninhibited expansion of capitalism." Sweezy considered the substantial importance of population growth in countering the crises of overproduction, together with the creation of new industries, unproductive investments, increasing consumption and public spending:

---

18 The Alliance nationale contre la dépopulation, also founded in 1896, opposed the spread of information on birth control on pronatalist and patriotic positions.

19 The call for a birth strike resurged in other times, as in Finland in the 1980s when the "No birth—no nuclear" campaign was launched to demand a change in the country's energy policy (Waring 1988).

> The share of accumulation which can go into variable capital without depressing the rate of profit depends in large part on the rate of population growth; the more rapid the growth of population, the larger the share going to variable capital; hence the more rapid the increase in consumption; hence also the smaller the danger of underconsumption. This means that, the strength of the tendency to underconsumption stands in inverse relation to the rapidity of population growth, being weak in periods of rapid growth and becoming stronger as the rate of growth declines. [...] If we drop the assumption of a closed and completely capitalist system, the scope of this law is extended. From the standpoint of capitalist production, new population includes not only natural increase in numbers but also the absorption of groups which for the first time become available for employment as wage workers. Particularly in its earlier phases, capitalism expands largely on the basis of a labor force recruited through more or less violent destruction of more primitive economic relations. In this stage of development, the "population problem" is primarily a question of the obstacles which have to be overcome in making wage workers out of peasants and independent handicraftsmen. (Sweezy 1956, 223 and 224)

For Eric Hobsbawm (1999, 36): "The mass market hardly has a faster increase than the population growth rate." For Stephen Hymer (1979), too, an additional workforce is necessary for capitalist expansion.

A renewed clash between Marx's and Malthus's ideas came about in the "Brenner Debate" from 1976 to 1982 (Aston and Philpin 1989). Marxist scholar Robert Brenner refuted the Malthusian thesis of economic historians Emmanuel Le Roy Ladurie and Michael Posnan regarding the "demographic crises" in the second half of the fifteenth and seventeenth centuries. The first crisis, following the depopulation that resulted from the Black Death in the fourteenth century, affected only the feudal lords and not the people, because wages increased and the price of wheat decreased. In Eastern and Western Europe, the outcomes were opposite due to the different cohesion among elites and the different power relations between the classes. In the East (Prussia and Poland) servitude was reintroduced with the Second Serfdom. Instead in the West (England and France), the renting of land in exchange for money spread, without any return to medieval constraints on the workforce, like in the East. It was the class struggle that had two different outcomes, not a demographic automatism. Brenner also noted that, according to Malthusian theory, depopulation in the fourteenth century should have triggered an immediate growth of the population, but this did not occur until over a century later. The working classes continued to enjoy high wages without multiplying dramatically. For Brenner, what happened was an attempt by the ruling class to extract more surplus per capita from the diminished population, a fact that affected production levels and "stagnated" the population. Historians Edward Anthony Wrigley and Roger Schofield (1981), of the Cambridge Group for the History of Population and Social Structure, agreed with Brenner. They also denied that within the English population there had been any Malthusian dynamics with positive checks like hunger, war or disease. It was actually the preventive checks that regulated the system, mainly with the fluctuations in marriage age, which was lower in the eighteenth century when the population began its incessant growth. Wrigley and Schofield attributed the bigger part of the population increase (70 percent) to the lowering of the age for marriage, with the consequent increase in the birth rate, and the smaller part of the increase (30 percent) to lower mortality.

### 3.6 Malthus Today

The Malthusian interpretation of history is still alive. Apart from the prevalence of Malthus's views in the discipline of demography, there are schools of thoughts that use the concept of population pressure when evaluating macrohistorical changes, taking for granted that population pressure would occur and force society to change. The microhistorical level is a common omission, as Robert Denemark writes: "One of the problems faced by structural analyses is that they are incomplete. They do not usually trace the microfoundations of macro-level activities" (Denemark et al. 2000, xviii). But the reasons to procreate cannot be considered as a black box (unless it is provisional), postulating population pressure as a constant force.

Christopher Chase-Dunn and Thomas Hall (1997) also analyzed population dynamics by combining their method of comparative analysis of world-systems with the cultural materialism of Marvin Harris (1979) and the approaches developed by Mark Cohen and Robert Carneiro. For these authors, population pressure is a force acting on all world-systems. It is not an absolute concept defined by numbers, but is related to the resources and technologies in a specific and circumscribed area. When population density approaches a territory's carrying capacity limit, greater sustenance can be drawn from the land only with irrigation, deeper plowing, extension of the cultivable area by reclaiming swamps and cutting down forests or by conquering new territories. In 2000 Chase-Dunn and Hall elaborated a feedback model in which population pressure is the cause of systemic expansion, hierarchy formation and technological development:

> In turn these changes intensify population growth. The process repeats cyclically. With each "iteration" the process repeats on an expanding scale. This is a world systems model because it necessarily involves processes that occur among societies as well as within them. The main forces are population growth, ecological degradation and population pressure. Population pressure results when scarcities cause people to increase the effort necessary to meet their needs. This often results in emigration, if new regions are available. Circumscription occurs when new locations do not geographically exist or are already filled with other populations who resist. Thus population pressure causes competition among societies for land and other resources and this is necessarily an intersocietal phenomenon. One possible outcome is increased conflict, especially warfare, as groups contend for scarce resources. In some systems, endemic warfare functions as a demographic regulator by reducing the population density and alleviating (temporarily) population pressure. But in other cases new hierarchies or larger polities emerge to regulate the use of resources, and/or new technologies of production develop that allow larger numbers of people to live within a given area. (Chase-Dunn and Thomas Hall 2000, 98)

Jack Goldstone (1991) proposed structural-demographic theory as an alternative to considering class conflict as a fundamental force of history, and Peter Turchin and Sergey Nefedov (2009) followed his footsteps. For Goldstone, structural-demographic theory provides a better summary of economic and political history than the Marxist model, introducing the dynamic factor of the numerical composition of classes, which modifies their relations:

> The latter which has come to be called "*the* social explanation" of early modern revolutions, argues that the motivation for change came from shifts in the relations of production, identified as the growth of capitalism which produced the conflicts between social classes that undermined states. I argue instead that the motivation for change came from the ecological shifts in the relation of the population size to agricultural output, which produced diverse conflicts between elites and states, among elite factions and between popular groups and authorities. These conflicts revolved around a variety of axes, including national and local political authority, status, and economic and religious issues. (Goldstone 1991, 37; italics in original)

Cycles occurred in agrarian-bureaucratic states during the historical period before capitalist relations of production took over, though feudalism had already disappeared (see Chapter 5). This period of modern history starts roughly with the age of explorations and contact with the New World and ends with the Industrial Revolution, before which fossil fuels were used massively only by the United Provinces, which had peat swamps and used turf in their industrial processes until they exhausted it. The scope of structural-demographic theory is extended to contemporary political dynamics by these and other authors (e.g., Goldstone 2010, 2011; Korotayev and Zinkina 2011; Turchin 2016).

Authors such as Phyllis Deane, W. A. Cole and Eversley (all quoted by McNeill 1982, 206n42) and Habakkuk (1974) attributed the triggering of the Industrial Revolution in England to population growth. Richard Wilkinson, whose view of technological change does not equate it to progress, but instead to a degradation of the human condition, also sees these dynamics as being spurred by the growth of population. McNeill instead pointed out the importance of the Napoleonic war efforts for the beginning of English industrial development.

Considerations about population have been used against world-systems analysis and its emphasis on the plundering of the resources of the periphery by the imperialist core. In an article written with a young Thomas Hall, sociologist Daniel Chirot critically examined world-systems analysis, concluding that population growth, which in the Malthusian viewpoint implied a decrease in per capita GDP, is the mechanism that best explains the poverty of peripheral countries, rather than the theory of dependence.

For Grimes (1999, 22), it is demographic pressure that drives innovation. He studied in particular the case of the Green Revolution, which had amplified effects on procreation and "delayed the completion of the demographic transition" (for a contrasting view of the Green Revolution as stimulating population growth—see Section 7.1), because, "For peasants without enough money to buy new machines, the easiest solution was to have more children to increase the family's workforce."

Boserup, as mentioned, considered that new technology, requiring more human effort, is adopted only under population pressure. She did not connect technology and population pressure to systemic and supra-local dynamics, which in the history of the capitalist world-economy have become increasingly influential. Her observations and ideas in contrast to those of Malthus were found by Ronald D. Lee (1986) to be not so incompatible. Lee unified them in a single theory in which the interaction between population growth and economic growth is an alternation of the two situations: in different phases in history population pressure spurs technology and growth, or technology allows for population growth. Lee's ideas were further developed by Wood (1998) who generalized the "Malthus–Boserup model" with a mathematical formalization. George Modelski (2000, 26), applying a world system perspective, wrote in favor or a multicausal model:

> We might wonder about the direction of the causal arrow between population growth and social organization. Is it the rise in population that caused changes in the social organization and the emergence of world system potential? Or is it that new forms of social organization, epochal innovations such as the rise of cities, or industrial revolutions, made possible the rise of populations? We would tend to argue that both types of causation are in fact relevant, at different points of human social experience.

In addition to noting that Boserup's vision was "cornucopian" since it did not contemplate the depletion of the earth, Abernethy (2005) suggested a feedback mechanism that leads to reduced fertility due to a perceived or hypothesized scarcity of resources for the future. Conversely, Abernethy (2000) attributed the increase in the number of children per woman to improved socioeconomic prospects, as in poor countries in the 1960s and 1970s during the decolonization period. On the basis of this and other empirical material, Abernethy invalidated the theory of demographic transition, which mistakenly considered urbanization and modernization the causes of the decline in fertility.

# Chapter 4

# DEMOGRAPHY AND ITS MYTHS

## 4.1 Naturalizations and Reifications

As a discipline, demography is a late emanation of the liberal division of intellectual work (Szreter 1993; Livi Bacci et al. 1994) and like the other disciplines derived from this division, it is limited in its perspectives and politically oriented in a conservative sense (Wallerstein et al. 1996). Barbara Duden (1993) denounced the intellectual creation of a dehumanized population-object by this discipline.

The word "demography" appeared in European dictionaries in the mid-nineteenth century, and demographers looked to Thomas Robert Malthus as their founding father. As discussed earlier, the English economist thought that the excessive procreation of the poor is the cause of the perpetuation of their misery, a theoretical position that at his time had very strong political repercussions, and is still politically used today (Section 8.2).

Demography often regards its concepts and laws as natural. Malthus himself claimed that instinct is the cause of procreation, and the social dynamic that keeps it in check is its confinement to marriage giving children legitimacy. Undoubtedly, the power of marriage to regulate births through a lower or higher age at which the bride enters it, is based on the social norms that punish women who become pregnant without being married. As Harris and Ross (1987, 88) wrote, "Age at marriage, however, regulated population growth only because it was embedded in a distinctive complex of sexual taboos, marital exchanges, family organization, wealth inheritance, celibate orders, and infant death control."

Following Malthus's footsteps, demographers also tend to ignore class analysis and reify the variables they work with. Marriage rates, intervals between children, the use of contraceptives in the modern era are all considered as causes of social phenomena, while instead these variables must in turn be explained. Demographers are inclined to ignore the role of practices that in the past represented the functional equivalent of contraception: abstinence, prolonged breastfeeding, procured abortions, relinquishment of newborn babies and infanticides. For example, Richard Easterlin, an economist who applied his disciplinary tools to demography, presented the concept of Mortality Revolution, pointing out that decreasing mortality spreads faster than economic growth. He thus deduced that the Mortality Revolution was independent from the Industrial Revolution. Easterlin (2009, 9) wrote: "The immediate effect of the Mortality Revolution was an acceleration of population growth, as death rates fell and birth rates remained constant or even rose as health improved." It is clear, however, that if couples who have children raise them instead of abandoning, neglecting or subjecting them to endurance tests for their selection (documented for some tribes), it does not entail any change in natural mortality, but in the reproductive behavior of the subjects. The change could well be connected with the Industrial Revolution and economic growth, that is, the growth of the M-C-M' spiral.

The concept of demographic regime (see, e.g., Reinhard et al. 1971; Livi Bacci et al. 1994) suggests that what happens to birth rates, mortality, migrations and marriage (as discussed, in past centuries births occurred almost exclusively within marriage) is independent of the other aspects of social life. However, these variables are affected by class membership, participation in the world of production and roles assumed, progressive commodification in the capitalist world-economy, and the gender roles relative to the economy. A "demographic regime" cannot explain anything. Indeed, redundant concepts are used to describe demographic facts with terms like birth rate, mortality and migration that do not *explain* the population trend but are simply the measures of its components. An example of this prose comes from the demographer Flinn (1981, 65), commenting on the use of contraception reported by Flandrin in the seventeenth and eighteenth centuries:

> It was immediately evident that some limited fluctuations in marital fertility rates could not in themselves constitute sure proof of an intentional control of fertility: as we have seen, there were too many chances that these rates were influenced by economic or demographic factors.

A measure like the marital fertility rate cannot be a "demographic factor," it does not have explanatory power but only a descriptive value. Population dynamics described by a "demographic regime" are structured by the social rules of procreation that, in turn, reflect the homeostatic or expansive characteristics of both the mode of production in general and of a particular domestic group as an economic unit, in an intertwining of macrohistorical and microhistorical levels. "Demographic regime" can instead be used in a simple descriptive sense, like in the books edited by David Kerzer and Tom

Fricke (1997) and by Eilidh Garrett, Alice Reid, Kevin Schürer and Simon Szreter (2001).

Demographers generally use the nation as their unit of analysis, to which they apply the key concept of demographic transition. This refers to the diminution first of the death rate and then of the birth rate: the lag between the two is due to a late realization by parents that more of their children could survive. The demographic transition arose from better standards of living and improved medicine in Europe after 1750 and in other continents later on.[1] The transition was from a so-called traditional demographic regime in which high fertility and high mortality were determined by Nature, to a modern demographic regime with low fertility and low mortality, characterized by the conscious and rational choice of the number of children to beget. In the modernization process, families slowly reach rationality and adapt the number of children to the decreased mortality rates, introducing a conscious calculation in the place of the customary passive acceptance of every pregnancy. The period of demographic transition therefore starts with population growth due to the maintenance of the natural, high birth rate with a contemporary decrease in mortality.

The fundamental concept at the basis of the demographic transition theory is natural fecundity (Henry 1953), which is typical of the so-called traditional societies, in which families do not have a precise procreative goal and welcome every new conception without countering fertility (and without abandoning the newborn). In natural fertility, "the behavior of couples is not influenced by the number of children already born, as is the case of populations that plan births" (Livi Bacci 1994, 128). Natural fertility is therefore the number of children reached in the absence of voluntary birth control and depends only on the woman's age at marriage. Naturalizing procreation is in turn based on the naturalness of the sexual practice resulting in new generations: coitus (see considerations made in Chapter 1). But procreation generally cannot depend on so-called natural fertility nor on chance, given that the continuance of human societies (world-systems) depends ultimately on a balanced relationship with the environment. Even before the environmental forces can exert their selecting influence, human groups must *consciously* take care of their offspring. It is here that the choice to take charge of a child or abandon him or her always comes into consideration.

1 This is commonsense also for world-systems analysts, e.g., "Technology revolutionized medicine, and the world's population exploded" (Bosworth 2000, 275).

## 4.2 Notestein's Demographic Transition

By 1890, the so-called decline of fertility in Europe was well known and had become the subject of political debates. The English geographer E. G. Ravenstein mentioned this phenomenon favorably and considered it as the solution to the problem of balancing population and arable land (Bashford 2014, 46). Adolphe Landry in *La Révolution Démographique* (The Demographic Revolution, 1934), observing the birth and mortality trends, attributed them to a "demographic transition." The first comprehensive theorization of this concept appeared in 1945 in an essay by Frank Notestein of the Office of Population Research of Princeton (Kirk 1996). In the same year Kingsley Davis (1945) also used the expression "demographic transition."[2]

Notestein interpreted the phenomenon described by Landry with the theory of modernization. Modernization equates to economic development, industrialization and the cultural and political changes associated with them, such as the establishment of liberal democracies and the extension of human rights. It is a typically progressive vision, that is, one that considers history the realization of Progress. During the demographic transition the average life span increases thanks to improvements in medicine, hygiene and nutrition, that is, to Progress in its various material and cultural aspects. Notestein stressed the importance of the cultural structure in dictating to individuals' behaviors in accordance with the interests of society as a whole. However, this cultural structure is subject to delays in adapting to new economic conditions. In the specific case of procreation, a high birth rate is the behavior imposed when mortality rates are high, in order not to risk the extinction of the society in question. During the cultural and material shift toward the goal of modernization, in spite of the lengthening of the average life expectancy—which in practice means that more children survive among the many who are born—individuals and families are still not able to make procreative decisions that would result in a balance by decreasing births.

Modernization theory is based on an assumption of the irrationality of so-called traditional behaviors, as in the quadripartition of the motivations in Max Weber's theory of social action, wherein tradition is opposed to rationality. In other words, families do not immediately try to reduce the number of their children because they do not pay attention to the decreasing mortality rate and continue to have as many children as possible as in the traditional demographic regime. When families finally realize that a much greater number of children reach adulthood than in the past, they finally apply

2 In *Food for the World*, edited by T. W. Schultz, Chicago: University of Chicago Press, 1945.

the rationality they learned during the modernization process and adjust the number of births according to the decreased mortality rate.

Modernization theory is however highly unsatisfactory. It traces a rough division, deemed as fundamental, between all the premodern societies and the only modern one, characterized by institutions such as market economy, schools and legislation for equal rights of women and antidiscrimination in general, which operate in conjunction with the industrialization and urbanization processes. This concept is not useful according to world-systems analysis. Modernization is actually equivalent to Westernization and is a word introduced in place of the latter to make the concept more acceptable and less racist, by masking its implications of the superiority of the West. "Westernization" and "modernization" are however simple synonyms of "capitalism expansion." As Wallerstein (2000, 171) wrote, "We do not live in a modernizing world, but in a capitalist world." However, if we were not dealing with capitalism but with modernization, the idea would be that sooner or later everyone, thanks to this process, will reach the West with its freedom, wealth, very high standard of living and wasting of resources. The use of the term "modernization" instead of "development of capitalism" obscures the unequal exchange and the fact that inequality is functional to growth: the development of one area implies the underdevelopment of another, which is the central message of world-systems analysis.

For Notestein, persistence of the old ideological apparatus explains the period of low mortality and high birth rates of the nineteenth-century West. However, the demographer took into consideration not only culture becoming "rational" but also the material driving factors behind it:

> Urban life stripped the family of many functions in production, consumption, recreation, and education. In factory employment the individual stood on his own accomplishments. The new mobility of young people and the anonymity of city life reduced the pressures toward traditional behaviour exerted by the family and community. In a period of rapidly developing technology new skills were needed, and new opportunities for individual advancement arose. Education and a rational point of view became increasingly important. As a consequence the cost of child-rearing grew and the possibilities for economic contributions by children declined. (Notestein 1953, 16)

Notestein also observed the changes in the role of women, who leave domestic production and enter the world of education and the labor market, emancipating themselves from the family and its oppressive traditionalism.

The new female role in the formal economy makes it more difficult for women to fulfill their role in raising children (Lindahl-Kiessling and Landberg 1994). The position of women and their growing power in deciding whether to bear the costs of pregnancy and childcare is certainly an important cause of the decline in fertility that is occurring in almost all of the contemporary world, and is related to women's growing degree of education and participation in paid employment.

## 4.3 Economic and Cultural Irrationality?

One implication of the demographic transition theory is that large families are not economically rational, so high fertility can be reduced by overcoming peasant ignorance. But family planning programs based on this pedagogical approach have failed. Mahmood Mamdani (1972) studied the Manupur village in Punjab, where there were no reasons to control fertility, always calculated at zero cost, in situations where women have no decision-making powers. Despite the fact that NGOs and the government had deluged the village with pills and other contraceptive methods, they were simply not used. Just a few years later, however, the same village began to enthusiastically use those devices which at the time of Mamdani's visit were thrown away or used as material for artistic creations. Moni Nag and Neeraj Kak (1984) visited Manupur 10 years after Mamdani and found that the conditions of production had profoundly changed. The fragmentation of agricultural properties had diminished the use of child labor. There were few pastures left, while the land was converted to farmland, so there was no longer any need for kids to look after the cattle. Chemical fertilizers were used in the plots and fossil fuels in the house, so the collection of dung that children had formerly done for these uses was no longer necessary. Even weeding had been replaced by herbicides, so the boys no longer did it. They usually attended secondary school.

However, the idea of the existence of a pronatalist cultural apparatus had already been rejected by Kingsley Davis and Judith Blake (1956), who wrote that one could not ignore the fact that in traditional societies children worked. The extended family easily and willingly covered the costs of short childhoods because its economic and political strength would be increased by the number of family members. The ancient French proverb was still valid in the Third World: *à pauvres gens, enfants sont richesse* (for the poor, children are riches). John Caldwell stated in the 1960s that each additional child brought economic advantages to the societies with a familial mode of production (see Section 4.8). He affirmed that none of the research he and his teams conducted in Nigeria or Ghana had ever found traces of cultural delays, in the sense that behavior was irrational with respect to the current economic and social purposes for that society, being rational toward the goals of the earlier period. Caldwell writes:

> I should remark that nothing I have experienced in West Africa suggests that there is any cultural lag—any delay in recognizing how to achieve new objectives arising from traditional ways of looking at things and an inability to do things in a new way—in adjusting to new economic ends that are determined by changed social ends. The rate of social change determines economic change, and this in turn determines the value of children, and hence fertility change. (Caldwell 1982, 72)

On the supposed "irrationality of traditional societies," Richard Wilkinson (1973, 17) said the following:

> In practice, the biological structure of man in the period in which we are interested [the last centuries] is so constant that it would be a good methodological rule not to invoke increases in intelligence, individualism or inventiveness to explain development, unless we can provide cultural explanations for these increases.

Considering high premodern fertility rates as rational behavior is a position shared by the "New Home Economics" founded by Gary Becker and Theodore W. Schultz of the Chicago School that first theorized neoliberalism. They apply their microeconomic theory to the demographic transition by stating that the driving force behind the transition was the reduced demand for children propelled by changing income, prices and tastes. For Becker and Schultz, the so-called decline of fertility is based on rational choices. Their economic theory of the family proposes models on the supply and demand of children (Becker 1981). Nancy Folbre (1986) criticized this theory because of its unrealistic hypotheses: in particular, that children are comparable to consumer goods and that in the family the altruism of the breadwinner reigns. As Folbre shows in *The Invisible Heart* (2001), Becker and his followers assume a clear division of moral work: perfect selfishness reigns in the market while perfect altruism reigns in the family. These are ideological assumptions, which are not descriptive but prescriptive of the behavior of men and women. Furthermore, for Becker as well as for demographers, the cost of having children for women is just the opportunity-cost of the paid work they could undertake.

Richard Easterlin (1978) integrated the Beckerian scheme with a sociological approach to procreation, considering it as a choice that the family makes with regard to the number of children, thus leaving the internal and external power relationships around procreation decisions in a black box. Like Becker, Easterlin wanted to calculate the discounted value of children, recognizing that the net value of work contributions an offspring can offer is an important consideration in procreative decisions.

## 4.4 Theory and Data

A major research project on the demographic transition has been the European Fertility Project coordinated by the Office of Population Research at Princeton (Coale and Watkins 1986). The Princeton group began a research program in 1964 to establish the timing of what they called "the decline of fertility in Europe." They gathered and analyzed the demographic data of Europe divided in more than 600 territorial units, corresponding to provinces. The head of the research, demographer Ansley Coale, stated that a decrease in fertility occurs when it "becomes part of the calculation of conscious choice," thanks to the availability of contraceptive means, that must be known to those who perceive that limiting fertility will have beneficial effects. These statements are still pillars of demography.

The all-time high of "natural fertility" was achieved between 1921 and 1930 by the Hutterites, a rural Anabaptist community established in the central-northern United States and southern-central Canada. A typical Hutterite woman married at 20 years of age and gave birth to 11 children, while the total fertility rate of the population was 9 children per woman. These values were the reference point for the measurements of the Princeton group, which pinpointed fertility transition in a province to the moment in which its fertility rate was reduced by 10 percent without ever increasing again to the previous level.

The results of the European Fertility Project were that the decrease in births was linked not so much to socioeconomic modernization as to diffusion processes in homogeneous linguistic or religious areas. The share of the population who worked the land was not useful to predict with statistical models the beginning of the decrease in births, infant mortality and literacy ratios, but language or religion shared with neighboring areas where births rates had already dropped were highly significant. Many examples of this can be found in Belgium (Kohler 2001).

France was the first country to start the demographic transition, which at the national level happened around 1827 but in some provinces was already occurring before 1800. In France, the socioeconomic structure consisted of small peasant property, which was much more widespread than in England, the country that was at the forefront of modernization and was expected to lead the so-called decline. Births were therefore not encouraged in the same way by the socioeconomic structure in France as compared to England, where the peasants had been dispossessed and had already obtained employment opportunities in proto-industry (see Section 6.3). After France, Hungary—also an agricultural and "backward" country—was the second nation in Europe to decrease fertility, having laws and customs that divided the land equally among the children in a family. One should therefore wonder why fertility was so high in the past in these agricultural countries prior to the transition: this is the real anomaly.

The demographic historian Marcel Reinhard wrote in his introduction to *History of the World Population*: "The rough vision of a demographic revolution that would have suddenly interrupted a long series of centuries of the so-called natural regime [...] had to be relegated to the rank of the mythical good savages and similar men of Nature" (Reinhard et al. 1971, 11) even if in the course of the text the authors again expressed their tribute to modern rationality:

> A centuries-old regime dominated by nature—that is, by climate, instinct, biological aspects—tends to give way to a regime controlled and wanted by man, which now slowly begins to master diseases, if not death, and the number of births, if not instinct. Thus begins what we might call the "conscious" history of the population. Can we imagine a revolution deeper than this? (Reinhard et al. 1971, 283)[3]

Livi Bacci, who participated in the research at Princeton, drew up the following critique of the demographic transition theory:

> Its weakness is not so much in the numerous deviations from the scheme (in many cases the decline in fertility began before that of mortality; the transition of fertility in rural France began a century earlier than in industrial England, and in many cases values and rules that governed individual choices seemed not very permeable to economic or social changes, and so on) as in the presumption that "before" and "after" the transition, there would be a state of demographic balance, in which

3 On the very next page the authors contradict themselves again: "In the various civilizations, the demographic regime, far from being a natural regime, was subject to the conditioning and control of beliefs and social institutions" starting with the rules on marriage. The only way out of the contradiction is that the conditioning and control of premodern civilizations upon their "demographic regime" was nevertheless irrational.

> birth and mortality are very close and growth is zero or negligible. (Livi Bacci 1994, 17)

Despite his criticism of the postulations of the theory, the Italian demographer continues to refer to it in his writings for a wider audience (e.g., Livi Bacci et al. 1994, 17; Livi Bacci 2016). He always uses other concepts of doubtful validity such as "reproductive instinct" and the "Malthusian trap," which blocks economic development due to the fact that if the lower class earns more than it must spend in mere subsistence, it will use the difference to raise a greater number of children, without ever being able to improve its well-being. The image of the Malthusian trap suggests that the exceptional nature of British and then European economic development was due specifically to variations in reproductive behavior. These propositions are untenable: England's population expanded at pace with industrialization. In fact, looking at global data and also national figures, the curves of population growth are highly correlated with the use of fossil fuels (Hall and Klitgaard 2018; see Section 8.1). Pomeranz, and others, disproved the correlation between low procreation and industrialization:

> The arguments positing that Western Europe's economy was uniquely capable of generating an industrial transformation generally fall into two clusters. The first, typified by the work of E. L. Jones, argues that beneath a surface of "preindustrial" similarity, 16th- through 18th-century Europe had already moved far ahead of the rest of its world in the accumulation of both physical and human capital. A central tenet of this view is that various customary checks on fertility (late marriage, a celibate clergy etc) allowed Europe to escape from the otherwise universal condition of a "pre-modern fertility regime" and thus from a similarly universal condition in which population growth absorbed almost all of any increase in production. (Pomeranz 2000, 27)

Eric Jones ([1981] 2003) in fact believed that the difference between European and Asian demographic regimes was due to the frequency of natural catastrophes, due to climate and geography. The European population could develop homeostatic mechanisms, but self-limitation of new generations in Asia would have jeopardized normal reproduction because of the frequent need to recover human losses from hurricanes, floods, earthquakes and the like.

The second cluster of Pomeranz's review focuses on the institutions present in Europe. Pomeranz partially welcomed this thesis, favorably mentioning Wallerstein's explanation in terms of capitalist development in a world-economy.

## 4.5 Tribute to Demographic Expansion

Even demographers who view it critically continue to use the theory of demographic transition, almost like exoteric knowledge.[4] But if the theory is not valid, why propose it again and again, and even teach it in textbooks? Demographers are the very first to complain about "too low" fertility rates and urge European states to adopt pronatalist policies, suggesting that this balance should be achieved at the contemporary all-time high levels, unprecedented in the history of the human population.

This high-level stationary state that nations should aim for, with a replacement rate of 2.1 children per woman, is the demographic equivalent of the mythical equilibrium point of neoclassical economics. But concepts of equilibrium as a social objective are extremely misleading in capitalism, since the growth of capital is the engine of the economic system that satisfies human needs (and this growth could be partly obtained from an increase in the population).

Reinhard et al. (1971, 410) pointed out that the "populationist" mindset was an integral part of the bourgeois culture of the French Revolution. "The ideal of population growth belongs to the whole marching wing of the revolution and contrasts with concerns about population limits by counter-revolutionaries" (see also Kesper-Biermann 2012 on Germany). This is precisely the ideal of the discipline of demography, which always sees growth in a positive light, fears "stagnation" (which might rather be called "balance") and demonizes regression (e.g., Del Panta et al. 1996). This type of prose is typical of population history literature.

> By the early 18th century the population of Europe was significantly greater than it had been two hundred years earlier, but even so, it is doubtful whether it had *recovered* its levels of the 14th century, so severe had been the damage caused by the first century and a half of the plague pandemic. This implies annual growth rates averaging *barely* 0.2 percent—less than one tenth of the growth rates *achieved* by some developing countries in the later 20th century. (Flinn 1981, 76; my italics for the words passionately connoting growth)

History appears to be a race to expand the population, in which only its quantity counts, never its quality of life, which depends on the class structure

---

4 More recently, this contradiction appears, for example, in the various works of Jennifer Johnson-Hanks, professor of demography at University of California, Berkeley. The demographic transition is mentioned or not, depending on whether the work is aimed to a more or less specialized audience.

and in many instances also on its size. It is not only demographers who uphold population growth and express anguish over its "decline." When dealing with population, almost all of the other social scientists speak in the same way. The Department of Economics and Law of the Sapienza University in Rome (Pizzuti 2017, 261) described the slight drop of the Italian population in 2015 and 2016 (139,000 and 142,000 inhabitants less, out of a total around 60 million) as "decline," "hemorrhage" and "depression," forgetting that the growth had been almost constant from 1861 onward, with the addition of an average of 220,000 inhabitants per year.

Italian historian Athos Bellettini (1987, 8–9) remarked:

> The alternation of phases of stagnation, limited development, and regression in which the history of populations is resolved up to the contemporary age is therefore due to the continuous erosion resulting from the high rate of mortality and its sudden accentuations, which often destroy in a very short time the increase of population slowly and laboriously accumulated.

Bellettini (1987, 22) connotes population decrease as "depopulation and economic and physical degradation" of the territory which becomes "the swamp, the uncultivated, the forest." These are the places where wild species live and it makes no sense to represent them as "degradation." Indeed, wild areas represent, in the words of Sheila Newman (2013), the infrastructure of biodiversity, which is necessary for our biological structures and therefore also for social ones. In permaculturalist terms it is called zone 5, where all that is indispensable to human life happens outside our control.

Is demographers' fascination with population increase a natural love for their object of study or an expression of nationalism? In the case of the three eminent scholars who wrote the first world population history, the former alternative seems to be valid, as they describe life in sub-Saharan Africa and Madagascar in the following way, with the usual enthusiasm about growth:

> These investigations have highlighted the restraining function that customs and various prohibitions have in this field. Indeed, despite getting married very early—so that at 20 years of age female celibacy is practically an unknown phenomenon—from 15 to 49 years of age women give birth on average only [!] six to eight times in the best [!] cases. (Reinhard et al. 1971, 32)

The examples could continue ad libitum.

## 4.6 The Second Demographic Transition

The alleged end of the demographic transition—the attainment of population balance—did not come about. In the countries that have "made the transition," the tendency instead is toward decrease, and a balance between births and deaths has not been achieved. Observing the continuous decrease in the number of children per woman, demographers developed the concept of a second demographic transition pulled by a value shift toward individualism (van de Kaa 1987; Lesthaege 2010), which happened while the first transition was still underway in underdeveloped countries (Cleland 2001). In the second half of the twentieth century, developed countries have thus moved on to a second demographic transition in which fertility is lower than the replacement rate, that is, lower than 2.1 children per woman, while the age for marriage has continued to rise. Moreover, marriage no longer "monopolizes" births as in the years before 1968: an increasing proportion of children is born to couples who do not marry, even if they sometimes do so later. Immigration from the periphery and semiperiphery keeps the number of inhabitants of the core steady, or increases it.

Demographers have wondered if the second demographic transition will become as universal as the first, if it really only has "demographic causes" (whatever they are) and if perhaps there is no necessary connection with the transformations of the family structure. Such questions could make sense only if demographic phenomena, for example the size of the family, were independent and dissociated from what happens elsewhere in society. Of course this segmentation is the basic vice not only of demography but also of all the disciplines in which liberal philosophy has fragmented social science.

However, Table 3 is interesting because it summarizes the opposing social characteristics associated with the first and second demographic transitions according to its two main theorists, Ron Lesthaege and Dirk van de Kaa. They refer to Inglehart (1998), who in the World Value Survey he coordinated found a transition to postmaterialist values of self-realization and individual autonomy. There have been two important cultural transformations in the second demographic transition. The first is the placing of the child at the center of the family's emotional life, becoming the object of enormous emotional and material investments. The second is the affirmation of the values linked to the self-fulfillment of adults, who limit their willingness to become parents in increasingly individualized societies. Procreation nevertheless is still considered by sociologists and demographers to be a normal step in the life cycle—clearly a prescriptive rather than a descriptive proposition. According to studies in Germany, it seems that currently men in particular reject parenthood (Mareen Spranz 2008).

**Table 3** Overview of demographic and societal characteristics related to the first and second demographic transitions in Western Europe

| First demographic transition | Second demographic transition |
|---|---|
| **Marriage** | |
| Rise in proportions marrying, declining age at first marriage | Fall in proportions married, rise in age at first marriage |
| Low or reduced cohabitations | Rise in cohabitation (pre- and postmarital) |
| Low divorce | Rise in divorce, earlier divorce |
| High remarriage | Decline in remarriage following both divorce and widowhood |
| **Fertility** | |
| Decline in marital fertility, via reduction at older ages, lowering mean age at childbearing | Further decline in fertility via postponement, increasing mean age at first parenthood, structural sub-replacement fertility |
| Deficient contraception, parity failures | Efficient contraception (exceptions in specific social groups) |
| Declining illegitimate fertility, but not necessarily among teenage women | Rising extramarital fertility due to parenthood within cohabitation |
| Low definitive childlessness among married couples | Rising definitive childlessness in unions |
| **Societal background** | |
| Preoccupations with basic material needs: income, work conditions, housing, health, schooling, social security; solidarity is a prime value | Rise of higher-order needs: individual autonomy; self-actualization, expressive work and socialization values, grassroots democracy, recognition by others; tolerance is prime value |
| Rising membership in political, civic and community-oriented networks; strengthening of social cohesion | Disengagement from civic and community-oriented networks, social capital shifts to expressive and affective types; weakening of social cohesion |
| Strong normative regulation by the Church and State; first secularization wave, dominance of political and social factions ("pillars") | Retreat of the state, second secularization wave, sexual revolution, refusal of authority, waning influence of political factions ("pillars") |
| Segregated gender roles, familistic policies, embourgeoisement, promotion of economic autonomy, breadwinner family model | Rising symmetry in gender roles, female economic autonomy |

**Table 3** (*Cont.*)

| First demographic transition | Second demographic transition |
|---|---|
| Ordered life-course transitions, prudent marriage and dominance of a single model of the family | Flexible life-course organization, multiple lifestyles, open future |

*Source*: Lesthaege (2010, 246).

However, these changes can also be seen as a shift from the values of the working and peasant classes to those of the middle class. They correspond to the main economic and social (rather than cultural) changes in the countries of the center, with the tertiarization of the economy and the generalized increase in the standard of living measured by GDP. Indeed, it is not true that income, work, housing, school, health and social security have ceased to be central concerns of the new generations. Only during *Les Trente Glorieuses* (the Glorious Thirty), from 1945 to 1975, were material problems more easily resolved, while currently one sees that conditions have deteriorated for the working class, with rising inequalities: 1 percent of the global population possesses 44 percent of global household wealth, while 2.8 billion adults possess wealth below 10,000 USD (Crédit Suisse Research Institute 2019, 2).

Since the beginning of the 2000s in many Western developed economies, the relationship between women's work or income and fertility has become positive: women who have higher income also have more children. Not only with birth allowances but also with policies of reconciliation between work and family, fertility has increased in Belgium, France and the United Kingdom, while in Estonia and Slovenia it is much higher than the European average (Matysiak 2011). Politicians still worry about the so-called decline in the birth rate, considering it a future shortage of the labor force (McIntosh 1981; Gauthier 1996) or purely for nationalistic reasons (Danna 2012).

## 4.7 Why Did Mortality Fall?

The capitalist world-economy has its own geoculture (Wallerstein 1999b), of which myths and narratives on demographic history are a part. The theory of demographic transition should demonstrate the advancement of Reason in the world, in a narrative of progress propelled by Europe that brings technological innovation and rationality to the rest of the world. It is another aspect of the white man's burden—the rhetorical figure which ideologically should justify colonialism as the bearer of civilization to savages. Civilization is linked specifically to the progress of medicine, to which the drop in mortality in the initial phase of the demographic transition is attributed, for example, "the rapid declines in infant and child mortality that were the main cause of the population explosion" (Lam 2011, 1250).

But that mortality decreased due to the application of better medicine is denied by multiple studies. *The Rise of the Modern Population* (1976) by Thomas McKeown is a rigorous examination of the possible reasons for the phenomenon, dealing mainly with England and Wales, thanks to the official records of the population numbers preserved there since 1838. At that time, population increase was already in progress and the decrease in mortality, observed in particular since 1838, dates back to the previous century. However, McKeown could not explain this decrease with the techno-enthusiastic vulgate that considers the progress of medicine at the base of it all. Far from acting as a defense, early vaccinations could trigger a given disease in the vaccinated and even infect other people: "The fall of mortality was not influenced substantially by immunization or therapy before 1935 when sulphonamides became available" (McKeown 1976, 153). There was not even a spontaneous regression of infectious diseases, excluded by careful examination of available documents by the British historian and physician. Hygienic measures such as "water purification, efficient sewage and improvement of food hygiene, especially milk" may have worked only from the mid-nineteenth century onward: "It is unlikely that such influences [hygienic measures] were effective before that time, since initially industrialization led to crowding and deterioration of hygienic conditions" (McKeown 1976, 153). The greatest contribution to the overall decline in mortality is found by McKeown in the decrease of the heterogeneous class of deaths attributed to "prematurity, immaturity and other early childhood diseases," together with the decrease in deaths from gastroenteritis, almost all of which occurred within the first year of life.

According to McKeown, there is no doubt that this trend depended to some extent on improvements in obstetric services, before and after labor, but it is also likely that it was mainly due to progress in maternal nutrition and better child nutrition and childcare. Ultimately, according not only to McKeown, the ceiling for the population is determined by the ability of a society to expand food production. He concluded that "the most acceptable explanation of the large reduction of mortality and growth of population which preceded advances in hygiene is an improvement in nutrition due to greater food supplies" (McKeown 1976, 153). Resistance to infections, thanks to the improved nutrition of the English population, decreased mortality. However, presumably what changed was the decision to use those food supplies for infants instead of neglecting them. It is rather unlikely that industrial workers' living conditions and nutrition had improved with the Industrial

Revolution, as McKeown also admitted upon describing the terrible situation of the early industrial workers. Even Reinhard, Armengaud and Dupaquier, not suspicious of anti-capitalist positions, wrote that at the time of the Industrial Revolution there was no progress in terms of hygiene in working-class homes and workplaces. On the contrary:

> Let's start with the houses: "sewers open on the road and below its level [...] where the air is humid and cold as in a cave"; the stench reigns in it and in the darkness the beds are piled up to welcome whole families. These hovels are rented at a very high price which often represents 10 percent of the salary. We come to the workplace: the premises are cheaply built with light material and where the land costs less. Every attention was paid to protecting the machines, never the workers. In winter, the cold was terrible, the heating was poor and unhealthy, and the lighting system poor and faulty. In summer the heat was intolerable, nothing mitigated it. In any season the dirt was incredible. In some processes the thick dust suffocated the workers causing pernicious diseases. "This is not piecework"—wrote Villermé —"it is torture." In similar places, women and children also worked from 5 in the morning to 9 in the evening. In the upper Rhine valley in 1847, out of 61,000 wage earners 13,000 were children. In 1838 the female workforce represented 56 to 70 percent of the total, depending on the branch of the textile sector in question. (Reinhard et al. 1971, 474)

The authors noticed that the workers were prolific:

> Villermé calculated an average of 4 or 5 living children per worker family. The geographical distribution of the birth rate [in France, as paradigm for the rest of Europe in the industrialization phase] proves that the industrial regions were at the top of the ranking: the North, Alsace, the Lyon region.
>
> Indeed, we must think that children represented a burden for families only for a short time, since they started working very early, at 7 or 8 years old. [...] "The worker proliferates in proportion to his misery," Buret observed. "Having as many children as possible is a fundamental principle since each child means a future salary," noted Mareska and Heyman. On the contrary, a certain limitation of births occurred between artisans and skilled workers who had a higher standard of living. (Reinhard et al. 1971, 476)

The same occurred in Latin America with a population explosion that coincided with its Industrial Revolution at the beginning of the 20th century (Viel 1976, 204), and this also occurred in India at the beginning of industrialization there in the 1880s:

> The industrial era was initially characterized by the same abuses and the same sufferings that had characterized its start in Europe. In the years around 1875, the use of children aged 5 to 6 was reported, as well as women, forced to work for 15 and 16 hours each. (Reinhard et al. 1971, 657)

The same connection between industrialization and development and population growth was shared by the so-called opposite totalitarianisms. Stalin planned the USSR's demographic development by providing for aid and rewards to families as they became more numerous. This political turning point was officially proclaimed in his speech of May 4, 1935: "Man, the most precious capital," he said, echoing Mussolini's speech of May 26, 1927, in the Chamber of Deputies, remembered as the "Discourse of the Ascension" in which *il Duce* launched the pronatalist policy of the fascist regime with the aim of counting 60 million Italians.[5] (This threshold was crossed in 2014.)

This also happened in Sicily, according to Jane and Peter Schneider (1992): the increase in population occurred in correspondence with the rise of the mining sector with the export of large quantities of sulfur, together with the increase in exports of wine and wheat. They write that the pace of capital formation and investment in Sicily corresponded with some precision to the pace of population growth. The population grew by 19 percent between 1814 and 1861, from just over 2 to about 2.4 million. Over the next 40 years, which was the golden age for the expansion of sulfur and wine production, the population on the island grew by almost 50 percent, reaching more than 3.5 million in 1901.

Local research in southern Anlo, Ghana, showed that "the period of the great leap forward for industry (1930-50) coincided with a population explosion in the area which resulted in mass migrations from neighboring villages to Abidjan, Badagri, and Cotonou" (Nukunya 1975, 215). The author also disconfirms the Boserup theory: "population pressure and an inclination towards farming are not sufficient conditions for agricultural intensification" (Nukunya 1975, 216). In Ethiopia, McCann (1995, 96) noted an increase in

5 On the debate and demographic policies of the 1930s in the more developed countries where the population slowed down its growth, see Teitelbaum and Winter (1985).

the birth rate after 1916 during a period of social peace in which the state facilitated the exploitation of new agricultural lands.

In general, considerations about African demography in the text edited by Cordell and Gregory (1987) mirror McKeown's doubts about the prominent role of medicine in the growth in population in Africa in the twentieth century: "two problems are apparent in this common sense approach. First, there is little evidence to support the supposition of major improvements in health, hygiene, standards of living or nutrition. Second, the analysis suggests that the demographic variables of mortality and fertility can be examined in isolation" (Dawson 1987, 201), while this is not necessarily true.

The hypothesis that McKeown does not take into consideration to find the cause of the fall in mortality is the willingness of people, particularly the industrial workers, to reduce mortality by providing food and caring for more children. The context is their extreme poverty plus an industrial demand for children's labor, in the absence of which the "excess" offspring would have consciously or unconsciously been eliminated. Jean Louis Flandrin[6] also believed that reduced child mortality in the eighteenth century may not have had medical or hygienic reasons, but was achieved by simply ceasing the practice of letting infants die. To my knowledge, and of course with the exception of the historiographic literature specific to infanticide, the real question which no scholar has ever faced upon reflecting on population is: when did it really become difficult to practice the infanticide of children who could not be supported? States have always considered it a crime—so did this difficulty come about because of greater controls or because of a cultural change, united with change in economic conditions? This is the real turning point regarding the mortality rate.

On the one hand, anthropologists recorded many observations of self-regulating behaviors. Traces of such behavior were also found in the writings of travelers and missionaries during the period of European expansion starting in the sixteenth century. On the other hand, demographers generally deny that before the "contraceptive revolution" there had been effective birth control, which they consider as the only possible method to consciously regulate the population. Only some demographers agreed on giving importance to the "death control" carried out consciously and voluntarily for the purpose of stabilizing population numbers. For example, Karen Mason (1997, 448) called the infanticides she observed in East Asia "postnatal means of family limitation." Ansley Coale defined both infanticides on other continents and

6 In an intervention at a conference mentioned in the introduction of Ariès (1960).

child abandonments in Europe as forms of population control, although only in a note to his introduction to the European Fertility Project (Coale and Watkins 1986, 4).

In *Death, Sex and Fertility* (1987), anthropologists Marvin Harris and Eric Ross showed how so-called traditional societies intervened as much as they could on fertility in an attempt to maintain the demographic balance, but managed to intervene more on mortality. They also observed that in Europe's past there were frequent deaths by suffocation of infants in the beds of parents who crushed them when turning in their sleep. Were they accidental events or intentional negligence? In the Middle Ages, the laws of many countries banned mothers and infants from sleeping in the same bed. However, at that time, parents of infants who died in their sleep were never punished. To return to the case of Denmark, deaths from the crushing of infants were indeed not so rare. In the diocese of Ribe in 1712–73, there were 140 trials before the bishop for this reason, half of which resulted in the punishment of the mothers. In all, there were 200 cases of infanticide in Ribe during this period, almost four cases per year. In northern Jylland, 89 women were tried in the period 1719–1805, 62 of whom were sentenced to death by the High Court, while the rest were tried a second time by minor courts. The last execution took place in 1861: a woman who for the fourth time had been found guilty of infanticide was put to death. The women who were discovered were probably a small portion of those who abandoned or killed their newborn babies, since many gave birth in secret. To find out if women had recently given birth, many authorities periodically checked whether unmarried women were able to breastfeed.

Another way to eliminate the "excess" offspring was to send the children to live with a wet nurse, a stay from which few returned. Even orphanages, rather than saving children, greatly reduced their numbers. For example, Langer (1975) reported that out of 4,779 children admitted in 1818 to the Paris hospital, 2,370 died in the first three months of their stay.

However, some social facts are just the unintended consequences of actions with a specific purpose. Indeed, population scholars of Tibet believed that polyandry in Kyirong and the custom in Sama to reserve a daughter for the Buddhist monastery to take care of parents when they grew old had no purpose in limiting the population, so this diminution occurred in a completely unintentional way (Childs 2008).

## 4.8 Caldwell's Review

John Caldwell (1982, 158) wrote critically about the theory of demographic transition: "Each mode of production has its own economic laws, and dependent demographic laws." Caldwell noted that Marx's modes of production (primitive communist, ancient, Asiatic, feudal, capitalist, socialist and communist) are rather mostly modes of administration or distribution. There are instead "three major modes: hunting and gathering, farming, and capitalist/industrial. Admittedly, a case could be made for treating both shifting cultivation and nomadic pastoralism as separate modes" (Caldwell 2006, 6). The Australian demographer adopted an anthropological perspective which, as he himself stressed, was rather unusual for his discipline, and recognized that procreative decisions were made prior to the transition to modernity. However, Caldwell did not adhere to an economic theory of fertility: procreative decisions can be rational only within the framework established by social objectives. Modernization (changes in economic organization) and Westernization (processes of cultural imitation) were for Caldwell increasingly powerful thrusts to establish low fertility even in poor countries.

Caldwell's first research studied migration from the countryside to the city in Ghana from 1962 to 1964. The interviews he carried out highlighted that the economic conditions of large families were in reality on par with those of small ones, and that even their future prospects were not worse:

> As I came to know them, the societies that first shook my belief in the universal burden of children were in the remote parts of Ghana and Nigeria. There, no indigenous person understood what I meant when suggesting that the largest families might be the worst off and might have been happier and richer had childbearing been more restrained. Children had few needs other than food, for there was no formal education and few clothes. After infancy, children growing up in small villages where everyone kept an eye on them, required only limited care. Conflicts over inheritance and farm subdivision were unknown because land ownership was communal. (Caldwell et al. 2006, 90)

(This excerpt also highlights a typical male vision of children's needs, presumed to be so limited.) This clearly contrasted with the then dominant demographic theories centered on the disadvantages of having numerous children. The research also stressed a negative correlation between the number of children and the schooling of parents, especially mothers. In 1966, Caldwell performed another study on the economic conditions of older people in rural areas of Ghana and found again that low fertility had not brought families any advantage over high fertility. The main source for improving one's economic conditions was the education of one's children. A survey he conducted in Nigeria in 1969 found that the inhabitants of the countryside who had contraceptive means available rarely made use of them, preferring not to limit their fertility. Finally, the experience of the Sahel drought in 1972–73 made him see the importance of family ties in the conditions of life in the Tropics, where populations lived under the constant threat of environmental disasters.

Caldwell's controversy with his academic and political environment, which refused to recognize the benefits of having numerous offspring in the countries where the population explosion was taking place, culminated with his speech at the World Population Conference in Bucharest in 1974. On that occasion, he denounced the emphasis on the presumed benefits of the decline in fertility as being simplistic and unrealistic—but this was exactly the message of almost all the other speakers.

Caldwell tried to get his discipline to make a paradigm shift and consider the usefulness of children's work as the economic variable that influenced choices on fertility, which also had political and social aspects. Finally, he formulated a theory of intergenerational wealth flow. In his view, the rise of the market economy and its worldwide spread meant first the transition from various familial modes of production (i.e., modes of production having in common the family as the fundamental economic unit, both in production and consumption) to non-familial modes of production. This included the industrial mode of production in the West and the modern sector in developing countries. In Caldwell's conception, changes were not sudden, and different modes of production could coexist for long periods. For Caldwell, the distinctive feature of the capitalist economy is the existence of a labor market independent of both kinship ties and traditional labor obligations. Industrial economy is considered a recent manifestation of this mode of production. In familial modes of production, the family constitutes the basic economic unit of production and organization, and is the main employer, whether it is a family of farmers, artisans, nobles or even workers without land, he writes. The extended family is typical of societies functioning with a familial mode of production, due to the widespread need to have long-lasting safety guarantees and protection links, in a measure inversely proportional to the protection obtainable by other institutions.

Caldwell noted a profound difference between the familial and non-familial mode of production in the direction of intra-family wealth flows. The term "wealth" was applied by Caldwell with some hesitation, because wealth is normally considered a stock. In relation to the analyzed flow, the term "income" would nevertheless be even worse, as it suggests a monetary flow. Caldwell considered it important to conceptualize it as a "flow of benefits." Wealth was thus defined as comprising goods and services, work and money, protection and guarantees, social and political support. If the basic economic unit is the family, wealth flows from children to adults (parents and other relatives). In contrast, where an impersonal market based on monetary exchanges has developed, the flow goes in the opposite direction. This is mainly due to the cost of education, necessary in a complex society, and to the emotional nuclearization of the family, concomitant with the dissolution of the extended family as a unit of production, which changes the position of children in the eyes of parents:

> The nucleation of the family will not of itself make high fertility unprofitable. This required the adoption of a system in which the lifetime net flow of money is from parent to child rather than in the opposite direction and a rise in children's costs which makes a large number of them prohibitively expensive. (Caldwell 1982, 111)

In familial modes of production, on the other hand, especially female children contribute from early childhood to their maintenance by working for the family. The children are entrusted with a substantial part of the housework, the transport of food and messages, the lighter jobs in the fields and the role of shepherd. Regina Smith Oboler (1985) noted how child labor was made invisible among the Nandi of Kenya, according to the usual practice of exploiting the labor of those who are denied any symbolic recognition for it, as admitting its importance would be tantamount to admitting the exploitation.

As for monetary earnings, children do not wait for their parents' old age to pass on at least part of the wages received or to hand over the entire amount. In addition, children continue to work on their parents' lands even after establishing their own production unit. The importance of the services rendered by offspring should not be underestimated: an easier life is identified, understandably, with being relieved of the repetitive tasks of household chores. Procreation provides the necessary workforce ("cheap labor instead of machines," wrote Caldwell), as also established by the traditional division of labor, which makes a man consider it humiliating to perform the jobs his children should do. Moreover, a large family confers political advantages. A large family is in itself synonymous with power, thanks to the physical strength it can employ and the numerical influence it has on the decisions of the village. It confers the opportunity for the patriarch to increase his influence through numerous marriage ties, although in general there is more trust in blood relatives than in acquired ones.

Children also constituted an investment channel: their education was considered a good alternative to buying new land. The earnings from the growing social mobility of children, in addition to remittances, included byproducts such as having contact with urban life. These could represent benefits for the whole village, in the form of gadgets of the modern economy that entered the village as gifts, or of the support given by the firstborn to the education of the other children. This investment never turned out to be excessively expensive: "It is, of course, common that it is the children, or they and their mother, who do the most belt tightening, and hence there is no real cost for the decision maker" (Caldwell 1982, 227). This exploitation was masked by the widespread ideology that emphasized the duties of children toward parents and other adults. Even this type of investment must however be considered from the perspective of traditional societies: it was an investment in security rather than in wealth. Caldwell insisted that what was economically rational in traditional societies was aimed at ensuring long-term protection rather than maximizing profit in good times, in agreement with Aleksandr Čajanov's analysis of the peasant economy ([1923] 1991).

Therefore, in procreation decisions it was not so much the future per capita earnings (the terms in which Western researchers generally thought) that were important, but it was the advantage that the dominant members of the family, the older males, could derive from more children. Male dominance in marriage was also ensured by the age difference between the spouses. In the case of sons, potential conflicts were kept at bay by the possibility of them enjoying the same benefits in adulthood. Nonetheless, the fact that family economic relationships were based on exploitation meant that there was potential for conflict and transformation, especially at the hands of women.

As to costs, most of the respondents in the surveys reported in *Theory of Fertility Decline* (1982) bluntly replied that children cost nothing. Food and clothing did not represent prohibitive costs (food was prepared in large quantities and adding an extra dish was barely a noticeable cost); the costs of compulsory education were still low; and younger children did not constitute a huge commitment for mothers, since they were cared for by older siblings. Furthermore, it was the extended family, and not just the parents, that took care of the new child. This implied that family planning decisions often were not in the hands of parents, but of the patriarch.

Since greater social mobility is generally desired by families, when does the economic motivation for having children cease? It ceases when education becomes compulsory, even if only socially. When this happens, parents invest in the brightest child to enable him or her to reach the highest possible level of education. At that point the cost of raising children increases and in parallel women begin to have power to speak up in procreation matters, via their proletarianization.

Production processes that use more advanced technologies require a skilled and formally trained workforce. The spread of mass schooling was an expression of both this need and the aspiration of families to obtain social mobility through access to higher education for their children. Fertility transition, in the words of Penn Handwerker, who elaborated on Caldwell's wealth flow theory, begins in places and at a time when it becomes possible for formally educated people to find work even without personal connections:

> Fertility transition is brought about by (1) changes in the moral economy of reproductive behavior and parent-child relationships, which change because (2) the expected wealth flows from children and the social relationships they create is negative, which occurs when (3) the relative importance of personal relationships in accessing key resources declines, which declines because (4) changes in opportunity structure are accompanied by the ability to make effective use of an independent criterion—most commonly but not exclusively, formal schooling and skill training—to create and maintain acceptable standards of income, which occurs when (5) competitive nonagricultural economic opportunities proliferate. (Handwerker 1986b, 404)

Handwerker differs from Caldwell in that he underlines how formal schooling is not a cause per se of less fertility, but because of the lesser importance of personal relationships that its introduction entails. He mentions situations where schools indoctrinate for high fertility, as it happened in Ireland. Changes in values cannot be a primary cause either, but those in the opportunity structure can:

> Hence, fertility transition does not follow from the onset of mass education, as Caldwell claims, but from the conjunction of mass education with changes in opportunity structure that increasingly reward educationally acquired skills and perspectives. Education or literacy by itself can have no important effect on fertility. On the contrary, because parents who are limiting their fertility are those who conceptualize their responsibilities to their children to include preparation for the new opportunity structure, the pace of fertility transition is likely to influence the pace with which public education, especially secondary education, becomes prevalent in a population. (Handwerker 1986b, 402)

In bureaucratized societies, as the authors of the wealth flow theory call them, the benefits of investing in formal education for children consequently made them less affordable, although some of these children, especially girls, were excluded from education (Handwerker 1986a).

This dynamic seems to be taking place today in poor countries: the universal reduction in birth rates is linked to increasing levels of education and, as Caldwell argued, greater employment opportunities in sectors in which non-peasant specializations are sought. Handwerker remarked though that in cities throughout tropical Africa "employment opportunities are dominated by government. Government employment depends heavily on personal relationships" (Handwerker 1986b, 402). Nevertheless, the condition of women is also improving; women are experiencing a greater power to limit their commitment to procreation and raising children (Danna 2007). This process seems irreversible: we can see that widespread poverty and the cutting of almost all welfare provisions in post-socialist Eastern Europe have not favored a return to high birth rates (Rajkai 2015). On the contrary, people can hardly afford the costs involved in raising children in that completely proletarian context with low demand for labor.

The costs of procreation, as mentioned above, have progressively increased due to mass schooling and changes in intra-family relations, which today are also characterized by greater equality in spending among its members. Indeed, capitalist production relations do not require the inequality of members of the family as the familial mode of production does, observes Caldwell. In the Third World, moreover, "the messages from the media and educational systems are largely western and tend to teach age and sex equality" (Caldwell 1982, 178). Egerö and Hammarskjöld (1994) observe that the media had enormous power in reducing the normal size of the family to two children. The establishment of close emotional ties between parents and children (which the extended family tried to detach) also increases the cost of raising children. Costs indirectly linked to schooling are often the highest ones: better clothes, shoes and a bicycle to get to school. However, the diffusion of schooling was gradual: despite the laws establishing it, compulsory school attendance generally took a long time to be accepted, and in the initial stages of the new production mode the ethic of austerity kept the cost of children low. Children will cease to contribute to family income, even if they are able to do so, only with the disintegration of the ideological structures of the extended family, and perhaps through changes induced by urbanization, writes Caldwell.

During and after the transition to a non-familial mode of production, children can no longer immediately contribute to economic well-being. The market economy and urbanization gradually expand, eradicating family production units. At an ideological level, the individual is driven to direct his or her loyalty toward larger aggregates: the large industrial company with its rigid regulations, and the national state, which increasingly ensures security in times of crisis. Initially, however, if the consumption of children is kept low and if they start earning early, high fertility will not be very disadvantageous:

> This is especially the case under two conditions: first, where the wife and children can offer a great range of household productive services without effective competition from the market; second, where the wife is uneducated or little educated, where she is not affected by ideologies urging her to demand a greater place in the sun, and where she accepts her place in the household with its implications for low consumption, hard work, and responsibility for keeping child-care problems away from her husband. (Caldwell 1982, 175)

This explanation should be valid both for the high fertility of the urban middle class in most of the Third World and for Europe in the mid-nineteenth century. In summary, for Caldwell, the essence of the demographic and economic transition must be identified in the transition from a traditional society, with a high and stable fertility rate justified by the economic value of children (who, after an extremely short period in which they represent a cost, will ensure a wealth flow to parents and adult members of the extended family in general) to a society in which the flow is reversed, and children represent a net cost in economic terms. Therefore, there are no appropriate or rational dimensions of the family in societies with different production modes, but only two demographic regimes that appear rational according to a strictly economic calculation. In familial modes of production there should be unlimited fertility, while in non-familial production modes there is no need for any children at all. Caldwell criticizes Easterlin (1978, 130) who puts the desired number of children at the center of his models—a function that is actually nonexistent. In industrial societies the only possible economic rationality is to not have children:

> Industrial societies have two outstanding features: they do not need the "traditional" family required by agricultural societies for production, and they are capable of producing immense riches that can facilitate myriad lifestyles. Agricultural families needed to reproduce themselves and so have children to remove the physical load from their aging parents and ultimately to inherit the land. In industrial societies there is no need at the level of individuals or couples to reproduce, although states may consider themselves obligated to make an effort to do so. (Caldwell et al. 2006, 314)

This analysis is further complicated by the intervention of other variables than the value of children, determining the range of intermediate situations. Factors that limit the number of children can include concern for their health and that of the mother, old age at the time of marriage, difficulties in establishing a new independent production unit, the wait to take over an already existing one, the problems in controlling more numerous offspring and the desire to avoid emotional conflict between children and grandchildren—concerns which motivated the Yoruba to control and stop further pregnancies upon the birth of the first grandchild. Finally, of course, the key forces that drive procreation when children represent an economic burden remain the pleasure of having them, the confirmation of virility and femininity and the simple compliance with social norms (Watkins and Danzi 1995; Behrman et al. 2002).

Dorothy Stein (1995, 64) reviewed the studies that put Caldwell's hypotheses to the test, such as the ability and willingness to consider children in terms of investments to be calculated. They did not always find confirmation of this vision or of the effective economic usefulness of children, who were most often seen simply as a kind of insurance for old age.[7]

In conclusion, the focus that the discipline of demography makes on periodization, causes and consequences of the demographic transition is misleading. The concept of demographic transition leads social scientists to focus primarily on the decrease in fertility and the reasons for this. Indeed, many authors, including Caldwell, *only* analyze the decrease in fertility, which they usually call "decline" in a pejorative way. The real questions should instead be why after 1750 in capitalist industrial society did population begin to grow everywhere in an apparently uncontrollable way, and why after this did the number of children per woman drop in successive waves, from the core to the periphery?

The general principle that answers these questions, in the context of an exponential trend in the use of fossil fuels, is that the capitalist world-economy pushes for unlimited growth of the labor force, which women produce for free, outside the monetary circuit. Children have been advantageous for families in semiproletarian and proletarian conditions. But this situation has been reversed. First, there is now compulsory education of children. Second, the demand for labor has greatly changed from unskilled to specialized. Third, as a consequence of proletarianization and education, women have increasing political power and have at least partially emancipated themselves from the male heads of families. All these developments are currently slowing population growth.

7 Stein quotes in particular the comparisons by Tim Dyson and Michael Vlasoff in *Child Labor in the Indian Subcontinent*, edited by Ramesh Kanbargi, New Delhi, Sage, 1991.

# Chapter 5

# DYNAMICS OF PRE-INDUSTRIAL POPULATIONS

## 5.1 Ancient Populations

If a single human being can subsist through hunting and harvesting crops in 10 km$^2$ of exploitable area, or 2–3 people per surface of 100 km$^2$ (or 0.01–2 people per square mile), agriculture has multiplied the number of people who can draw sustenance from the same areas. It is estimated that in the Neolithic Age, the density rose to 10 persons per 10 km$^2$, ten times as much as before (see also Kander et al. 2014, 46).

The rise of civilizations has always been marked by population growth, which increases the complexity of societies. Population growth in terms of density and absolute numbers distinguished the great powers of ancient times. According to estimates, around 400 BC the complex of the Classical Greek city-states had 3 million inhabitants, which decreased with the loss of its strength and unity upon the death of Alexander the Great. Meanwhile, the Italian peninsula conquered by the Romans was in geopolitical rise with 4 million inhabitants. Its population reached 7 million at the beginning of the Christian era, when the Roman Empire lived on the tributes received from dozens of provinces, which enabled it to feed and maintain such a large number of citizens. The population of all of Europe was 31 million inhabitants at the time, always according to estimates. Egypt was the most populous province in the Roman Empire, with 7.5 million inhabitants in the first century AD, a number estimated to have grown to 10 million in the following century. According to Reinhard, Armengaud and Dupaquier, this was "thanks to improved irrigation systems" but, as Boserup would say, these systems might have had to be adopted precisely to accommodate the growing population. This dilemma could be solved only with a microhistorical analysis—if we had the relevant data. The number of Egyptians declined to around 3 million in the fourth century. The Roman Empire had 46 million subjects at its height, which, with its decline, was reduced by one quarter.

The Chinese empire, later the republic, has always been the most numerous politically united human group, starting from its unification under the Han dynasty two centuries before Christ. There were only two periods when the record of being the most populous empire was snatched from China, according to the synthesis drawn up by McEvedy and Jones (1978, 127). The first time in the third to the fifth century AD by the Romans, the second in a very short period on the eve of World War by the British Empire, which population peaked at 531 million people.

Still the most populous country today, China has had enormous fluctuations in its population. China's Han population almost doubled from 40 to 70 million inhabitants over the course of four centuries (from 206 BC to 220 AD). It was reduced to 16 million during the crisis of the 3rd century AD, and grew to over 120 million in the 12th century (China 1987). The fluctuating figures of the Chinese population were mostly parallel to those of the European one, with the exception of the latter's decrease at the end of the Roman Empire. In the fourteenth and seventeenth centuries, the plague decimated all the peoples of the Old World. In Europe, population growth resumed around 1650 in the Netherlands, England and France: they were countries that dominated territories in the New World and had commercial companies in Asia, while a rural, or cottage, industry with a putting-out system had been established domestically. Although the workers were still not forced to regroup in factories but were employed at home, they were completely dependent on suppliers of capital and raw materials. At the same time, many independent artisans lost their place in the market, since the new domestic industry undermined the guild system (de Vries 1976). Domestic industry was also a system that stimulated the establishment of more families (Kriedte et al. 1988), as we will see in Section 6.3.

From 1750 onward growth accelerated everywhere, as can be seen in Table 4, which shows the most important trends, with exceptions that were local such as the Great Famine in Ireland (as written, 1 million deaths from starvation and 1 million emigrants out of 8 million inhabitants). After the crisis in the mid-eighteenth century, the Irish population continued to diminish until the twentieth century.

The rise in the French population was contained compared to that of other European countries. The French Revolution changed the social structure by distributing small agricultural properties. The farmers in this situation had to control their fertility, since only the firstborn was destined to succeed its pair of parents each additional child would have to look for alternative means of livelihood.

**Table 4** Populations of the Powers 1700–1800 (in millions)

| | 1700 | 1750 | 1800 |
|---|---|---|---|
| British Isles | 9.0 | 10.5 | 16.0 |
| France | 19.0 | 21.5 | 28.0 |
| Habsburg Empire | 8.0 | 18.0 | 28.0 |
| Prussia | 2.0 | 6.0 | 9.5 |
| Russia | 17.5 | 20.0 | 37.0 |
| Spain | 6.0 | 9.0 | 11.0 |
| Sweden | — | 1.7 | 2.3 |
| United Provinces | 1.8 | 1.9 | 2.0 |
| United States | — | 2.0 | 4.0 |

*Note*: The primary sources of Table 4 are listed in note 40 on p. 742. Obviously, these are not exact figures but approximations.
*Source*: Kennedy (1988, 99).

## 5.2 Pre-Industrial Cycles

Population numbers have generally gone in opposite directions compared to those of the prices. Wrigley, in *Population and History* (1989), showed the inverse relationship between the trend of the population and of wages in England from the sixteenth century until the beginning of the nineteenth century, when wages began to grow and the population increased.

The "disastrous" fourteenth century, the "iron century" between 1550 and 1650, and what Hobsbawm baptized the Age of Revolutions from 1789 to 1849 were periods preceded by substantial population growth. These pre-industrial cycles of expansion and then contraction/stability of the population occurred in what Theda Skocpol (1979) called agrarian-bureaucratic states. In the footsteps of Skocpol, Jack Goldstone developed a structural-demographic theory to analyze these dynamics. Turchin and Nefedov then followed, calling these dynamics "secular cycles," whereas Goldstone sets a clear difference between cycles and secular trends that are long-term and linear. In structural-demographic theory, class analysis—that is, analysis of power relations and mechanisms of extraction of surplus—plays a very important role. The microhistorical foundation is still the tendency of the population to increase, as Malthus postulated.

Goldstone observed that from 1400 to 1800 European history did not respond at all to the simplified vision of a slow and uninterrupted expansion of capitalism, as Wallerstein and others had theorized. However, it would be a mistake to continue to call this a feudal period because more centralized states were formed, with a basis in bureaucracy. The agrarian-bureaucratic states were still agrarian: more than half of the population—often 90 or more percent—worked the land. Agricultural products were put on the market, which was the way to support cities, courts and the bureaucracy. The organization of the state through bureaucracy, generally recruited from an educated part of the landowning class, was much more solid than the feudal one, with a more pervasive power. It was the hereditary monarch who directly appointed the officials of his bureaucracy instead of investing the nobility with various government tasks. The degree of commercialization and urbanization varied in agrarian-bureaucratic states, as well as the degree to which the bureaucracy was subject to monarchial control, but they remained distinct from the preceding communities based on a subsistence economy and on only small-scale communications just as they would differ from the succeeding industrial states. The aristocratic elites and merchants were by no means divided but acted mostly in agreement with each other. These states formed in Europe, but the Ottoman and Chinese empires that were their contemporaries had followed the same pattern in Asia. Political uprising in the Ottoman Empire and China saw struggles within the elite, urban strife, peasant rebellions and the spreading of heterodox ideologies against a fiscally weakened state. Political crises in the West shared these characteristics. In fact, the cyclical view of history was first developed by the Chinese, who traditionally interpreted their history as a series of dynastic cycles. The Tunisian Ibn Khaldun, who lived in the fourteenth century at the time of the Caliphate, also described political cycles in the history of the Muslim kingdoms, attributing them to generational variations in the *asabiya*, or group solidarity.

This type of state was expunged from the reflections of both liberals and Marxists, because both sides were and are subjugated by the myth of linear progress and growth. These states instead went through cyclical dynamics between 1250 and 1850. According to Goldstone, it was population dynamics that gave impetus to the phases of their cycles: from the "medieval crisis," a time of weakness, to the stronger Renaissance states of the fifteenth and sixteenth centuries, that especially in the second half of the seventeenth century had to face simultaneous rebellions and revolutions, namely the English Revolution, the French Fronda, the anti-Habsburg revolts in Catalonia and Naples, revolts in Sicily and Bohemia, the Khmelnitsky revolt in Ukraine, the Celestial revolts in the Ottoman Empire and the collapse of the Ming dynasty in China.

The loss of power by the monarchs had not been smooth or linear. Absolutism followed in the late seventeenth century, especially in France and Germany. The agrarian-bureaucratic states weakened again in the late eighteenth and early nineteenth centuries: "absolutism was defeated everywhere, or forced to make concessions to some form of constitutional order (even in Prussia, albeit only slightly)" (Goldstone 1991, 41). From 1770 to 1850 the French

Revolution and turmoils elsewhere occurred, including Pugachev's revolt in Russia. In 1820–21, 1830 and 1848, Europe was crossed by rebellions and revolutions, while similar processes occurred in the Greek, Balkan and Egyptian zones of the Ottoman Empire. The "bloodiest revolt in history," that is the Taiping rebellion in China, erupted in 1850, lasted for fourteen years and claimed 20–70 million lives, according to different estimates.

Broadly described political cycles can also be found in the economy, with the blossoming of early forms of capitalism in the expanding cities of the High Middle Ages, that stopped abruptly with the outburst of the Black Death. Again the economy, especially trade, expanded in the sixteenth and seventeenth centuries, stagnated in the late seventeenth century and grew again in the eighteenth century:

> Even if we examine an index of "capitalism" as precise as the proportion of English farm laborers who were non-household hired wage-earners (as opposed to in-household farm servants), we find that this ratio rose markedly in the 16th century, then *fell* in the late 16th and early 18th centuries, before expanding in the late 18th and early 19th centuries.[1] And if we look at such vital factors as population and price levels, a similar cyclical pattern forcibly presents itself. Given this fundamentally cyclic character of so much of early modern history, how can we be content to focus primarily on *secular* changes? (Goldstone 1991, 42; italics in original)

However, demographic growth will eventually always meet a limit. Upon approaching this point, the prices of basic food items and rent increase, labor supply becomes extremely high and wages decline. In fact, there is a close correspondence between the historical series of real wages in England and population trends that vary inversely (see Turchin and Nefedov 2009, 36). Goldstone, too, connects England's prices and population time series from 1400 to 1500, concluding that "high mortality kept the population stable" (Goldstone 1991, 89), while prices had remained practically constant. When the population begun to rise again from 1500 onward, grain prices soared until 1640, when mortality again increased.[2] In the following century, from 1640 to 1740, mortality increased and England's population remained stable. Prices remained stable as well, even though bullion imports resumed after

1 Reference to Ann Kussmaul, *Servants in Husbandry in Early Modern England*, Cambridge, Cambridge University Press, 1981, 97–98.

2 References to D. C. Coleman, *The Economy of England: 1450-1750*, Oxford, Oxford University Press, 1977; see also Phelps Brown and Hopkins (1957).

1650 and actually surpassed their sixteenth-century level.[3] In short, from 1500 to 1750, price changes for basic food followed the pattern of English population change and not of bullion imports.

The succession of events in Goldstone's cycle had already been described by Wilhelm Abel in *Crisis and Agricultural Conjunctures: A History of the Economy of the Earth and Food in Central Europe from the Early Middle Ages* (1935)[4] with the first historical series of prices reconstructed for various countries in Europe. Peter Turchin and Sergey Nefedov (2009, 2) summarize price fluctuations in Europe in this way:

1. an upward movement during the thirteenth and early fourteenth centuries, followed by a decline in the late Middle Ages;
2. another surge in the sixteenth century, followed by a decline or an apparent balance (depending on the country) during the seventeenth century;
3. a third rise during the eighteenth century, which eventually converged toward a minimum rank in the beginning of the twentieth century;
4. the twentieth century saw another period of price inflation (the fourth in the last millennium).

## 5.3 Structural-Demographic Analysis

According to Goldstone, historical analysis should start from the population/resources ratio. Goldstone calls his theory of agrarian-bureaucratic states a "structural-demographic" one precisely because population growth acts indirectly, pressing on economic and social structures. Even a modest change in the population causes indirect and massive effects on prices, state revenues and income distribution. He is aware of the fact that the first modern populations controlled their fertility:

> Restrictions on marriage, and the practice of infanticide, meant that populations were not simply controlled by their "animal instincts." One may thus ask whether it is proper to consider population change as an exogenous factor in early modern history, or whether population change

3 References to Michel Morineau, "D'Amsterdam a Seville: De quelle realitél'histoire des prix est-elle le miroir?" *Annales: Economies, Societes, Civilisations* 23, 1968; Michel Morineau, *Incroyables gazettes et fabuleux métaux. Les retours des trésors américains d'après les gazettes hollandaises (XVIe-XVIIIe siècles)*, Cambridge, Cambridge University Press, 1985; William Doyle, *The Old European Order, 1660-1800*, Oxford, Oxford University Press, 1978.

4 Quoted from Turchin and Nefedov 2009 (original title: *Agrarkrisen und Agrarkonjunktur. Eine Geschichte der Land- und Ernährungswirtschaft Mitteleuropas seit dem hohen Mittelalter*).

> should itself be considered as dependent on changing economic or cultural conditions. (Goldstone 1991, 27)

Whatever their origin, these changes affected the socioeconomic structure of the agrarian-bureaucratic states because they acted on prices:

> The societies studied in this book differed from earlier agrarian empires in having widespread internal markets, so that the prices and distribution of goods were widely affected by supply and demand. Prices were meaningful in that they affected the access to goods and services for a wide variety of actors. Thus rulers had to acquire food for armies and many other services at prices set by the market, elites' earnings from rents or productive enterprises depended on the market price of their products, urban workers' incomes depended on a market-influenced wage, and peasants' access to land depended on market-determined rents. (Goldstone 1991, 7)

Population dynamics have an impact on economic, political and social structures, and thus lead to the fall or reorganization of agrarian-bureaucratic states and empires. In China, population boomed in the sixteenth and seventeenth centuries, and many tried to establish advanced commercial enterprises, so much so that Chinese historians now speak of that period as the time when "sprouts of capitalism" appeared:

> Under the Qing, Chinese trade was evidently regulated by local merchant associations whose enforcement of contracts, regulation of weights and measures, and freedom from state interference in commerce equaled or exceeded anything found in the absolutist West. [...] Specifically, increased centralization, uniformity of taxation, collapse of the power of local landlords and transfer of their authority to the bureaucracy, and abolition of serfdom and its replacement by formally free tenant cultivators exceeded the changes produced by the English Revolution and paralleled those in France centuries later. (Goldstone 1991, 7)

The causal sequence starts with population growth that causes the prices of subsistence goods to rise, which negatively affect not only the conditions of the working class in the cities but also the elite's incomes and recruitment, though it clearly becomes a better situation for the agrarian elite that receives rents. The changes affect ideology: the allegiance to established churches gives way to heterodoxies. This explanatory framework starts with demographic change but includes the ability of various social structures to respond to it. It is therefore not just a demographic model that explains the breakdown of states, but rather a demographic and structural model.

Even if his work cannot be framed as a world-systems analysis, Goldstone was well aware of the supranational dimension of the dynamics he studied. Fluctuations and crises are not local phenomena. Movements of the English population cannot be explained in terms of English agriculture, nor French political crises in terms of the development of the French absolutist state, nor the Chinese peasant rebellions in terms of dynastic cycles. Population movements, political crises and peasant rebellions have almost exactly coincided in all of these states. Another example of cyclical events is the "discovery of the poor," which first occurred in the Elizabethan era and led to the approval of the Poor Law. A new discovery of the poor, equally surprising for the contemporaries of the period, led to the modification of the law in 1834. And in eighteenth-century France, the problem of poverty was again "discovered" as *la question sociale* (the social issue):

> What is going on? The answer to this paradox is again resolved by a focus on cyclic forces. In the 16th century, population growth flooded labor markets, leading to previously unknown, widespread unemployment among the able-bodied. This new social problem then attracted attention. It faded after 1640, when population stagnated throughout Europe and labor markets tightened. It returned in 18th-century France, and in 19th-century England, when population growth renewed and again flooded labor markets, producing again a wave, not seen for several generations, of massive unemployment and underemployment among the able-bodied. In short, the problem of unemployment, not merely poverty, was not "discovered" by this or that society. It was a *real* problem that periodically recurred as a consequence of cyclic forces, in this case, population growth. (Goldstone 1991, 44; italics in original)

The title and theme of Goldstone's research is *Revolution and Rebellion in the Early Modern World*. His findings highlight the three conditions needed to trigger a revolution: (1) a financial crisis of the state, that is, the insufficiency of revenues to cover expenses; (2) divisions in the elite, caused by the growing insecurity of elite positions and increased competition; and (3) a high mobilization potential of popular groups caused by growing grievances (e.g., about high rents or low wages) along with social characteristics that predispose or promote popular groups to action, such as a high proportion of young people in the population, an increasing autonomy of rural villages and increasing concentrations of workers in weakly administered cities. The combination of these three conditions generally produces a fourth difficulty for the rulers: an increase in the salience of heterodox cultural and religious ideas. Heterodox groups provide both leadership and organization to attack the state (Goldstone 1991, xiv). The dissolution of an agrarian-bureaucratic state depended entirely on the reaction of the elite, becoming litigious and possibly fragmented: under population pressure the elite also increased their numbers, therefore needing to increase their overall wealth. But there was a limit to the possibility of extracting surplus from the working class, especially when it was already suffering from a rise in the prices of subsistence goods, again due to overall population growth. During a crisis, if the elites are divided by internal struggles, innovators who relied on popular discontent could achieve their revolutionary goals by being co-opted by the part of the elite that became revolutionary. In short, "the crucial factors that lead to state breakdowns are state fiscal crisis, elite opposition, and intra-elite conflicts" (Goldstone 1991, 86). Contrary to Marx's expectations, Goldstone believes that the mobilization of the popular classes in the absence of a split within the circle of the elite would be in vain. Marx, however, did not deal with states of the modern age but with the dynamics of industrial society.

In modern times, Goldstone wrote, the parallelism in the fall of absolutist states both in the East and in the West is evident from the sequence of events that starts from the states' fiscal crisis linked to inflation. This leads to divisions and intra-elite struggles due to social mobility and popular uprisings (partly autonomous and partly orchestrated by the elites) that push to pass their basic economic demands, namely the reduction of prices and rents. The crisis is often followed by changes in political, social and economic organization, and whether or not the post-revolutionary stabilization will last depends on the underlying demographic forces and on the culture of the winning faction among the elite. Goldstone argued that "state reconstruction offers elites a variety of possible choices, and whether such reconstruction will result in radical change or the strengthening of traditional institutions *depends primarily on the specific cultural framework and the development of elite ideology*" (Goldstone 1991, 27). The English Revolution was one case of return to traditional institutional forms, as the population there "declined" in the half century after 1640, and England then revived the monarchic, aristocratic and religious high prestige. The (comparatively moderate) population growth in France after 1789 is seen as a concause of the crises in 1830 and 1848.

After 1850, railways and steamships brought American and Russian wheat to Europe cheaply. Had Europe been isolated, it would have had to again face famine and political upheavals due to its growing population. Goldstone added that "in Russia and China, however, population growth continued to outweigh agricultural expansion, and hunger in the countryside contributed to the collapse of the state in both countries in the second decade of the 20th century" (Goldstone 1991, 26).

## 5.4 New Studies

Following Goldstone, the ecologist and biologist Peter Turchin and the historian Sergey Nefedov (2009) analyzed long-term cycles starting with population growth and increased labor supply. The cycle is divided into four phases: two of integration and two of disintegration. In turn, these phases are double: integration has an expansion and a stagflation phase, while disintegration presents a crisis and a depression phase, also called an intercyclical phase. Turchin and Nefedov applied these theoretical schemes to ancient Rome (Republican cycle 350–30 BC and Principality cycle 30 BC– AD 283), medieval England (Plantagenet cycle 1150–485), early modern England (Tudor-Stuart cycle 1485–730), medieval France (Capetian cycle 1150–450), early modern France (Valois cycle 1450–660) and modern Russia (Moscovia cycle 1460–620 and Romanov cycle 1620–922). The result is a strong correspondence between theory and historical reconstructions.

The following are the phases of the cycle: when population grows, the plots left in inheritance are divided among the offspring until they become insufficient for the sustenance of a family. A wave of migration therefore starts from the countryside to the cities, offering cheap labor that allows the expansion of trade and crafts. Often this work is used in the construction of monuments. In this phase, the numbers of the elite grow, and hence their economic pressure on the working class. Their ostentatious consumption also increases thanks to the low cost of labor and the flowering of trade. Inequality proliferates. In the countryside, reserves to tackle bad harvest years decrease, and malnutrition causes innumerable deaths from illnesses. The prices of basic necessities, primarily wheat, rise. Food riots and wage protests erupt in the city. When social conflict explodes, it can either be kept at bay by the cohesion of the elites or lead to revolutionary changes. In any case, the population decreases due to wars and diseases, in turn triggering a decrease in wheat prices (the authors suppose that crops can remain abundant even if the population decreases, and that labor can be cheap when the price of wheat is high). At this point, due to the growing scarcity of workers, wages also gradually increase. Then the population begins to grow again as Malthus theorized, repeating the cycle. As Turchin and Nefedov themselves have noted, their theorization is essentially the same as Malthus's and Ricardo's theory on diminishing returns: with the increase of the population, rents will rise, subsequently the price of wheat rises and finally the prices of industrial production goods will follow the same upward trend.

Turchin and Nefedov included in their analysis several variables that approximated population numbers, which are difficult to reconstruct. Population historians agree on relative movements, that is, on the trends, while the exact absolute numbers, impossible to reconstruct, are the subject of disputes, which are probably unsolvable. The measurements of the stature of the skeletons of people who lived during the modern era confirmed the alternation of periods of "Malthusian crisis" and relative prosperity, with the increase or decrease of population pressure on resources. When resources were abundant and inexpensive, people could be fed better in childhood and therefore grow taller—Turchin and Nefedov considered this trend a good proxy for the population trend.

Turchin commented on Goldstone's writings about industrial England (Goldstone 1986 and 1991), where he found that economic expansion via industrialization and empire-building helped the country to deal with its rising population. Population growth is therefore clearly considered by both as the triggering mechanism that industrialization helped to cope with—or as just one among several coping mechanisms, as Peter Turchin believed:

> Thus, while Goldstone stresses the role of an expanding and industrializing economy in *absorbing* 19th-century England's demographic shocks, we accept this analysis but argue alongside it for similar attention to the vector of emigration, settler-colonialism, and imperial state expansion into which at least some of *the exhaust fumes of the population explosion were vented.* [...] *without the industrial jobs they made possible*, the society could not have coped with the new demographic reality, which would otherwise have brought *untold misery*. Thus, Goldstone again emphasizes his inversion of Marxian thinking on this topic: the problems of the era were not caused by proletarianisation or by the Industrial Revolution; rather, given the population explosion in progress, the huge glut of new industrial jobs was the society's *saving grace*. (Davis and Feeney 2017, 185 and 198; italics added)

My italics emphasize the passages that show the causal direction from an independent growth of the working class to industrialization solving the crisis (a consequentiality that, incidentally, does not take into consideration the question of the resources needed to satisfy the needs of the extra population). We still have Malthus against Marx, blaming the poor for their condition that industrialization helped to solve—while factory work and related living conditions were exactly the untold misery brought to the working class by capitalists. This shows the danger of considering demography as an independent force: the interplay of the economy, class relationships and gender are flattened in the pursuit of solutions to the "problem" of population growth. Conversely, population growth could instead be the solution to a lack of workers, enacting a positive feedback between new energy resources and more workers to chain to machines to produce goods that are requested in other (demographically expanding) also world-economy areas.

Goldstone reviewed the steps of his theory construction in 2017 and acknowledged the scholars that followed his theory and enriched it applying structural-demographic analysis to contemporary history.[5] Population has not been subject to cyclical movements in the last decades, but there have been different trends in the different areas of the world-system, thereby changing proportions of age cohorts. When the total fertility rate (TFR) diminishes to below replacement level, the older part of the population becomes more numerous, while the younger segment of the population is prevalent when the TFR is high. Therefore, there have been attempts to include population dynamics among the causes of rebellions and revolutions on the basis of the occurrence of a youth bulge, as in the countries of the Arab Spring in 2011, where in fact a mass of youth surged up. Likewise, Peter Turchin (2016) wrote about the political cycles that started in 1780 in the United States to underline the demographic components of class relationships.

## 5.5 Climate Cycles

In a review of Turchin and Nefedov's *Secular Cycles*, Brian Berry (2010) criticized the structural-demographic theory together with the work of Jared Diamond (1998) because they do not identify social causes, but everything can be traced back to climatic oscillations deriving from the variability of solar activity. A correlation between climate and population change had already been found by Patrick Galloway (1986) for China and some other countries in Western Europe.

Goldstone indeed pointed to environmental causes, considering that the demographic and political cycles were found in the early modern era, not only in Europe but also in Ottoman Turkey and China, which were moreover non-capitalist economies. If these cycles can be found on an intercontinental scale, then their origin cannot be connected with the growth of capitalism that occurred only in Europe. The market can obviously control the prices of subsistence goods beyond national borders, but to explain the synchronization of cycles between distant areas, we must think of independent mechanisms

---

5 See the articles published in the special issue of *Cliodynamics* vol. 8, n. 2, 2017, titled *25th Anniversary Publication of Goldstone's Revolution and Rebellion in the Early Modern World.*

that synchronize the cause of price fluctuations. The only factor that could be responsible for these changes is the drop or rise in average temperatures (Vittori 1989), which causes increases or decreases in harvests and therefore affects the population, regardless of the existence of commercial networks. The climatic explanation was also taken into account by Goldstone, when he wrote that "a combination of favorable climate and receding disease led to a doubling of the population in most regions between 1500 and the early 1600s." Diseases returned when the climate turned cooler by the mid-seventeenth century: "There followed a century of high mortality, in which population in most regions stagnated or declined. Yet for those who lived, conditions paradoxically improved" (Goldstone 1991, 25–26). This is still the Malthusian theory, seeing the cycle as starting with greater food availability at low cost, thus allowing people to raise children that would have otherwise starved or died from disease.

Berry also affirmed that the cycles analyzed by Turchin and Nefedov corresponded to the historical reconstructions of the climate: the rise of Rome took place in a warmer period that favored agriculture, whereas its decline took place during a colder period. The next period of greater heat culminated between 1100 and 1250, followed by a period of decrease in global temperatures from 1280 to the Wolf minimum in 1350. It was precisely at that time that the Black Death and the crises of the Plantagenet and Capetian cycles took place. The parallel timeline of climatic and historical changes continued with the lowering of temperatures until the Spörer minimum between 1460 and 1550. There was then an ascent and then a descent of temperatures called the Little Ice Age, which culminated in the Maunder minimum between 1645 and 1715. It was the time when the bubonic plague returned and the parallel crises of the cycles of Tudor-Stuart, Valois and Moscovia occurred.

The parallels of climate and social turmoil do not invalidate the theory of structural-demographic cycles, because not all the causes of social changes must necessarily be endogenous to the social world. Society is not at all independent of Nature, and social scientists must be versed in elementary biophysical facts, like changes in climate, influencing collective human life. Recent research moreover hypothesizes that the Little Ice Age, beyond reduced solar activity, might have had as a concause the renewed growth of forests that followed the demographic decline in the New World, diminishing the concentration of $CO_2$ and the corresponding greenhouse effect (Dull et al. 2010).[6] In any case, Goldstone's attention to nonhuman factors in history cannot in principle

6 Of course, the previous deforestation, in the New as in the Old World, had contrary effects on the $CO_2$ concentration, making appreciable temperature rise (Dull et al. 2010).

be wrong; it is Berry's critique that is surprising: did he really believe that everything happening in human society should have a social cause? This is again a fruit of the liberal division, or fragmentation, of knowledge. Indeed, August Comte, the inventor of the word "sociology," theorized that social science should deal only with society (Bonneuil and Fressoz 2016). But climate is indeed influential. If maintained over the years, a drop of 1 degree Celsius in average temperatures results in a 10 percent diminution of the kilocalories of solar radiation, translating into a three-week decrease of the growing season for crops and pastures. The decrease in microbial activity in the colder soil also results in less fertility. The altitude at which land can be cultivated goes down 80–200 meters (Kander et al. 2014, 40–41). This is knowledge that any social scientist should have in order to really be able to understand the social world with its biophysical foundations, based on food and energy obtained by the people, generally appropriated in some measure by a ruling class, and then put (or let) at people's disposal in various quantities and with various class mechanisms.

# Chapter 6

# LABOR DEMAND AND THE INDUSTRIAL REVOLUTION

## 6.1 The Demand for Labor Theory

Adam Smith observed that "poverty seems favourable to generation," a phrase that Marx quoted from *The Wealth of Nations* (1776).[1] The whole Smithian passage is as follows:

> Poverty, although it undoubtedly discourages marriage, does not always prevent it. It even seems that it is conducive to procreation. A poor undernourished woman from the Highlands often gives birth to more than 20 children while an elegant lady gorged with food often fails to give birth to one, and generally runs out of two or three. (Smith [1776] 1995, 117)

Smith also observed that in the free-market economy under his scrutiny, "the demand for those who live on wages therefore naturally increases with the growth in national wealth, which could not otherwise increase." In the eighteenth century, children worked in factories, so Smith connected the demand for their labor with their multiplication:

> Work is compensated so well that a family with many children does not represent a burden for parents but a source of well-being and prosperity and therefore, the liberal remuneration of work is as much the effect of wealth as the cause of population increase. Protesting against it means complaining about the effect and cause (both necessary) of greater public prosperity. (Smith [1776] 1995, 111–12 and 119)

Since the division of labor boosts the social product, the remuneration for all production factors can increase, thus allowing population growth (Smith takes

---

1 Book 1, Chapter 8, quoted in Marx ([1867] 1992, 797n22).

for granted the necessary food). As we have seen, also Malthus (1836) said that in the Speenhamland system, labor demand is the cause of population increase, which in turn increases subsidies and other expenses for dependent children.

The root of population dynamics in labor demand was therefore recognized by classic economists but was then forgotten by the neoclassic authors, with the exception of Alfred Marshall. Curiously, in a letter from 1909 (cited in Folbre 2001, 12), Marshall attributed the "problem" of reduced births in England to the selfish desire of women to resemble men—which proves how even apparently aseptic macrohistorical reasoning about the population can be based on visceral feelings related to women's sexual difference and the sex's social role, or gender.

In *Population Theories and the Economic Interpretation* (1957), the English economist Sydney H. Coontz expounded a demand for labor theory by starting off from Marx[2]—although, as we have seen, Marx spoke about population and labor demand in a contradictory way. Marx clearly said that it was unrealistic to attribute population growth to the demand for labor, because children remained dependent on their parents for too long before they could contribute to the family budget. Nevertheless, this evaluation contrasted with his more general statement that capital needed the growth of the labor force, occurring according to its "cost of production": Did this growth occur because it was natural, as Malthus postulated, or because the household could improve its economic situation?

Coontz's theory is based on the economic value of children in the different social classes and for different jobs. This economic value obviously depends on the legal framework and on the relations of production, that is, on class struggle. Unions wanted to introduce restrictions on the work of women and children who competed with men by being paid less—even if at that time, female and child labor in the factory guaranteed the survival of many working families. It is a typical composition effect: the microhistorical subjects, that is, the individual families, benefitted from choices that damaged them at the macrohistorical level as a class, the working class. The unions acting at the macrohistorical level managed in the end to change the rules and protect children from exploitation.

The situation favorable to population growth is the moment in which the demand for low-skilled labor increases: "The more unskilled the labour, the shorter is the period of time required for it to reach the market, and the lower

---

2 A non-Marxist author that advanced the same hypothesis on population growth as being due to labor demand was T. H. Marshall (1965).

its supply price. An extreme example of such a situation was the utilization of child labour at the time of the industrial revolution" (Coontz 1957, 169). It was a historical moment in which the labor market was not regulated and educational obligations were absent. According to Seccombe (1995, 35–36), in England in 1816, more than half of the cotton mill workforce was under 18; in France, in 1841, 12 percent of the industrial labor force was under 16, while in the textile industries in the mid-1840s the percent was 15; in Belgium in 1846, 21 percent were under 16.

According to Coontz, the quantitative and qualitative changes in labor demand explain both the initial population growth in conjunction with industrialization and the subsequent decrease in the birth rates since the last quarter of the nineteenth century. In particular, he argued that the "decline" in births at that time in England, the United States and other developed countries was linked to the declining or rising need for unskilled laborers or qualified workers. When the countries of the core needed specialized workers for their productions, the capitalists directly persuaded the legislators to finance compulsory public education (Green 1990). This was viewed with suspicion by the working class who did not want their children to be exposed to religious and ideological influences in favor of the capitalist order (Seccombe 1995). The key mechanism for population trends, according to Coontz, was the rise or fall of wages, which marked the scarcity or abundance of a certain category of workers, giving rise to its "production" as with any other commodity. Fertility rates in England peaked around 1815, shortly after real wages hit their lowest point.

Economic stimulus was for Coontz the only mechanism that linked macrosystemic requirements to the reproductive behavior of families. He corroborated his theory with a broad historical account of the economic functions of the family, gathering historical and contemporary data on the cost of labor in various sectors. Changes in the labor demand were in turn due to the increase in accumulated capital and technological progress incorporated in the machines. The workforce was scarce and therefore expensive in the United States in particular, prompting the owners of the means of production to use the machines that were built with cheaper labor. The American politician Alexander Hamilton, recognizing how difficult it was to find men who were willing to work in factories, urged industrialists to hire women and children:

> In his famous *Report on manufactures* written in 1791, Hamilton noted that thanks to industrial jobs "women and children are made more useful, and the latter at an early age." Indeed, not only employers could find workers, but also "the husband himself found a new source of profit and help in the increased industriousness of his wife and daughters..." The owners of

> the factories however, continued to have problems finding workers. When General Humphreys opened his wool factory in Connecticut in 1803, he nearly went bankrupt before introducing the "innovation" of hiring mostly children. Similarly, Samuel Slater in his spinning mill on Rhode Island was forced to hire mostly children. And in the famous factories in Lowell, Massachusetts, there were young women and girls recruited from Yankee farms from faraway places like Maine. Newspapers like the *Massachusetts Spy* were full of search ads for "families with five or six children" working in the factory, and recruiters had to go further and further to attract new workers. (Bowles and Edwards 1993, 111)

Microeconomic rationality, as Bowles et al. (2011) explained, necessitates the use of any tactical means to decrease the cost of the factors of production, upon the threat of bankruptcy and thus withdrawal from the capitalist market. Discrimination of sex and ethnicity *must* be used in the absence of sanctions imposed by political powers, due to the divide and rule policy applied to the working class. Joel Bakan (2004) also highlighted very clearly the inevitable exclusion of ethical consideration from the actions of any corporation that pursues the goal of profit. The only correct way that management can fulfill its profit maximization task is to minimize expenses by outsourcing as many costs as possible. The economist Karl William Kapp (1950) thus argued that *all* profit derives from outsourcing, so there would be none if entrepreneurs paid the business costs that they pass on to others: pollution, deterioration of worker's health, exhaustion of renewable and nonrenewable materials and energy, and the like. This explanation can be criticized because externalities do not have a precise price, but the general idea is correct. Marx, too, had written on the metabolic rift with which capitalism, besides workers, exploits Nature:

> Moreover, all progress in capitalist agriculture is a progress in the art, not only of robbing the worker, but of robbing the soil; all progress in increasing the fertility of the soil for a given time is a progress towards ruining the more long-lasting sources of that fertility. The more a country proceeds from large-scale industry as the background of its development, as in the case of the United States, the more rapid is this process of destruction.[3] Capitalist production, therefore, only develops

3 Original note: "See Liebig, *Die Chemie in ihrer Anwendung auf Agricultur und Physiologie*, 7th ed, 1862, and especially the 'Einleitung in die Naturgesetze des Feldbaus' ('Introduction to the Natural Laws of Agriculture') in Vol. I. To have developed from the point of view of natural science the negative, i.e. destructive side of modern agriculture, is one of Liebig's immortal merits." See also Foster (2000).

> the techniques and the degree of combination of the social process of production by simultaneously undermining the original sources of all wealth—the soil and the worker. (Marx [1867] 1992, 638)

Coontz's work thus integrated demography into economic analysis: "population is the dependent variable reflecting both long- and short-run changes in demand for labour" (Coontz 1957, 183). He wrote, "at one time women and children were prized economic possessions," implying the power of the male head of the family to "own" his family (Coontz 1957, 139). As an orthodox Marxist, he distinguished between productive and unproductive labor, and stated that "purely as wife and mother in the home, woman is divorced from direct productive activity" (Coontz 1957, 152). Unproductive activities are all the "female" tasks that are not paid with money and do not use the means of production, or capital, employed to obtain a profit. Coontz also thought that the association between high female status and low fertility was spurious, because both depended on the economic value of women's paid work. However, besides this value, called "opportunity cost" in New Home Economics, children are always a cost for women, both in terms of physical well-being and commitment to raising them: the material aspects of pregnancy, childbirth and the unpaid care work necessary for the growth of the new generation are in fact still mainly borne by women.

Compulsory education was introduced in most Western countries in the period 1860–90, and the response in terms of a decline in fertility was not long in coming. For example, in Denmark, from 1889 onward, it was no longer the work of the children that decreed how much free time they had for school, but the opposite. With the restriction on justified absences from work that was introduced in 1889, school attendance increased, immediately followed in 1890 by a drop in births.

The value of children is very different from one class to another, and so is the typical family (Bengtsson and Mineau 2009). In 1880, the differences in the procreation between the classes, as already seen from the nineteenth-century research by Rubin and Westergaard (1890), did not proceed in a linear way from a richer class with few children to the proletarian one with numerous child-workers. The Danish upper bourgeoisie was associated with the lower classes by a high number of children, while the petty bourgeoisie limited fertility. This showed that the limitation of births was not something that everyone wanted and that depended only on the possibility of buying expensive contraceptives. Rather, it was specifically the role of the children in the different classes that differed and made families opt for a high or low number of them. The world of the upper middle class, like that of the aristocracy in the previous period, was made of close alliances between powerful families. The children added power to the dynasty and were employed in the paternal enterprise, while the petty bourgeoisie drew its sustenance from an urban economy that had lost almost all familial features.

The corroborating observations are manifold (e.g., Wrigley 1969, 186, Mueller 1976). In contemporary Bangladesh, the economist Mohammed Sharif (2007) observes that landless workers have low numbers of offspring, whereas the fertility of land-owning families is linked to the size of their properties: on small properties it is proportional to the need for hands to work the land, while the owners of medium and large parcels of land have low fertility, since their children do not work and represent a net cost. In any case this is not a universal law: fertility data on the various social classes in India, Pakistan, Bangladesh and Nepal showed no correlation between poverty and high fertility (Rodgers 1989).

Proletarian dynamics also exist in the informal economy and in sexual abuse paid for by men:

> In the burgeoning Third World cities vast numbers of urban people are unable to find regular wage employment. For many who are forced to survive in the so-called informal sector, children are still assets. Many urban slum communities are supported largely by "street children." In Sao Paulo and Bangkok, child prostitutes are often the sole supporters of families. (Bandarage 1997, 162)

Even in the field of the Unified Growth Theory, proposed by economists who apply Malthusian concepts such as the poverty trap of premodern societies, it is recognized that the approval of laws against child labor and the decrease in birth rates have coincided with the industries' demand for more skilled labor (Doepke and Zilibotti 2005; Galor 2011). Matthias Doepke (2004) confirmed the importance of compulsory schooling by comparing South Korea to Brazil in the period from the 1950s to the 1980s. The rates of economic growth and industrialization were similar in the two developing countries but the effectiveness of the laws against child labor and compulsory schooling differed greatly. Population growth was much greater in Brazil than in South Korea, reflecting these differences.

## 6.2 Modes of Production and Reproduction

At the end of the 1970s, Marxists started to reflect on the connections between the modes of *production* and modes of *reproduction*, in terms of procreation and not of social reproduction as it was and is usually meant. Is the mode of reproduction an independent process, or is it bound to the mode of production?

A school of anthropologists in the 1970s and 1980s adopted the explanation for population growth based on the demand for labor (Mamdani 1972; White 1973; Folbre 1977; Gimenez 1977; Wasserstrom 1978; Kleinman 1980; Franke 1981; Gregory and Piché 1981; the works of Steven Polgar). Richard Franke, who followed Coontz's demand for labor theory, named the school Mode of Production and Population Patterns. Like Coontz, these authors believed that labor power is produced in response to the increase or decrease in wages, as occurs for any commodity, provided that children can work. In addition, especially in the colonies, there is labor demand arising from the imposition of taxes and forced labor. A low-skilled workforce was requested and used in the production and extraction of raw materials to be exported, stimulating procreation. Franke (1981, 365) quotes specialists of West Africa that considered it underpopulated while its fertility rate was among the highest in the world, starting from the 1930s in the colonial French irrigation project of the Niger River Inland Delta, which failed because of lack of manpower, until the 1970s in Senegal and Mali. Samir Amin (1971) also considered all Africa to be underpopulated in the 1970s. The reasons for not recognizing this lack or ill-distribution of labor force in development projects were for Franke purely ideological and geopolitical:

> The birth control ideology of the past thirty years in the West has held back our understanding of the interaction between demographic factors—including birth rates—and the type of social and economic organization that accompany these variables. The West African data supply substantial evidence that fertility rates, migration, and other demographic factors may be the result of a series of production systems that have had the effect of continuously pulling labor power out of local economies, thus imposing severe labor shortages. These shortages were made up by high birth rates, migration, or, in some places, inability of the population to respond, leading to massive breakdown of the production systems. (Franke 1981, 384)

The situation that encourages population growth is an increasing demand for low-skilled labor, observed in the neocolonial peripheries still subordinated to the countries from which they have obtained political but not economic independence. Franke, like Caldwell, recognized that in these peripheries the circumstances were changing and families wanted to invest in the education and/or emigration of their children, decreasing their number and usually choosing the most promising one to invest all their resources in him or (at times) in her. James Faris (1975, 260) expressed the position that the system's requirements of population growth would be automatically satisfied, without examining the microhistorical mechanisms underneath:

> The important fact is that IN SPITE OF population control programs and IN SPITE OF decreasing infant mortality (which allows larger families to be maintained with few children born) and in spite of death in war, no demographic change can alter the dynamics of population growth significantly until the productive system necessitating such dynamics is changed.

Anthropologist Claude Meillassoux (1975) instead believed that in simple societies the mode of reproduction is equivalent to the mode of production of complex societies. In minisystems, the control of the dominant group is not exerted on the means of production but on the means of subsistence and on women as workers and as producers of the next generation of workers. He overlooked the fact that male control is not peculiar to minisystems, but rather a constant in the transition of simple societies to more complex ones. Indeed, in the 1970s sociologist Christine Delphy analyzed marriage as an employment contract—a servile one, not paid—a contract that women are culturally driven and economically forced to sign in favor of a man.

Anthropologist Marvin Harris postulated instead that the mode of reproduction should be analyzed independently of the mode of production, in the same way as the presumed "demographic regimes," thought by demographers to be independent from other social features. The theory and research strategy that Harris illustrated in *Cultural Materialism* (1979) distinguishes three sectors of society: (1) the *infrastructure*, made up of the mode of production (technology and the forms of organization of the economy) and the mode of reproduction, that is, both of the productive forces and of the reproductive (demographic) forces, considered separate and of equal importance; (2) the *structure*, that is, the domestic and political economy; (3) the *superstructure*, made up of aesthetic, symbolic, philosophical and religious beliefs and practices. The pattern is hierarchical, with the imperatives or needs of the more material levels guiding the policies and beliefs of the overlying cultural levels. This is Harris's Principle of Infrastructural Determinism. Within the infrastructure, the mode of reproduction entails the following: the care and treatment of fetuses (i.e., mainly, of the bodies of pregnant women), infants and children; the care and treatment of girls and women as concrete agents of procreation, and, to a lesser extent, of boys and men, because the general reproductive potential is based on the number of fertile women and not on the number of fertile men; the frequency and duration of breastfeeding; the frequency of coitus.

But this approach revealed major problems in its empirical implementation. First, Marvin Harris and Eric Ross (1987) formulated the hypothesis of a collective rationality that unwittingly aligns actions with material needs, allowing the reproduction of the system. To postulate unconscious intersubjective processes such as this collective rationality, which does not seem to exist, is clearly a functionalist stance by these authors (belonging to this school). But even if such a collective rationality existed, it would be structured by the evolution in the natural environment and not by a social system. Even the alleged independence of the mode of reproduction was short-lived. In *Death, Sex and Fertility* (1987), written by Marvin Harris with Eric Ross, this theoretical framework was not substantiated. Harris and Ross (1987, 2) stated that they wanted to leave open the causal direction of the relationship between production and reproduction: "We are not prepared to make any categorical assertion that either mode of production or mode of reproduction is dominant over the other." Yet precisely in a passage appearing shortly after the one mentioned, preeminence was given to the means of production:

> Modes of reproduction consist of practices which directly or indirectly affect reproductive processes, which, in particular, can modify fertility and mortality rates over a wide range of values according to the optimizing pressures imposed by particular modes of production under given techno-environmental circumstances. (Harris and Ross 1987, 5)

In the analyses and examples given in the text, the causal arrow invariably moves from the mode of production to the mode of reproduction, and never in the opposite direction. The control that societies strive to exercise, and to some extent achieve, on fertility and mortality allows a generational renewal usually in line with the system's needs, as evidenced in the examples Harris and Ross provide. The knowledge obtained by observing the effects of common human behaviors in a given society is sufficient to understand its modes of reproduction, even if the subjects declare other motivations for their actions or even deny them:

> thus, when most men in a New Guinea society engage in intense and exclusive homosexuality, severely limiting the marital coital rate, one does not need to know whether or not individuals consciously intend to "control" their wives' fertility rate to conclude that their homosexuality is a population-regulating mechanism. (Harris and Ross 1987, 14)

Harris's method gives priority to behavior and not to declared intention, which often can be sincere but self-deceiving, as in the issue of not killing bovines in India, where the oxen are more present in the areas that need to be ploughed while cows prevail where they are needed for dairy products, despite the taboo on killing bovines of both sexes (Harris 1974, 28). People are unreliable in describing what they do, because they usually utter socially approved statements to explain the reasons for their actions. Both factual actions and socially approved explanations are worth studying, but one cannot substitute the other.

In the history of Europe and Asia, scholars prevalently failed to recognize the importance of infanticide to keep the population in check. Harris and Ross attribute this fact exactly to the scholars' inability to see the diffused discrepancy between moral precepts and behavior. Many people claim to act in accordance with such precepts, while their actual behavior proves otherwise: anthropologists, contrary to historians, see this every day. This discrepancy, they add, is not just a footnote of history appearing on particular and rare occasions, but its main issue. People may or may not be sincere, therefore only direct observation can give an account of how a society is organized. However, as noted, the study of motivations alone has its own scientific worth as an inquiry into culture, values and mentalities.

Other authors who affirmed the separation between mode of production and mode of reproduction, such as Wally Seccombe, instead recognized the problems in the interactions between the two:

> Modes of production facilitate and foster the reproduction of certain family forms, and preclude or hamper the development of others. The crucial factors in this regard are the ways labour-power is harnessed and consumed, and producer families obtain the means of their member' subsistence. If modes of production shape family forms, the obverse is also true. Family forms are active elements in the constitution and development of modes of production, above all because they are central in the production of people and their capacities for work, compliance and resistance. (Seccombe 1992, 9)

For Seccombe, the limited rationality of the subjects of reproduction can lead to actions that contrast with the collective needs, just as all conscious choices can have unexpected and counterproductive consequences for the social system (and therefore also for individuals) when they are aggregated, passing from the individual level where they are undoubtedly rational to the collective one, where they can have unintended consequences, also called composition effects. In this way, producer families may for entire periods inadvertently manage to conform their demographic regime to that of the demand for work by the socioeconomic system, through a flexibility that manages to adapt the relationship between arms and mouths to be fed within the households. In other periods, he finds, family formation strategies conflict with the workforce requirements of the system as a whole. Thus inefficiencies build up, and if left unresolved they can lead to stagnation and crisis (Seccombe 1992).

As feminists did, Seccombe (1978, 1983), too, urged Marxists to stop considering the work done within the family as unproductive. For the Canadian historian, all human societies are necessarily involved in three interrelated productions which cannot be subsumed one to another: the production of the means of production; the production of the means of subsistence; the production of the workforce. The advent of capitalism disrupted the balance in this last field. Seccombe found that the relationship between workforce consumption and population replacement is absolutely crucial for all modes of production. Under feudalism there was a close connection between the lords' exploitation of peasants and their demography through marriage and inheritance. This matrix was broken in the transition to capitalism, since the extracted surplus was separated from the place of domestic reproduction. In its place, a much looser form of balance took shape, mediated by the labor and housing markets, that constitute a quasi-market for future marriage partners (Seccombe 1995). In the capitalist labor market, the relationship between the demand for labor by the capitalists and the prolificity of the working class is mediated by non-capitalist mechanisms: spouse selection and marriage; coition rules and contraceptive practices; values passed on by parents to children; welfare state provisions; international migration patterns.

Seccombe believed that families made procreative decisions by rationalizing their predictable life cycles. Child labor made it possible to maintain an acceptable level of income just when parents began to earn less due to aging. For most of the nineteenth century young people belonging to the working class began paid work from the age of 10 or 11 (if not earlier), earning more than was necessary to cover the costs of their maintenance. When their mothers entered the final phase of their fertile years, the income earned by the oldest child could ease the family's economic distress. In the Edwardian era, older children still attended school rather regularly when mothers reached an age around 35 and had to decide whether to continue getting pregnant or try to stop it.

## 6.3 Proto-Industrialization and Industrialization

The "unlimited" (up to now) expansion of the population began with cottage industries, that is, commissioned domestic production, generally of textiles, with the help of simple machines powered by the workers themselves. This system of distribution of raw materials and tools for weaving or spinning in homes, with the collection of the products by fabric merchants who then sold them to consumers, spread both in England and in many Central European countries from the seventeenth century onward (Braun 1966; Landes 1966; Gillis et al. 1992). Dates and places coincided: wherever industrial production was established, the population began to increase (Wrigley 1969; Kriedte et al. 1988). The presence of commercial outlets for proto-industrial production triggered a positive feedback mechanism for the workforce. According to Pomeranz, this proto-industry reached a dead end because the "Malthusian trap" came into play soon after. Only the use of techniques to obtain energy from fossil fuels could have increased the population. Industrialization with steam power and the factory system in fact made this correspondence with population growth even more evident: Wrigley (1961, 72–73) published a series of graphs showing the parallel trends between increase in coal production and increase in population in eight regions between the late nineteenth and early twentieth centuries.

Jonathan David Chambers studied the Vale of Trent[4] in England in the eighteenth century, and discovered the same correspondence:

> In the county of Worcester, the two halves of the [18th] century are clearly distinguished as to the number of children generated per marriage. During the first half, this number remained at 3.6, with a depression around 1730 (3.3) and an increase in 1740 (3.8). During the second half, however, it was higher than 4, except around 1760 (3.9) and 1790 (3.7). The highest rate is found exactly in the middle of the century. However, there was no appreciable progress thereafter.
>
> In the Vale of Trent the caesura occurred more clearly in 1740, but it only applied to industrialized villages. In these villages there were slightly less than 4 children per marriage before 1740, and in the following period from 4.4 to 4.8; on the other hand, during the entire century agricultural villages recorded an average of 3.3 to 3.7 children per marriage, a marked depression between 1730 and 1750. (Reinhard et al. 1971, 298)

4 Jonathan David Chambers, *The Vale of Trent 1670-1800. A Regional Study of Economic Change*. Cambridge: Cambridge University Press, 1957 (*Economic History Review supplements*, n. 3) (some passages in Glass and Eversley 1965, 327–34). For a review of studies on the subject, see Tilly (1984, 40 ff).

The result of these differences was that in the villages where industry was present, the population doubled between 1764 and 1801, whereas in the agricultural villages it increased by less than 40 percent. Charles Tilly (1984) performed a detailed analysis of the proletarianization process, which he defined with two variables: the separation of producers from the means of production and the degree of dependence on wages for the satisfaction of workers' needs. The two components of the process can vary with some independence from each other. Poverty does not appear in the variables; Tilly did not consider it a necessary component in defining membership in the proletariat.

How did proletarianization take place? Did the Marxist dynamic based on the expropriation of peasants with enclosures really account for this whole historical process? Tilly summarized the trends that emerged from many studies of local history, which was new at the time, proving that descent from other proletarians was the main component in the establishment of the proletariat in Europe from 1500 onward. The growth of the proletariat by descent was particularly evident from 1800, also due to the decrease of early mortality in this class. The sector of the proletariat coming from the dispossession of the peasants and from migration from other areas was numerically less important, though Seccombe (1995, chapter 3) disagreed with this summary, finding more variation in time and space.[5] Tilly wrote the following about the European regions with rapid acceleration in population growth and increase in landless labor:

> In fact, most such regions probably did begin their proletarianization with a stock of underemployed, cheap labor; that made them attractive to entrepreneurs. But once the process had begun, rates of marriage, childbearing, and migration all seem to have responded actively to employment opportunities. (Tilly 1984, 22)

A new demand for goods and services to which entrepreneurs responded was the essential component for setting the mechanism in motion. *Cherchez le capitaliste* (look for the capitalist) Tilly said (1984, 53), "The activity of the capitalists, not the abstract mechanics of population growth, was behind all the growth components of the proletariat." Proletarianization had responded to labor demands from the large estates of the seventeenth century, from the cottage industry in the eighteenth century and from factory production in the

5 Tilly also notes that in the case of the Soviet Union, proletarianization happened by government's decision.

late nineteenth century. The establishment of a class that did not have to wait for the "freeing up" of workplaces, or niches, stimulated the marriage rate and boosted the birth rate. While non-proletarians adapted their fertility to the availability of land and capital for cultivation, proletarians adapted it to the availability of wages. This class was undoubtedly more represented in the more industrialized countries where population growth began: France's resident population grew about one-third between 1820 and 1900, Germany's more than doubled and that in the United Kingdom almost doubled, according to the Maddison Project (Bolt et al. 2018).

Harris and Ross observed that this unprecedented increase in the English population, which had its highest growth in the century following 1759, when it tripled, was accompanied by changes in power over colonies. It was then, they wrote, that distant parts of the planet "became part of a *single* demographic system" (Harris and Ross 1987, 106; italics in original), in which the labor demand increased everywhere under British hegemony. Between 1700 and 1780 there was a doubling of English foreign trade: the new markets opened in the colonies were practically unlimited, and this demand for finished goods paved the way for the establishment of large urban factories where imported cotton was processed. In particular, this happened as Indian textile production was choked by the tariffs imposed after the battle of Plassey, which in 1757 brought the entire Indian subcontinent under the British colonial administration. India was then forced to produce only raw materials to be exported to the British textile factories.

The push for population growth came not only directly from the labor demand by industry but also from the demand for agricultural products to feed the workers. It was particularly the introduction of potatoes from the New World that allowed greater density also of the peasant population, a process that progressed slowly starting at the end of the eighteenth century. Indeed, these tubers were initially rejected because Europeans did not eat what was buried in the soil, finding it disgusting, although potatoes have greater caloric yield than wheat and are richer in other nutrients.

In England, the factory system caused premature deaths, as Marx ([1867] 1992) and Engels ([1844] 1972) and many others denounced, and therefore a part of the population increase was reabsorbed by the mortality of old and new generations exhausted from work or victims of accidents in factories. Life expectancy was strongly differentiated between the classes, more than today, as can be seen in Table 5 for three English industrial cities.

In Preston, England, in 1841, mortality before 5 years of age was 18 percent among nobles, 36 percent among merchants and 55 percent among industrial workers (Harris and Ross 1987, 120). The difference in nutrition was reflected in stature:

**Table 5** House of Commons data: Average age at death by class

| | Liverpool | Manchester | Rochdale |
|---|---|---|---|
| Gentry and professional | 43 | 38 | 34 |
| Trade | 19 | 20 | 26 |
| Operatives | 15 | 17 | 18 |

*Note*: Original source: *House of Commons Reports from Commissioners*, vol. 8: *State of Large Towns and Populous Districts*, 1845, 358.
*Source*: Harris and Ross (1987, 120).

> As far as the somatic characteristics are concerned, the existing studies on the subject, albeit too scarce, allow us to identify two basic characteristics. On the one hand—and this is especially true for city populations and the bourgeoisie—there was an increase in their statures as a consequence of the higher standard of living and better nutrition; on the other hand, among the working classes and especially among the poorest and during periods of crisis, there were a smaller physical size and a lower weight than in the past. (Reinhard et al. 1971, 450)

In Western Europe, at the end of the nineteenth century, coinciding with the decline in births, the statures of the populace improved in a generalized way. According to world-systems analysis, the advantages of colonial appropriation of labor and raw materials then began to spread to the population of the countries of the center. Wallerstein (1979) posited the redistribution of the surplus obtained with the extraction of labor and materials from the periphery to the lower classes to have occurred around 1873, with the beginning of a Kondratieff Phase B. Redistribution was used to relieve social tensions and was facilitated primarily by the increase in the consumption of fossil fuels, because the new energy available to the center had expanded the social product.

# Chapter 7

# POPULATION GROWTH IN INCORPORATED AREAS

## 7.1 The European Expansion

In this chapter, the focus is on what happened to the population of external areas after their incorporation into the capitalist world-economy. European expansion since the Long Sixteenth Century simply intensified long-established contacts with world-empires such as India and China, initially only through increased investments in trade. The balance of power between these world-empires and the capitalist world-economy changed with the ever-improving European armaments resulting from the incessant state of war between large and small powers on the continent ( Kennedy 1988; Cipolla 1999). In particular, effective artillery gave European military forces superiority over these ancient civilizations, not only at sea, as before, but also on land. The Portuguese, Spanish, Dutch, French and English thus assumed political control of ever-larger portions of foreign territories even in the Old World, not only in the New World, where Europeans had established colonies exterminating the natives in wars and with diseases.[1] The decline of Native American populations is estimated to be from 54–61 million in 1492 to 6 million in 1650. In North America, settlers gradually took over the territory of the sparse populations of hunter-gatherers and the few agricultural settlements, defeating them militarily. In Central and South America, depopulation resulted mainly from the contagion of diseases from which Europeans were relatively immunized because they were endemic to the Old Continent, but against which the natives had no defenses (Crosby 1988). In colonial Mexico there was a "desperate lack of workforce"[2] as illustrated in Table 6.

1 David Graeber (2011) put forward the hypothesis that the debts incumbent on *conquistadores* such as Pizarro and Columbus had played a part not only, obviously, in their craving for enrichment, but especially in the ferocity with which they obtained it.

2 Francois Chevalier, *Land and Society in Colonial Mexico: The Great Hacienda*, Berkeley: University of California Press, 1970 (quoted in Finley and Lepore 2000, 19).

**Table 6** Decline in the inhabitants of Central Mexico when the Spaniards arrived

| Year | Inhabitants |
|---|---|
| 1519 | 25,200,000 |
| 1532 | 15,800,000 |
| 1548 | 6,300,000 |
| 1568 | 2,650,000 |
| 1580 | 1,900.000 |
| 1595 | 1,375.000 |
| 1605 | 1,075.000 |

*Source*: W. Borah and S. F. Cook, "The Population of Central Mexico in 1548. An Analysis of *Suma de visitas de pueblo*," in *The Indian Population of Central Mexico, 1531–1610*, Berkeley, 1960 (quoted in Reinhard et al. 1971, 203).

In Africa, on the contrary, it was the Europeans who were defeated by diseases, until the discovery and use of drugs against the sleeping sickness (African trypanosomiasis), which killed men and cattle. The imperialist race was then unleashed, with the partition of the continent in 1878 during the Congress of Berlin, when the European powers drew boundary lines across unexplored places. Before 1750, the emigration from Europe to other continents was small, due in part to the cost of transport. This cost dropped after the Napoleonic wars, as the wood trade between England and North America grew due to the Continental Blockade and led to the accruement of shipping capacity for intercontinental transport (Belich 2009, 106 ff.). European settlers migrated especially toward the Americas while Russians moved into Asia. Before 1900, emigrants were mainly British, including the Irish. From 1800 up to World War I, migrations were massive: as many as 50 million Europeans left the continent:

> Between the end of the Napoleonic wars and the beginning of the First World War, the European population went from less than 190 million souls to more than 400 million. As if this was not enough, an emigration thrust of exceptional breadth led to the birth of "new Europes" all over the world, the development of which soon took on a prodigious rhythm: just think that, more or less in the space of time considered, the population of North America increased tenfold. (Reinhard et al. 1971, 447)

A contrary migratory flow toward Europe started only after World War I.

Governments encouraged the occupation of lands. For example, in North America, the price of wheat was subsidized by the states of the Union in order to make their settlers occupy the territories of the Native Americans, subjected to physical and cultural genocide. After the US census of 1790, in many parts of the country the population decreased because cultivation systems suitable for soil conservation had not been adopted. The introduction of cotton brought prosperity and rapid development for about three decades, after which the fields were exhausted and had to be abandoned as they were covered with weeds, the only plants that survive on impoverished soil. This depletion of land led people to emigrate to the west.

Fertility rates in border areas reached more than 7 children per woman in 1800, a figure similar to that of the late nineteenth century in the newly colonized areas of the Russian Empire: southern Russia and parts of Asia. In Quebec, the expansion of the colonists was particularly remarkable: few families gave rise to millions of *québecoises*.[3] The colonists had a high birth rate because families were using their children as free labor, and when they grew up they became partners, occupying more and more extensions of land taken from the native inhabitants. The birth rate was pushed up by the expansion of peasants into territories previously occupied by nomadic and scattered hunter-gatherers, whose mode of production could not support a dense population, which ensured they were always a minority among agriculturalists. Children's work in hunting-gathering societies did not have value contrary to the work of those in sedentary societies:

> on the cost side, sedentarism relaxes the need to transport neonates and toddlers; while on the benefit side, children's labor plays a more important role, especially in tasks such as bleaching, grinding, and pounding of nuts and seeds, in the procurement of molluscs and small fish and game, and in varied house- and child-care activities. [...] Up until the time of the emergence of sedentary communities and their "broad spectrum" economies, to judge from recent hunter-gatherer societies, the economic role of children was slight. (Harris and Ross 1987, 39)

The expansion of the capitalist world-economy broke every homeostatic mechanism of population control that could exist in the conquered areas outside Europe. Everything changed in the relationship between mortality and fertility, but not in the way described by the demographic transition theory. Capitalism reversed what was previously mainly a direct relationship between

3 Hubert Charbonneau, Bertrand Desjardins, Andre Guillemette, Yves Landry, Jacques Légaré, François Nault, *Naissance d'une population. Les Français établis au Canada au XVII siècle*, Montréal: Presses de I'Universitéde Montréal, 1987 (quoted by Livi Bacci et al. 1987, 20).

high birth rates and high mortality to keep the population stable: under capitalism the greater the mortality, the more fertility had to compensate for the loss of present or future workers (Murdoch 1980). Agriculture intensified. More work was applied to obtain the low-cost products that supported the workers of the central countries, as well as the surplus that the local ruling class appropriated. The need for labor force in the colonies was met through mechanisms such as the separation of workers from the means of production, taxation, indentured labor (i.e., work to repay a debt, usually contracted by workers to be transported to the place of immigration), slavery and other forms of violence.

As the German colonial administrators wrote, "a healthy and numerous indigenous population is the requirement for a real and lasting exploitation of tropical lands."[4] The response of the exploited workers to the imperatives of capitalism was to expand the family workforce in response to the labor demand. This was the cause of population growth: the number of children increased to stay on par with the demand for labor (Nardi 1981). The marketing of agricultural products favored increased fertility (Weil 1986) and even soil degradation gave its contribution—especially the fragile soil in the tropics (Cleveland 1986)—because more workforce was needed to produce the same quantity needed for subsistence: this was indicated by local studies conducted precisely with the intent to test the theoretical framework of the demographic transition (Handwerker 1986a). Even the Green Revolution had a stimulating effect on procreation: the labor demand grew because only work performed by men was mechanized while the unpaid work of women and children continued as before for tasks that even increased in labor intensity such as the weeding of fertilized fields—as weeds grow faster than crop plants. In fact, complaints were still made in the 1960s regarding the shortage of manpower in the former colonies:

> Now demographic development is needed in Black Africa. It is the indispensable condition for creating a modern and balanced economy. Too often large companies have significant difficulties in recruiting the necessary manpower. (Reinhard et al. 1971, 933)

Nevertheless, it is mainly in the documents of the colonial era that the lack of workforce is frequently lamented.

4 Archive documents mentioned by Schaefer (2012, 35). To understand the error of such a thought, which ignores the frail nature of tropical soils, see Grimes (1999).

## 7.2 The Two Stages of Incorporation

When an external area is incorporated into the capitalist world-economy, population dynamics undergo two phases. Anthropologist Steven Polgar explained:

> In the first substage, the population of the colonizing peoples grew enormously (at average annual rates of 5 to 10 per 1,000), while the population of many subject societies was decimated through imported diseases, slavery, war, and forcible removal. In the second substage, in the metropolitan nations population increase slackened, while among subject peoples it generally surged. Thus, as I will elaborate below, the Third World is obviously not "starting" now demographically where Europe was in the 16th century. (Polgar 1972, 205; see also Foucrier et al. 2007)

In *World Population History* the authors reflect on the psychological aspects of conquest:

> The first reaction of the conquered peoples was profound discouragement, the belief that the fight was now a hopeless battle, and a sort of abandonment that sometimes even allows us to glimpse the renunciation of procreation. Such a phenomenon is less strange than one might believe: it was repeated on other occasions, for example in Oceania in the 19th century. (Reinhard et al. 1971, 204)

However, the three demographers relentlessly idolize Development:

> But the scarcity and low productivity of manpower constituted a constraint on the development of the New Continent: this was the reason why they resorted to forced immigration of the Negroes torn from their African homeland by the slave trade. The Spaniards began, followed by the Portuguese, the Dutch, the English and the French, all competing for such a lucrative trade. (Reinhard et al. 1971, 205)

The first phase of incorporation therefore saw a drastic decline in population due to the impact of the diseases brought by the Europeans, along with massacres and ruthless exploitation. In the second phase, the birth rate rose, mortality dropped and the population increased under the pressure of the labor demand. From the demographic point of view, what happened in the areas incorporated during European colonial expansion was not the first phase of a demographic transition, involving the spread of rational control, first of mortality and then of fertility. The first phase instead started with population decline followed by the violent exploitation of indigenous labor to benefit the core countries of the capitalist world-economy. This exploitation was imposed on the working class of the central countries in the early stages of the capitalist world-economy, and then on the periphery. The labor demand increased the population even in places where the initial depopulation phase did not take place:

> The rapid growth of the Egyptian population during most of the 19th century (from 2,500,000 to 9,000,000) occurred while the country was being reoriented to international trade, but before outright British annexation. (Polgar 1972, 207)

The problem of the settlers in the New World, who wanted to produce for export both foodstuffs and raw materials for the textile industry (cotton, tea, sugar, coffee and wheat were the principal exports), was the lack of sufficient workers for the lands they had appropriated. The workforce shortages were remedied by drawing laborers from other external areas.[5] This occurred in particular with the Africans who were enslaved and deported by the millions, and the Indians and Chinese, who also by the millions emigrated with indentured labor contracts: from China two million people emigrated in the second half of the nineteenth century alone. The Americas were the main markets for slaves bought in Africa. This trade dragged 900,000 Africans to the Americas in the sixteenth century and 2,750,000 in the next, probably cutting down the population of Africa by subtracting youth of reproductive age. From the eighteenth century onward England played a major role in slave trafficking: the Treaty of Utrecht, with which the Spanish War of Succession ended in 1712, gave England monopolistic control of the trade in human beings in Hispanic America.

Colonial administrators had the means to induce procreation, as they could raise taxes so that natives had to sell their workforce to get the cash needed to pay them. They could also exact corvées in lieu of taxes (e.g., Guérin 2008, 220). In the meantime, subsistence work was to be carried out by an increasing number of children. This is why the voluntary component of infant mortality decreased and more sons and daughters were raised and not neglected, abandoned or killed. The practices of abandonment and infanticide were also repressed by Christian missionaries, who exalted the demographic increase as

5 For Chase-Dunn and Hall (2000, 95) this meant that the process of incorporation into a political-military net was accomplished.

it fulfilled the biblical commandment to be fruitful and multiply. The capitalist imperative of population growth was thus translated into the reproductive imperative of Christianity, spread by missionaries and colonial authorities. The Christian religion certainly was the most important means of cultural influence for the capitalist world-economy, not without the threat of concrete sanctions (Ittmann et al. 2010).

Reinhard, Armengaud and Dupaquier recognized the existence of two demographic phases in European colonization, that is, in the incorporation of external areas in the capitalist world-economy:

> The first consisted of a serious and sometimes fatal crisis. At one time, everything was questioned. The colonizers were in a hurry to "exploit" the local wealth: weren't these colonies of exploitation? The natives were reduced to a more or less disguised condition of slavery, openly, or through the forced labor system, or because of the need to pay a certain number of taxes. It was the natives who had to provide the indispensable manpower to complete the great works: roads, ports, and canals. They were also responsible for working in the mines and cultivating commercial plantations. (Reinhard et al. 1971, 670–71)

In the second phase, the colonies were transformed into producers of raw materials and into markets for European manufacturing, discouraging and destroying local industries and imposing taxes that put pressure on subsistence production. In the colonies, the demand for labor was great in four sectors: construction and maintenance of infrastructure, development of commercial agriculture, mining, and military and law enforcement agencies. For the authors of the *World Population History*, however, the demographic increase must be attributed to the health and welfare measures activated by the colonial powers, and not to the labor demand in these sectors.

## 7.3 Colonization and Population

The two-stage mechanism of incorporating external areas is clearer on islands. For example, in Java, during the Dutch domination misery expanded, and some with a Malthusian vision attributed it to irrational and uncontrolled population growth. The Dutch arrived in Java in 1596 and in 1602 founded the United East India Company (VOC), which resorted to forced labor to exploit the sugar and coffee plantations they had established there. Another way of extracting work from the Javanese was taxation. New sources of income therefore became necessary for families and villages subjected to taxes, and the use of child labor expanded in subsistence agriculture to replace the adults working on plantations or in other paid jobs. The population grew, but its most massive increase occurred after the island was annexed to the Dutch Provinces as a Domain in 1816. Agribusiness then intensified agricultural production for export. The number of inhabitants increased by 2 percent, thereby doubling every 36 years, so that during the nineteenth century the population of Java grew from 4 to 30 million. The growth was made possible by more intensive rice cultivation, but its cause were the exorbitant requests of the Dutch for work and crops, in particular sugar derived from the cane, for export. Steven Polgar wrote that

> Java in the 19th century is perhaps an extreme example, but it may be taken to illuminate this general phenomenon. Governor General van den Bosch introduced in 1830 the requirement that the Javanese were either to raise crops for the government on one-fifth of their own land or work for 60 days on government land. Geertz (1963, 69) feels that this "culture system" [*cultuurstelsel*] was significantly correlated with population growth. (Polgar 1972, 207)[6]

In 1825, the Javanese reacted to their oppression and exploitation with the war for independence, which ended with their defeat and the sacrifice of 200,000 lives. The *cultuurstelsel* against which they rebelled was the obligation for villages to pay taxes in kind: mainly sugar and coffee—which is not actually just a sumptuous item, but a necessary stimulant, like the tea that British workers needed to cope with the rigid, long and exhausting schedules of the new factory system. As written, the Dutch authorities had requested that a fifth of the land in each village be planted with sugar cane, but later required it to be one-third:

> A village forced to cultivate sugar on one-third of its land had to increase agricultural labor inputs fifty percent by virtue of that fact alone; a task made much more difficult because of the simultaneous labor peaks in the cropping cycles of the two cultigens.[7] In addition, if the village was to maintain rice production at former levels, it had to increase labor inputs on the remaining two-thirds of its land. And this was only the beginning: villagers also had to transport the cane, provide labor for

---

6 But see Geertz's retractions to his statement in Alexander (1986).

7 Reference to Jennifer Alexander and Paul Alexander, "Sugar, Rice and Irrigation in Colonial Java," *Ethno-History*, vol. 25, 1978, 207–23.

> the mills, muster men for construction of roads and extensions to the irrigation systems, and meet corvee obligations to both Dutch and indigenous rulers. (Alexander 1986, 254–55)

During the commodification and intensification of agriculture, the work of children had become precious, since they increased the family income. White (1973, 172) estimated that in contemporary Java girls from 9 to 11 years of age did 38 hours a week of economically viable work, while boys from 12 to 14 years did 33 hours. It was not an exceptional situation: Cain (1983) found that in the Bengali village of Char Gopalpur males became net producers from the age of 12, and had compensated for all their past consumption by the age of 15. Mamdani (1972) made identical observations regarding the farmers of Punjab, for whom the only variable costs of production were labor costs: putting the children to work as soon as possible was therefore the only way to lower payments, as it made it possible to avoid having to employ other laborers. Caldwell (2006, 93) wrote:

> My findings from early Ghana showed that children who did not go to school produced enough to compensate for their own consumption at age 14–15 years in central and southern Ghana but at age 10 years in the less developed north. Mueller (1976, 129, note 16) cited our unpublished Nigerian Value of Children Survey data to show that unschooled sons and daughters were producing more than they consumed before age 15 years, while compensating returns for children who had been in school were delayed by two or three years.

Debra Schumann (1986) saw that there was a "prize for large families" in Chiapas, though families did not intentionally generate a large number of children. Whatever the circumstances, families with more children benefitted from the economic opportunities that required a greater contribution of family labor.

In summary, the Javanese events were similar to those taking place in other colonial and ex-colonial territories. A world-systems analyst, Georg Elwert, believes that the population increase in West Africa was probably caused by the greater labor demand at the time of its incorporation into the capitalist world-system: "After 1890 the reproductive pattern changed: all brothers obtained equal access to women, and the numbers of children increased" (Elwert 1984, 278). Also dealing with population history in West Africa, Richard Franke found that both in colonial times and in the neocolonial era, population growth and migrations were primarily reactions to changes in the production system. Franke noted:

> These overall lower fertility statistics for two of the major nomadic herding groups in West Africa [Fulani and Tuareg] could be explained by the lower demand for labor required in animal herding as opposed to agriculture and by the fact that the herders were less susceptible to the labor demands imposed by the colonial regime. (Franke 1981, 367)

Pastoralism, a nomadic mode of production, is related to low fertility, lesser than among farmers.

In West Africa, too, violence ushered in the new order:

> Workers were literally kidnapped from their villages and forced to become porters. Villages which resisted French-imposed taxes or labor conscription were burned down and the inhabitants killed. Porters themselves were underfed and overworked to such an extent that they died in large numbers. [...] But, to the effects of massive population loss and increased demand for labor by the colonial government, was added yet another policy destined to generate labor shortages: the forced migration of thousands of West African workers to plantation sites where their labor could be more efficiently exploited for cash-crop production. (Franke 1981, 375–76)

Congo, and Africa in general, also had a first phase of depopulation according to Catherine Coquery-Vidrovitch and Henri Moniot:

> The distant past does not seem to testify scourges analogous to those that marked the discovery of the American continent, because Portuguese penetration in Africa was less extensive and at the same time, generally, more peaceful. If a demographic scarcity was present, it came later, starting at the end of the 17th century, being provoked indeed by the slave trade, and then by wars of conquest: big famines and epidemics appeared mainly with the recent devastation born from colonial clashes. They caused populations to fall by at least a third between 1890 and 1925 in the regions that we studied. And the problem is that they developed among peoples already weakened and on a declining path.[8] (Coquery-Vidrovitch and Moniot 1977, 239)

8 Reference to Catherine Coquery-Vidrovitch, *Le Congo au temps des grandes concessionaires 1898-1930*, Paris: Mouton, 1972, 494–503.

Other sources on Congo during the time of Belgium's King Leopold II (the Central African country was his personal possession) testify to a decrease in the population that continued into the 1930s. In Tanzania, contemporary observers noted both low fertility and decrease in population, as well as its subsequent increase:

> Early 19th-century travellers, used to the high fertility rates of Britain, stressed the relatively low fertility of African societies. However, by the late 19th century, colonial officers who were accustomed to falling marital fertility in Western Europe, began to emphasize the high-fertility societies they came across in East Africa. [...] Colonial officers in the 1920s and 1930s took the view that population in Tanzania generally had been falling, since before 1885 up to 1920. (Lockwood 1998, 25 and 27)

In their protectorate of Kenya, the British carried out partial censuses for the purpose of exploiting the colony's "human resources," and estimated a very slight increase in the population between 1902 and 1931: from 4 million to 4.1 million inhabitants (Owino 2010). The huge population growth of the country began after World War II: in 1939, the population estimate was 4.8 million, while the 1948 census recorded 5.7 million inhabitants.

A study on Kavango, a region of Namibia under German colonization, reported the Germans' growing need for agricultural workers and miners in the early twentieth century. At that time, the dispatch of labor had to be negotiated with the tribal chiefs, who satisfied these requests only in periods when men were free from work in their fields (Eckl 2004, 224). Another study on Namibia by Jürgen Zimmerer (2001, 126) shows that the objective of controlling colonial subjects was "education to work" (*Erziehung zur Arbeit*), which involved a total transformation of indigenous societies, with the additional objective to guarantee the safety of the colonizers. Zimmerer (2001, 28) quotes Theodor Gotthilf Leutwein, colonial administrator of German Southwest Africa from 1894 to 1904: "a nice thought is to force the indigenous to work through this kind of tax," the head tax.

Europeans went on to colonize the Pacific Islands. These areas of the New World had been inhabited for 40,000 years, evidently maintaining the balance between population and resources (Pirie 2000). The clear exception was Easter Island, the civilization of which had already collapsed at the time of the Europeans' arrival, with few inhabitants living in misery among environmental destruction (Tainter 1989). Australia and Polynesia were invaded at the end of the eighteenth century, Fiji around 1810 and the last islands of western Melanesia around 1840. There was again a first phase of depopulation there:

> In Fiji, between 1840 and 1891, the population plummeted from 150,000 to 105,000 people, then to 87,000 in 1911; in Hawaii, between 1823 and 1893, from 142,000 to 39,500, and in New Caledonia, between 1853 and 1921, from 100,000 to 27,000. (Reinhard et al. 1971, 667)

In *World Population History*, the events of Tasmania were reported as follows:

> The Aboriginal population of Tasmania was methodically exterminated. It was believed to have amounted to 7,000 people. At the end of 1834, following a relentless hunt, the survivors found themselves concentrated in such an unhealthy region that within 10 years they all died [except for some who were deported]. The main culprit for this "cleansing" was celebrated as a hero and received a huge reward.
>
> On the [Australian] continent, destruction had been less complete due to the fact that some regions had been neglected by immigrants. Conversely, in the colonized areas the Aborigines had been totally eliminated. They survived only in reserves; it is believed that in the late 19th century their number was around 30,000 while in 1788 they had numbered around 300,000. (Reinhard et al. 1971, 611)

On the island of Reunion in the Indian Ocean, the French colonizers established measures to encourage births from the mid-seventeenth century onward: birth celebrations, exemptions from compulsory services for fathers of at least five children and a celibacy tax (Reinhard et al. 1971, 649).

Finally, the turn came for the circumpolar areas to be colonized, where the indigenous population succumbed to diseases brought by Europeans, such as measles: in the early twentieth century, there was an epidemic in the MacKenzie delta in Canada, after which only 120 out of 2,000 Inuit survived (Massa 1999, 129). The same thing happened in Paraguay, when contact with the Ache was established in 1970: half of the Ache died from newly introduced diseases over the course of the next eight years (Kaplan 1994, 756).

Two societies described at different points in time in their contacts with Europeans are the Tikopia of the Polynesian islands, visited by Raymond Firth in 1929 and 1952, and the Vunamami of New Britain, another Polynesian island visited by Richard Salisbury in the early and late 1960s.[9] At Firth's first visit, the Christians' opposition to traditional population control practices was

9 Sources: Firth (1939, 1959) and Richard F. Salisbury, *Vunamami: Economic Transformations in a Traditional Society*, Berkeley: University of California Press, 1970 (quoted in Wilkinson 1973).

beginning to take effect. The Tikopian people had practiced abortion, coitus interruptus, abstinence and infanticide consciously aimed at keeping the population in balance: "Contraception, celibacy, and infanticide are resorted to consciously by the Tikopia as a reflex of the population situation—*fakatau ki te kai*, 'measured according to the food' as they put it" (Firth 1939, 43). Responsible couples had to program the procreation of only two children. If they had more, only the older children of each sex could marry, whereas the others could certainly have sexual relations but were not permitted to procreate. In 1929, when Firth first came, the population was already beginning to increase under the influence of Christianity. The chiefs who were converted had stopped declaiming the traditional exhortations for people to limit the number of their descendants (Firth 1939, 44). Upholding interrupted intercourse to limit births in public prayers had been part of the Tikopia religion since time immemorial, but this has no space in Christianity. On his next visit in 1952, Firth found the Tikopians fully Christianized, and most of the traditional constraints on population growth had disappeared. Everyone had several children and all the children married. When the missionaries discovered a *liaison*, they tried to force the "guilty" to marry. The elderly who had not been converted judged the situation as insane, totally lacking the sense of responsibility and forethought of the recent past. Indeed, despite the adoption of more productive species or varieties of plants (which usually required more work), the crops were barely sufficient for the population, which grew by 35 percent between the two visits of the anthropologist, even though the Tikopians had begun to emigrate massively to neighboring islands in search of work. Between 30 and 40 percent of men of working age had already left.

As for the Vunamami, Richard Salisbury interviewed the elderly regarding older periods, and they claimed that around 1875 the population was balanced with resources, and that a relatively high standard of living was ensured through low mortality and a low birthrate maintained with late marriages for women. The land could have supported a much larger population, but part of it was lost by the Vunamami to a Christian mission founded in the 1890s. Moreover, other Europeans established cocoa and cotton plantations at the same time, settling on the lands of other natives who they pushed away. After some clashes, in 1896, the Europeans imposed a treaty forcing the Vunamami to give up all the territory they could not cultivate. The Vunamami began a populationist policy, reducing the bride-price to facilitate marriages. In the following years, their growth rate reached 3 percent, obviously reducing the amount of land available to everyone. They began to cultivate for export, but most of their income came from waged work on European plantations or from the remittances of workers who migrated to other islands. Finally, the arrival of Christian missionaries, with their cultural heritage forged under the influence of capitalist power with which they had allied, uprooted all practices aimed at limiting the population and also impeded the importation of contraceptives.

In the external areas the limitation of the population took place also by explicitly advocating the aim of equilibrium with the environment, as was applied to the Mining, the Aborigines of southern Australia: "The reason they give for this practice [infanticide] is that if their numbers increased too rapidly, there would not be enough food for everybody" (Howitt 1904, 748).[10] Regarding the inhabitants of Ellis Island in the Pacific, George Turner said, "Infanticide was prescribed by law; each family could only have two children, because they were afraid of food shortages."[11] This reason was countered by John Mathew ([1910] 2010, 166), with regard to the Australian tribes of Queensland: "The motive for infanticide with these tribes could not be to save food in times of dearth, for the food supply was constant and plentiful," probably reversing the causal link. Mathew—as usual—blamed mothers: "It would be mainly, if not entirely, that mothers might escape the irksomeness of nursing and caring for infants and of carrying them on their frequent journeys." Many other testimonies stated that scarcity was not a problem in many of these minisystems. Among the Hadza, still living as hunter-gatherers in Tanzania,

> In fact, there is never any general shortage of food even in time of drought. The range of foods in the bush is so great, if one knows what these are and how to obtain them, that if weather conditions should cause the failure of some type of root or berry, or the migration of some of the game, some other type of food is always available. For a Hadza to die of hunger, or even to fail to satisfy his hunger for more than a day or two, is almost inconceivable. (Woodburn 1968, 52)

For the Maori, Raymond Firth ([1929] 2011, 280) observed that "starvation or real want in one family was impossible while others in the village were abundantly supplied with food" (Firth 1959, 290) because in minisystems redistribution is a duty.

In other cases, there were no conscious mechanisms, but action was taken for ritual reasons or to respect taboos, which kept the population under control regardless of the persuasion of all members of the group. Furthermore, beliefs and superstitions were often vague and therefore could be used to justify opposing courses of action. The Ubena, a Bantu people, believed that a child

---

10 A. W. Howitt, *The Native Tribes of South-East Australia*, London: Cambridge University Press, 1904, 748 (quoted by Wilkinson 1973, 34).

11 George Turner, *Samoa*, London: Macmillan, 1884, 284 (quoted by Wilkinson 1973, 34).

whose upper incisors grew before the lower ones should be killed, but it could be allowed to live by practicing ritual acts. Arbitrariness was useful precisely because these rules aimed to keep the population stable: their validity was not absolute but depended on historical and family contingencies.

## 7.4 Famines and Looting

Even if the population always started to grow again soon after, famines did not end in the mid-eighteenth century. Their effects were greatly amplified by the international shipping of food, also on the basis of the instantaneous diffusion of price changes with the advent of the telegraph, widely diffused in the middle of the nineteenth century (Davis 2002). Indeed, in India under British rule there was an increase in the intensity and frequency of famines, which occurred on average every two to three years in the period 1860–1908. The Indian scholar B. M. Bathia (1967) pointed out that the famines of this period were not due to an absolute food shortage caused by bad harvests or other agricultural tragedies, but due to rising prices. They therefore did not hit an entire region as in the past, but made victims everywhere, even in the regions that had good harvests, killing those who could not afford to buy what they needed to feed themselves.

The barn system for public aid during famines was dismantled by the British, who introduced the total marketing not only of grains but also of the land, privatizing all the property that could be privatized. Where the market did not impose its laws, the British imposed the cultivation of plants for export by decree, because what they needed was cotton, more cotton and then again cotton, of course at the lowest possible price. The volume of international trade increased enormously with the inauguration of the Suez Canal in 1869, which halved travel time between England and Asia, thus reducing the costs of sea freight, physically and economically facilitating the movement of goods. This facilitation of the exports from India resulted in a shortage of food at home. The construction of railways on Indian soil had the same effect. So rents again increased and small farmers expelled from the land became agricultural proletariat, together with weavers and other artisans whose production was no longer competitive with English goods.

In *Capital*, Marx describes the famine of 1866 that struck the Orissa region with a million deaths. Famine raged after the British forced Indian farmers to grow cotton with laws restricting the area on which they could grow rice. What happened was not a mathematical relationship in which food did not keep pace with the growth of the population as Malthus advocated, but an expropriation of resources by the colonists and the Indian ruling class. Famines did not stop the looting:

> Warren Hastings, governor of Calcutta, had made this altogether clear when he wrote to the Board of Directors of the East India Company in 1772: "Notwithstanding the loss of at least one-third of the inhabitants of the province [of Bengal], and the consequent decrease of cultivation, the nett [*sic*] collections of the year 1771 exceeded even those of 1768." (Harris and Ross 1987, 141)

Under the new colonial and liberal regime, landowners no longer felt or actually were socially responsible for helping the hungry. The new market system had gotten rid of traditional bonds, while in the previous system the government of the Mughals controlled prices, and in the event of famine organized aid to the affected areas, with state supplies of food accumulated for this purpose during the good years. As mentioned, the community barns were dismantled: the British did not waste money on this or other public works that were not investments for their own income, and they did nothing, for example, to fight malaria in areas where it was endemic. Small farmers lost their land and became proletariat, and in order for them to be able to pay taxes subsistence crops had to give way to saleable production: jute, cotton, skins and dyes for the Industrial Revolution.

For Hornborg, these usurpations and unequal exchanges are the real meaning of industrialization—which has a meaning because its products are attributed a prestige that makes unequal exchanges culturally acceptable. In addition, industrialization allowed domination by means of modern weapons, which were also industrial products:

> Industrialization was fundamentally a strategy for Britain to appropriate, in terms of land area, an ecological footprint several times the size of its entire national territory, and in terms of embodied labor, the toil of a workforce several times larger than its national population. (Hornborg 2016, 22)

## 7.5 Inversion of the Growth Curve

The apparently unlimited population growth of the capitalist world-economy began to decrease not in absolute numbers but in terms of children per woman as early as the 1970s. World-systems analysts such as Michael Hout (1980), Peter Grimes (1981), Kathryn B. Ward (1983, 1984, 1985), Bruce London (1988), John G. Patterson and Nanda R. Shrestha (1988), who all had analyzed data of that decade, found that what they considered dependent development discouraged the periphery countries from practicing birth control in the same way as core countries had done at the same level of income. Kathryn Ward, in conjunction with scholars of the Mode of Production and Population Patterns paradigm, predicted that the birth rate would continue to rise in the dependent countries of the periphery. Instead, just after 1975–80, when it touched 2 percent, the global rate of population increase began to slow down, while the TFR began to decrease even in the least developed countries, according to data and estimates of the United Nations Population Division (see also Bulatao and Casterline 2001). In the end, growth in GDP pushed toward a decrease in fertility, since the advance of the market economy allowed women to find more job opportunities, and the cost of children rose due to child labor limitations (Anker et al. 1982; Bhattacharya 2006). Furthermore, the expanding opportunities to find employment in the cities and in industries as technicians and public employees required investments in education and therefore led to fewer children (quality vs. quantity, as it is said).

Other world-systems analysts have drawn a parallel between Third World poverty, where population growth was concentrated in the 1970s and 1980s, and the situation at the beginning of European industrialization (Ward 1983, 1984, 1985; Ingerson 1984; Schiel 1984). But there are important differences: the Third World half a century ago was the periphery of the world-economy, caught in the dynamics of dependent development, while nineteenth-century England had reached the status of a hegemonic country thanks to industrialization. But though their status in the world-economy was different, the labor-intensive technology used was similar in the two areas, which could account for the similar expansion of the population. The situation of the workers of the core at the time of the rise of England was not very different from that of today's periphery workers: where the labor market is expanding, dispossessed workers are subject to the same pressure to have more children to overcome their misery, hence alleviating uncertainty about the future and securing support in old age.

Other quantitative analyses have highlighted the direct correlation between inequality and fertility (Repetto 1979; Ward 1984). Menard (1986), however, criticizes these results, finding Repetto's methodology inadequate and stressing that female education is a much more significant variable in explaining the reduction of fertility compared to the degree of inequality. But indeed, the first poor countries that reduced population growth rates to less than 2 percent per year were Burma, Chile, China, Colombia, Cuba, Sri Lanka and the Indian state of Kerala. As Frances Moore Lappé and Rachel Schurman (1990) observed, these countries—except Burma on which information was not reliable—had low levels of economic growth, per capita income, industrialization and urbanization (the urban population is generally less prolific than the rural one), but also had effective redistributive policies that satisfied the basic needs of the whole population. China's rate of population growth and TFR had already strongly diminished when the one-child policy was introduced in 1979:

> The most fundamental reason for the decline in China's fertility rate is not the one-child policy. The most rapid decline in the fertility rate occurred in the 1970s before the introduction of the one-child policy. At the time, the fertility rate decreased from 5.8 children per woman in 1970 to 2.7 children in 1978. (Cai 2014, 16)

Nadia Diamond-Smith and Malcolm Potts (2010, 291) concluded their research on whether the population policies of India and China were responsible for their fertility "decline" negatively: "while the Indian 'Emergency' (with forced sterilisations) and the Chinese One-Child Policy were cruel abridgements of human freedom, they had relatively little influence on the fertility declines in both countries."

Asoka Bandarage (1997, 174) considered the demographic forces a result of capitalist social relations, concluding that the satisfaction of basic needs was the main mechanism in reducing birth rates:

> Fertility declines require alleviation of poverty and improvements in the living conditions of the poor, especially women. Where children's labor is not essential for family survival, and where women and children have food and nutrition, education, health care and gainful employment, they are more likely to accept birth control and voluntarily lower their fertility. (Bandarage 1997, 174)

Indeed, birth control policies began to be effective only when at least some of these conditions were met (Bryant 2007). The higher level of education, especially for women, has lowered the birth rate in at least some of these places, such as Kerala. According to Betsy Hartmann (1995, 283), the factors common to Cuba, the two Koreas, Kerala and Sri Lanka (all states that reduced the birth rate to low levels in a short time after World War II) were as follows: the redistribution of land and income; employment opportunities and social security; mass education; improvements in the condition of women, with a higher marriage age; availability of health care and contraception.

Indeed, in this third phase of incorporation, the advancement of capitalism with its commodification of female labor led to an increase in the economic and political power of women,[12] as in the West. Women became emancipated from the family, that is, from subordination to the male head of the family, massively entering into the labor market and organizing themselves politically.

---

12 For a review of (not recent anymore) studies on women and work in multinational corporations in the Third World, see the introduction to Ward (1990).

The second wave of the feminist movement (the first being the fight for the right to vote—among other goals—in the nineteenth century and into the twentieth) aimed to change the discriminatory laws and customs. Women could no longer be ignored as subjects of procreation. The theories that in the past excluded them as subjects, considering female procreative power as a "natural resource" bearing no cost (Folbre 2009), were not justified anymore: women had become influential in the decision-making process regarding their own bodies.

As, thanks to the computer, decades of increasingly refined quantitative analyses show, women's education is the variable most closely related to the global change in fertility (e.g., Cleland and Hobcraft 1985; Kravdal 2002; York and Ergas 2011). Generally, female education is clearly inversely correlated with the birth rate, but sometimes the relationship is found to be "humpbacked," with primary education associated to higher fertility compared to the absence of education (Hull and Hull 1977; Simmons 1988, 196). Furthermore, in countries where the indicators of equality between the sexes (e.g., the UN Gender Inequality Index) are higher, a very recent trend shows that employed and highly educated women have higher fertility (Esping-Andersen and Billari 2015). This is due to the more equal sharing of housework and child care at home in educated couples or to their outsourcing to maids and babysitters, and to the pressure by governments on employers to improve the conditions of working mothers.

In developing countries, the World Fertility Surveys found strong correlations between high education of women, late marriage, few children desired and the frequent use of contraceptives. Indeed, early marriages, often with older men, certainly denote a low status of women, as well as their lower education level compared to men, as adolescents drop out of school in order to get married. Demographers Federici, Mason and Sogner (1988, 13) are skeptical about these findings and write that "unfortunately, factual evidence relating to the mechanisms that connect women's situation to demographic change is weak," but this happens because it is difficult to detect the status of women, since there is usually an inverse relationship between female power and female prestige. A woman who is satisfied with the subordinate position reserved to women usually enjoys a high social prestige, whereas if she acquires economic and social power, mechanisms are triggered to deprive her of prestige. Helen Ware (1988) analyzed three aspects of the position of women: autonomy, economic power and prestige. She then identified nine areas in which women's status indicators were consistent in representing women's power. These were the control of property, power within kinship, value given to women's lives, value attributed to women's work, authority in household matters, ritual separation of the sexes, control over one's sexual life, ritualized fear of women and level of joint participation of the two sexes in basic activities.

Of course the proletarianization of women, their work for the market, does not necessarily emancipate women from the family, which, on the contrary, can completely take possession of the earnings of the daughters.

Furthermore, the increased power of women does not automatically translate into the choice of having fewer children. We can observe this in countries with high fertility: poverty is widespread whereas welfare services that decommodify and defamiliarize part of the needs of individuals are absent (Cain 1983; Pritchett 1994; Sharif 2007). Nancy Birdsall (1976) noted that reduced fertility is associated only with employment in the urban and modern sector, while in rural areas, as Caldwell's research also revealed, women and men have the same preference for numerous offspring. This may depend on women's adherence to male preferences, but also on their need for protection through children, preferably boys.[13] Birdsall (1976, 708) wrote:

> In the Middle East, North Africa, and the Asian subcontinent, fertility might decline more quickly if the wife had a greater stake in income generation, greater ability to provide for herself in old age, and a lesser stake in her children as a sole means to acquire self-esteem.

In sub-Saharan Africa high fertility persists, probably due to the minimal involvement of women in decision-making about childbearing. Harriet Presser (2001), for example, observed that women's awareness of their right to have time for themselves contributed to the decline in the number of children, but this right can be acknowledged and vindicated only being in a powerful position.

Alaka Malwade Basu (1992) instead operationalized the status of women in India as dependent on three indicators: exposure to the world outside the domestic sphere, interaction with the world outside the domestic sphere and women's decision-making autonomy. The demographer found that status, along with employment and education of women, affected fertility, which was higher in Uttar Pradesh and lower in Tamil Nadu. Other historically rooted cultural factors also contributed to a different status of women and therefore to the different size of families in Indian states. Female freedom was greatest in South India, where the number of children was lower.[14] Basu's research also showed that the high status of women guaranteed lower levels of infant mortality and a lower mortality differential between males and females (the measure is always to the disadvantage of females—see Das Gupta et al. 2009).

---

13 On the power of women in relation to men, see Safilios-Rothschild (1982).

14 On the importance of culture and religion in procreative choices in India, see Kumar (2000).

However, the women who declared to be the happiest were those who had the greatest number of living children. Lant Pritchett (1994, 2) showed how "desired fertility" is the key variable underneath reproductive choices:

> In countries where fertility is high, women want more children. "Excess" or "unwanted" fertility plays a minor role in explaining fertility differences. Moreover, the level of contraceptive use, measures of contraceptive availability (such as "unmet need"), and family planning effort have little impact on fertility after controlling for fertility desires.

Some authors believed that educated women have lower fertility simply because they marry at a later age (Therborn 2004; Jones et al. 2009). But there are other reasons, such as access to different ideas and/or practices with regard to the female role rather than that of the traditional role of wife and mother. When women work, there is the opportunity for higher wages for those with fewer career breaks due to pregnancies, and generally participation in wage labor is associated with a better ability to defend one's interests (Mason 1987). In the event of death of the husband or abandonment by him, security is ensured by employment even without a large number of children (Basu 1992, 230).

Finally, a victory of the women's movement should be mentioned. "Reproductive rights" were defined and recognized in 1994 at the UN International Conference on Population and Development, Cairo—even though women's empowerment was considered just a means of reducing population growth and not a value in itself. The attempt by the Vatican and some Muslim countries to remove from the definition of reproductive health the clause of free access to contraceptives and, in cases of their failure, to abortion at the request of the woman, was defeated (Goldberg 2009). It is argued indeed that in recent decades the biggest driver of a reduction in births has been the accessibility of contraceptives. The same reduction would happen everywhere if they were available (Potts 1997).

# Chapter 8

# DEVELOPMENT, POPULATION AND ENERGY

## 8.1 Adapting to the Environment or Changing It

Natural selection is a much slower mechanism of adaptation than the cultural shifts with which our species quickly faces changes in the environment (as well as causing them), or becomes more efficient and effective in a given environment. This efficiency is not Nature's imperative, rather the contrary:

> Nature "seeks" a high P/B [daytime net production/biomass] ratio, not a high P/B efficiency, so the tendency in the human use OF nature is opposite from that IN nature—or in other words, man reverses the law of natural ecosystems: the strategy of "maximum protection" (that is, trying to achieve maximum support of complex biomass structure) often conflicts with man's goal of "maximum production" trying to obtain the highest possible yield [...]. For example, the goal of agriculture or intensive forestry, as now generally practiced, is to achieve high rates of production of readily harvestable products with little standing crop left to accumulate on the landscape—in other words, a high P/B efficiency. Nature's strategy, on the other hand, as seen in the outcome of the successional process, is directed toward the reverse efficiency—a high B/P ratio. (Odum 1971, 262 and 266)

Cultural evolution is our way of adapting to different ecological niches. Better: it is the way of changing our niche quickly, without waiting for the biological mutations that make other species bodily adapt to the (slowly but ever changing) environment through natural selection through the generations: "Once man's behavior and mode of existence are determined primarily by his culture, then he is able to make adaptive changes to meet his environmental conditions by modifying his culture" (Wilkinson 1973, 9).

In natural selection, as in human culture, there is a preeminent force that relates to the fulfillment of the fundamental life needs. In basic agreement with Marx and Harris, Wilkinson (1973, 11) wrote: "Both individuals and societies will give priority to the maintenance of subsistence activities at a level at least adequate for survival. [...] The demands of production have a pre-eminent position which allows them to ride roughshod over other elements of a culture." Wilkinson overlooked that production can have purely economic motivations—the pursuit of profit—inverting the sequence he describes as going from need to production of what satisfies this need. Production and advertising of useless objects show that consumers' satisfaction is by no means the goal of those who organize the output in the capitalist world-economy.

According to Wilkinson, changes in the mode of production have generally led to a worsening of living conditions, due to the greater labor intensity that new techniques invariably require and the worsening quality of the products that are obtained (that nevertheless have the upside of becoming more diffused among the populace). New products are generally inferior to those that have become too scarce and (in a market society) expensive. This can be seen daily with the progressive replacement of quality materials or flavors of natural foods by poor and less expensive substitutes, soaked in toxic substances. New materials such as plastics, which have some superior qualities when compared to the natural ones, have the disadvantage of being very harmful when they become waste (Sacchetti 1985). Plastics present robustness, imperviousness and impermeability, deriving from a chemical synthesis that transforms oil into artificial materials that cannot be decomposed by any living organism, precisely because they do not exist in Nature (Commoner 1977). These are also the qualities that make them dangerous for life: their residues cannot be disposed of, while their fragmentation makes them easily assimilated by living organisms, causing physical degeneration starting with the delicate function of reproduction. All the substances humans invent are dangerous:

> After global warming, global toxic chemical pollution is almost certainly the next greatest environmental threat we face. Scientists since Rachel Carson have warned that human survival and the survival of many other species is increasingly at risk because of the growing assault on our bodies and the environment from the tens of thousands of different kinds of toxic chemicals pumped, dumped, leached, sprayed, vented into the environment every year by the chemical industry, polluting factories and farms, power plants, and so forth.[1] (Smith 2010, 36)

---

1 Original note: Rachel Carson, *Silent Spring*, New York: Houghton Mifflin, 1962. Theo Colborn, Dianne Dumanoski and John Peterson Myers, *Our Stolen Future: Are We Threatening Our Fertility, Intelligence, and Survival?* New York: Dutton, 1996.

Similarly, human inventions in the field of energy are dangerous: electromagnetic fields that accompany alternate-current electricity (a kind not existing in Nature) and data transmission in the invisible frequencies of the electromagnetic spectrum have negative biological effects (Blank 2014; Firstenberg 2020; Kostoff 2020; Pall 2020).

The only real growth evident in the processes we call "development" is for Wilkinson population growth, which he also believes to be the cause of the transformations in the techniques and technologies that "develop" societies:

> In English history there can be no mistaking the intimate connection between the periodic appearance of population pressure and economic development. Since the Norman conquest it seems that there have been three major periods of population growth leading to acute population pressure [around 1300, 1600, and the late 18th century]. Each one has, in its later stages, ushered in a period not just of agricultural expansion, but of agricultural innovation and industrial development as well. (Wilkinson 1973, 81)

Again, the basic concept at play is Malthusian population pressure. Wilkinson meritoriously draws our attention to the downside of what we call development, though his view of it seems exceedingly somber. For example, notwithstanding pollution, life expectancy has risen everywhere. On the other hand, his views are too rosy: power is completely missing in his theory. Power—also in the meaning of intensive use of energy—characterized European expansion with its incorporation of world-empires and minisystems, accompanying and allowing the development of capitalism on a global scale. The encounter with greedy and armed Europeans is interpreted by Wilkinson as a mere cultural disturbance leading to an increase in population because of the cultural disruption it caused. As we saw in the previous chapter, many other, stronger mechanisms were at work requiring population growth after its initial very concrete disruption. In Wilkinson's scheme it is the depletion of some resources, often caused by the increase in population, which triggers changes in the mode of production, and this invariably implies greater exploitation of human labor. Somehow in contradiction with these propositions, Wilkinson also believed that industrialization, that is, the introduction of machines to perform new tasks and also save on labor, was accelerated by the shortage of manpower. He neglected the fact that even in the presence of unemployment the use of machines in production continues to increase, as Marx observed explaining the fact with the law of value. Hornborg explained this mainly with the concept of a culturally determined unequal exchange, though access to new forms of energy is also of preeminent importance for his theory that considers machines as expression of inequality, that make possible their employment.

Inequality increases with available energy. The energy consumption of the richest countries is a thousand times greater than that of the poorest countries:

> Although post-1950 economic development reduced the relative gap between haves and have-nots, the disparities are unacceptably large. In 1950 industrialized countries consumed about 93 percent of the world's commercial TPES [primary energy found in nature and not transformed]; by 1985 the rich world containing one-quarter of global population consumed about 82 percent of all primary energy, and in 2005 its share fell to just over 60 percent versus about 15 percent for population. The United States alone, with 5 percent of world population, used about 22 percent of total energy, and the G8 countries, with 12 percent of the world's population, consumed about 46 percent of the world's energy. In contrast, the poorest one-quarter of humanity (sub-Saharan Africa, Nepal, Bangladesh, most of rural India) consumed less than 3 percent of the world's TPES. Few other comparisons illuminate more starkly the existential chasm separating the two worlds. (Smil 2008, 258)

Two billion people do not have access to electricity, while the average per capita consumption of rich countries is 10 megawatts per hour. Greenhouse gas emissions are concentrated in the countries with the lowest population growth, on the other hand, where the population grows more, its $CO_2$ emissions are lower (Satterthwaite 2009).

In the theories of some economists who have studied development, economic growth and population increase are inextricably related, so they always regard population growth positively.[2] Simon Kuznets (1990) attributed part of the economic growth to an increase in population, and Julian Simon considered the population as a source of innovation, in a scenario where resources can be practically unlimited thanks to technology:

> If we extend the horizon even further, we can see that the long-run effects of additional people are positive on balance, which is quite in contradiction the conventional wisdom. The most abstract outline of the central process that links population growth to long-run economic development is as follows: Increased numbers of consumers, and

2 Incidentally, this correlation is well known among businessmen: Vance Packard quoted a series of statements such as "This stork means business" in *The Waste Makers*, New York: McKay, 1960, 171–74 (quoted in Thomlinson 1965, 355).

> increase of income, expand the demand for raw materials as well as finished products. The resulting actual and expected shortages force up prices of the natural resources. The increased prices trigger the search for new ways to satisfy the demand, and sooner or later sources and innovative substitutes are found. Eventually these new discoveries lead to cheaper natural resources than existed before this process began. (Simon 1977, xii)

For this "Cornucopian" ideologue, technology is a pure expression of human ingenuity and multiplies in quantity and quality with the growth of the population, guaranteeing the solution of every present and future problem.

But a lack of correlation between the trends in GDP and population was ascertained in the 1970s and 1980s when an inverse correlation was expected (Bagchi 2010). Later analyses of the subsequent period show instead a clear correlation between population growth and GDP (Birdsall et al. 2001). More constant is the simple global correlation between population trends and energy use, as reported in Hall and Klitgaard (2018). The above quotation by Simon can be said to correctly describe the positive feedback system of the population-prices-resources cycle in the core of the world-system in the period of the availability of very high energy returns on energy investments (EROI).

A complementary vision of development stems in fact from biophysical economics, that highlighted many examples in which GDP per capita correlated very closely to the energy used, also per capita (Hall 2000; LeClerc and Hall 2008): "Where energy use has increased more rapidly than populations, people have become wealthier; where energy use has increased less rapidly than population, people get poorer" (Hall and Klitgaard 2018, 273). But this again fails to consider inequality and what happens at the microhistorical level.

## 8.2 Overpopulation?

In mid-May 2021, the Population Media Center reported that the world population amounted to 7,848,800,000 people, growing at a rate of about 1.18 percent per year, that is, a yearly addition of about 83 million human beings. The annual growth rate is slowly decreasing: in 2008 it was 1.24 percent, but humans are still on an exponential curve.

The contemporary version of attributing to the poor the cause of their own misery because they have too many children states that environmental degradation is caused by overpopulation (e.g., Alam 2012). It is instead caused by overproduction and overconsumption, because our social organization aims at incessant growth of the capital employed in the production of goods that must also incessantly increase: this is how energy has been and is being used. The ecosocialist activists Ian Angus and Simon Butler criticize what is becoming common sense in dealing with the problems humans cause to the environment: putting the blame on population increase without analyzing what the causes of pollution actually are. They write:

> The corporations that make disposable products [with their planned obsolescence here included] are responsible and should bear the cost: that concept is obviously just and could easily be applied to other products than electronics, but populationists don't see it. All that garbage, they argue, just proves there are too many people. A college-level biology textbook puts it this way: "Humans are not only using up limited resources. We are also damaging air, water, and other renewable resources by polluting them with industrial waste, garbage, and sewage. The more of us there are, the more pollution we generate."[3] The underlying assumption is that industry is just responding efficiently to consumer demands: garbage is inevitable, so the only variable is how many people buy and discard it. The authors ignore the simple fact that between 1960 and 2000, US garbage grew more than three times as fast as the population. Obviously something other than the birth rate is driving the throwaway economy. (Angus and Butler 2011, 159–60)

The World Resources Institute[4] has calculated the impressive mass of materials used for production in industrial economies that return to the environment as garbage within a year: it is three-eighths, excluding water, which alone would completely obliterate all other masses. The Green New Deal just adds new consumption items, dissipating even more energy (Parrique et al. 2019).

The current debate on ways to bring the human species back to sustainable interaction with our environment is marred by the free-market ideology of the elite, covering its greed. This "Davos spirit," as Wallerstein called it, clings to the axiom that markets are the best way to organize human relationships, despite countless contrary evidence. The theorem of Consumer Sovereignty, which says that consumers will decide how to (best) orientate production through their demand for goods, is used politically to put the blame regarding various forms of pollution on the consumers themselves. The indicated solution would be a change in consumers' tastes and preferences. But in reality the decisions about production are made by companies and states, which make certain

3 Authors quote Alla J. Tobin and Jennie Dusheck, *Asking about Life*, Belmont, CA: Brooks/Cole, 2005, 592 (3rd ed.).

4 Matthews et al.: *The Weight of Nations: Material Outflow from Industrial Economies*. Washington, DC: World Resources Institute, 2000 (quoted by Angus and Butler 2011, 185).

products or services mandatory. These policies are hardly in the interest of consumers or of life on the planet:

> That's why corporations are rarely mentioned in populationist writing: the producers of ever increasing quantities of goods are simply acting to fulfill consumer demand, which is growing because the number of consumers is increasing. If that's true, then the entire super-polluting system results from consumer decisions, and we have only three options: reduce the number of consumers, or persuade consumers to consume less, or both. (Angus and Butler 2011, 153)[5]

The responsibility for this super-polluting system lies in very few hands. A very small portion of the population works for the largest corporations: in 2000, 1 percent of the world's population worked for the two hundred biggest corporations, whose turnover was 27.5 percent of the world product in monetary terms.[6] Responsibility for the conduct of corporations obviously lies with the managers, not the personnel who have to obey them under threat of dismissal. Per capita statistics are widely used to demonstrate the environmental impact of individuals, but it would be more correct to talk about emissions per corporation and wars per government, as Angus and Butler wrote. The inability of citizens to set limits to the economic activity of corporations and to the aggressive military enterprises of states point to the real decision-makers and their responsibility for the world's current ecological disasters.

It is the law itself, the civil codes of the capitalist countries, which make profit or capital increase the sole objective of corporations. These are the rules of the capitalist game, codified and independent of the personal qualities of company managers. Those who have fewer scruples in fulfilling the corporate mission will be selected, as shareholders must see their investments grow (Bakan 2004). Ira Rennert, for example, leader of the Renco Group, ranked forty-fourth among the richest men on the planet in 2010 with a net worth of 5.3 billion dollars, according to *Forbes*.[7] One of the companies of the Renco Group, MagCorp, was the largest source of pollution on US soil in 1996, according to the Environmental Protection Agency (EPA):

---

5 See chapter 12: "The myth of consumer sovereignty" (Angus and Butler 2011).

6 The data is taken from David Rothkopf: *Superclass. The Global Power Elite and the World They Are Making.* Toronto: Penguin, 2009.

7 Quoted by Angus and Butler (2011, 166). In 2019, again according to *Forbes*, Rennert's fortunes dropped to a mere 4.1 billion.

> Wastewater ditches around MagCorp's plant are reported to be contaminated with dioxin at levels as high as 170 parts per billion: EPA rules require immediate cleanup action at one part per billion. Doe Run [another company in the Renco group] has frequently been cited by the EPA for exceeding legal emission limits, as well as polluting roads and soils around its facilities in Missouri. In February 2002, health officials found that 56 percent of children living near the Doe Run smelter had high blood-lead levels. An October 2009 EPA report says that soil on one-third of properties situated within a mile of the company's lead smelter contains lead at levels exceeding the legal threshold for mandatory removal and replacement. (Angus and Butler 2011, 167–68)

And this does not include what the Renco Group does abroad, such as poisoning the Peruvian town La Oroya with another foundry that disperses heavy and toxic metals into nearby rivers and lakes. According to the Blacksmith Institute and the Green Cross Switzerland, La Oroya is one of the ten most polluted sites on the planet.

The military is also a huge perpetrator of global pollution, especially the US army. Barry Sanders researched the environmental impact of the Pentagon, despite the fact that most of the data is covered by military secrecy. The Pentagon is the world's largest oil consumer. In 2009 the US military used 5,700 billion gallons of oil, just under 16 billion gallons per day, and its operations produced 73 million tons of greenhouse gases: for comparison, Italy's emissions amount to about half a billion tons per year. In the Iraq War, from 2003 to 2007, at least 141 million tons of $CO_2$ were emitted, equivalent to the annual emissions of 25 million cars.[8] But the United States has prohibited accounting for the emissions of the military in greenhouse gas reports.

Militarism and the polluting action of multinational corporations in search of profits are two sides of the same coin, because the core of the capitalist world-system needs military strength to keep the costs of the raw materials it uses low (Jorgenson and Clark 2012). Therefore:

> Those who claim slowing population growth will stop or slow environmental destruction are ignoring these real and immediate threats to life on our planet. Corporations and armies aren't polluting the world and destroying ecosystems because there are "too many people," and they won't stop if the birth rate is reduced. If Afghan women have

---

8 Barry Sanders, *The Green Zone. The Environmental Costs of Militarism*, Oakland: AK Press, 2009, data reported by Angus and Butler (2011, 174).

> fewer babies, the US military won't stop firing shells made of depleted uranium into their villages. Nor will military bases in Afghanistan stop dumping toxic wastes into open burn pits. If Iraq's birth rate falls to zero, the US military will not use one gallon of oil less.
>
> If the United States and Australia block all immigration, energy companies will continue burning coal to produce electricity. If the world's population growth stops tomorrow, Ira Rennert's companies will still poison indigenous children in Peru, Shell will continue killing people in the Niger Delta, and Alberta's tar sands will still be the worst ecological crime on earth. (Angus and Butler 2011, 176)

But if the demand for commodities decreases because new generations are fewer, the capitalist economy will go into crisis. At the beginning of the nineteenth century, Guglielmo Ferrero (1994, 895) thus described the needs of capitalism:

> Population growth is the necessary condition for any other growth: in industry, commerce, savings, state revenues and expenditures, and in the army, ranks of the ruling class, and number of places open to those who want a social rise. A civilization aiming for an indefinite increase in the quantity of all things must begin with the multiplication of men.

Although I agree that population growth is not the ultimate cause of ecocide, however an increased awareness of the current human impact on the planet leading to the choice to have fewer children does not seem a completely negative stance—always understood that the action needed is not on the microhistorical level of individual actions and procreative decisions in an unchanged capitalist framework, but on the macrohistorical level of collective decisions about the organization of society and economic policies: will we continue to put our destiny in the invisible hand of the market with its monetary profit spiral and in the visible hands of the ruling class or will we do away with both?

## 8.3 The Environmental Unsustainability of Capitalism

The concept of Anthropocene was launched in 2002 by the chemist Paul Crutzen in *Nature*. Global warming acts on tectonic and volcanic activity by modifying glaciers, and consequently their weight on Earth. Humanity became a geological force a couple of centuries ago, ending the Holocene, the geological era that lasted for the previous 11,500 years. The Anthropocene is a useful concept, contrasting the hitherto positive picture of Modernity and

Progress, albeit it expresses an alleged responsibility of our entire species for ecocide, the destruction of Nature. Bonneuil and Fressoz (2016, 212) devoted their book to unmasking this presumed collective responsibility: "Thinking the Anthropocene also means challenging its unifying and grand narrative of the errant human species and its redemption by science alone," which is the indicated solution, for example, with geoengineering. The biggest threat to Nature seems to be climate disruption, as the leading scientist studying the world climate, Jim Hansen of NASA, affirms:

> "Yes, most of the fossil fuels must be left in the ground. That is the explicit message that the science provides. This is the precise message of science." If we don't, we won't be able to contain global warming to within 2° Centigrade, and if we fail to do that, our goose is cooked. [...] If we want to save ourselves and many other species, then we have to give up the freedom of capitalists to produce and sell as they please and consumers to buy whatever they like and can afford—*in order to win the greater freedom* for humanity to breathe clean air, to have safe water to drink, to have safe food to eat, to live long and healthy lives free of toxics-induced diseases, to restore a forested, clean, safe, habitable planet we can pass on to our children. (Smith 2010, 36 and 39)[9]

But the immoderate use of fossil fuel energy with its dangerous repercussions for the climate is certainly not a decision made democratically by the majority of informed citizens. It was a precise choice of the ruling class of this capitalist globalized world, starting with the shift from water energy to coal during the Industrial Revolution (Malm 2016). Jason Moore (2017) therefore proposes another term for the era starting for him in the Long Sixteenth Century: Capitalocene. Andreas Malm and Alf Hornborg instead suggest the term "Technocene," marking the recent industrial era, from 1750 onward. The growing use of technology and fossil fuels energy in the daily life of the world's wealthy and middle class is made possible precisely by the growing inequality at the planetary level. For example, in 1820 the poorest 20 percent had 4.7 percent of the global income, while in 1992 they had less than half of that: 2.2 percent (Bourguignon and Morrisson 2002). It is thanks to the conditions of the poorest people who are forced to provide cheap labor for production and extraction that the core ensures the availability of the various raw materials and of the energy used to build high-tech objects that only the

9 Quoted in an article by Richard Smith titled, "Beyond Growth or Beyond Capitalism?" which appeared in *Review of Real World-Economics.*

core (plus the ruling class in all other areas) can afford to use. Had materials and energy not been cheap because of low wages in the countries from whence they were and continue to be extracted, technology would not have pervaded daily life in core countries:

> We would argue that, to the contrary, uneven distribution is a condition for *the very existence* of modern, fossil-fuel technology. The affluence of high-tech modernity cannot possibly be universalized – become an asset of the species – because it is predicated on a global division of labour that is geared precisely to abysmal price and wage differences between populations. The density of distribution of technologies that are ultimately dependent on fossil fuels by and large coincides with that of purchasing power. These technologies are an index of capital accumulation, privileged resource consumption, and the displacement of both work and environmental loads. (Malm and Hornborg 2014, 3)

The Swedish anthropologists thus conclude that the root of the "infinite" expansion required by capitalism lies in the organization of the flow of general purpose money for the achievement of profits. The internal logic of money, the M-C-M' spiral, is invincible: "Our only hope is to replace the logic with a new systemic orientation, which requires a transformation of money itself" (Hornborg 2001, 18). It is the characteristics of the money we use, being a "universal equivalent" created by banks at the condition of begetting an interest, that perpetuate the unequal exchanges in terms of matter and energy between center and periphery. This type of money permits the exchange of nearly everything with everything else on the planet. For Hornborg money is just a symbol which circulates for the value society ascribes to it, but nevertheless he affirms that capitalism is really general purpose money. When "capitalism" is blamed, the real culprit is this very concrete human manufacture with its characteristics, primarily its capacity to make everything exchangeable. Other types of currency can have different effects, such as the acceleration of economic activity with money that loses value over time (not a great idea in times of ecological crisis). A historical example of this effect is the money put into circulation in the city of Wörgl following the proposal of Silvio Gesell. This money had an expiration date and its circulation canceled unemployment in the mid of the Great Depression (Kennedy 2006). Hornborg instead proposes the introduction of a secondary currency, limited to the exchanges of production that occur locally to favor the economy at Kilometer Zero (Hornborg 2016). Urging us to change the rules of our money/capitalism, which clash with the finitude of our planet,

Hornborg repeats Fredric Jameson's quip: "Envisaging an end to capitalism is no doubt preferable to imagining the end of the world, even if it is more difficult."[10]

But it is not (only) money's expected property of yielding interest which compels firms to deliver a profit, rather (also) the institutional arrangements to actualize this property: the legal organization of firms, the obligations of CEO's to their shareholders, the imperative of profit inscribed in the civil codes, the competition to prevail in markets and reach economic power, plus the actions of the political power that guarantees profits for production, especially if it is useful for the military. These are the mechanisms that propel the pursuit of growth, which is the multiplication of monetary exchanges in order to accumulate capital. Underneath the multiplication of monetary exchanges, products and also people, lies the multiplication of energy at the disposal of investors. In the M-C-M' spiral: "the more fossil fuels and other resources capital has dissipated today, the more it will afford to dissipate tomorrow" (Malm and Hornborg 2014, 65), as our economy rewards the dissipation of resources and allows it to be perpetrated through profits, in the absence of which the economic subjects must leave the market going bankrupt.

But markets are not given, they are created by use, law and class struggle. Capitalism needs them to expand in all directions. For example, buying a child commissioned with the juridical institution of surrogate motherhood became legally possible in California in 1993. Another example is the appropriation by private firms of bandwidth in Earth's electromagnetic spectrum, which states sell, thereby once again attributing property rights to commons. These new markets are the object of current struggles—in the first case to keep money away from motherhood, in order to preserve the right of the newborn not to be sold and to have continuity in his or her family life, and in the second case in order to preserve the health of all living beings on the planet.

## 8.4 EROI and the Future of Capitalism

According to world-systems analysis, the end of the capitalist world-economy is in sight, because its expansion imperatives are reaching the limits in economic and especially social terms—as for Wallerstein (1999a) ecological problems affect society only through social actions.[11] The system is "oscillating" trying

---

10 Hornborg (2019, 140n5), from Fredric Jameson, "Future City," in *New Left Review*, vol. 21, 2003, 76.

11 See Wallerstein (2006), chapter 5: "The crisis of the modern world-system. Bifurcation, chaos and alternatives." For the critique of the nineteenth and twentieth centuries theories expunging Nature from the social science, see Bonneuil and Fressoz (2016).

to solve current problems with old solutions that no longer work. Capital accumulation cannot continue, because by now there are no more external areas to be incorporated, and production costs are rising, eroding profits. This happens because labor costs grow thanks to the organization and education of workers (proletarianization is considered by Wallerstein an irreversible process), so the cost of outsourcing rises because of the working-class demands, and also the costs of infrastructure and public services rise again because of people's demands and expectations. Moreover, the price of raw materials increases as they become scarcer and pollution is to be remedied at increasing costs. To this picture I have added a foreseeable downward population trend, with less consumption and less workers (all other things being equal) that is problematic for the perennial growth required by M-C-M'. But contrary trends push down state expenditures with the privatizing doctrine of neoliberalism, while globalization (i.e., competition among workers across borders because of free-trade and cheap transportation) pushes down wages in the core area, and—more urgently and importantly—fossil fuels are not just raw materials the cost of which is growing. The already presented EROI value is diminishing, and this diminution in the energy returns on energy investments is not reversible, as only carbon-based sources (i.e., sources that have already been mapped and exploited) can furnish energy with a high EROI. Nuclear energy also does it, but it can hardly be harnessed without damages to human and environmental health.

World conventional crude oil production peaked in 2008 according to the International Energy Agency (2018, 45). Oil production peaked in 1970 in the United States, when Wallerstein pinpointed the beginning of the descending arc of American hegemony, and real wages in the United States also peaked in 1973. Since then, peak oil production has been reached in at least 18, and probably in the majority of the 50 most significant oil-producing nations (Hall and Klitgaard 2018, 286).

The unprecedented quantity of energy at the disposal of the world-system in the industrial era (surely concentrated in core countries and ruling classes) has been used at the microhistorical level to multiply machines and make them work, but also to multiply the population, still encouraged to grow by religious and secular authorities. At the macrohistorical level, energy was and is used to build the infrastructure necessary for transporting raw materials, final products, people and energy itself, and to wage wars that have been more and more destructive. These positive feedback mechanisms can continue as long as the EROI of fossil fuels gives returns higher than one—all things being equal for the other resources, which must also be extracted with diminishing returns. As Lewis Mumford wrote, for mass production to be successful there must be mass consumption, and nothing assures this consumption better than organized destruction. War is the health of the Machine, he drastically concluded.

Knowledge of EROI, and in general about energy and its use, is still limited among social scientists and the general public: "Society has gone to great lengths to isolate most of us physically and intellectually from the energy sources upon which our food, our comfort, our transportation, and our economy depend," as Hall and Klitgaard (2018, 300) observe. Nevertheless, what is essential to industrialization, and to the changes in society and Nature it brought with it, is the use of fossil fuels. This fact has surprisingly not been recognized until recently by social scientists, including the founders of world-system analysis,[12] still pervaded by the Comtian imperative of reducing historical social science to human interactions. Only the perception of expanding resources has been considered as a motivation to procreate, principally by Virgina Abernethy and also by the anthropologist Brian Hayden (1986, 186), who wrote:

> The use of fossil fuels is therefore very relevant to contemporary population dynamics: Perhaps the most dramatic and pervasive example of increasing resources, however, took place during the Industrial Revolution, which opened up truly enormous and entirely untapped new reserves of energy resources, consisting of fossil fuels, water power, and electricity.

With market or state demand for goods (mostly) guaranteed, and the demand for labor stimulating procreation in order to have the necessary workforce, population and production could explode at the macrohistorical level as they did in the period following 1750. The end of this positive feedback mechanism has been identified by some with the end of profits, starting a debate about the extent to which our present economic system is still capitalist. As profits have continued to plummet since 2007 in what has been called The Secular Stagnation, only states can now guarantee contracts that give a monetary reward. Thus a new feudal era seems ready to dawn, with gains made only with rents and other transfers sustained by the political power, especially for firms producing digital platforms that manage information, as there are few possibilities of competition by other platforms once one of them has reached a critical mass of users for a certain purpose.

---

12 For example, in the excellent studies by Giovanni Arrighi (1996) and by Arrighi and Silver (2003) of hegemonic power in the long K-waves, the variables considered are just economic, in the sense of pertinent to the money circuit. Energy provision and use are never referred to. To the contrary, on world(-)system(s) as dissipative structures, see Wallerstein (1983) and Gunder Frank (2007).

States have indeed started to heavily intervene in the daily lives of citizens during the 2020 declared pandemic of COVID-19, enacting very similar plans to force citizens to stay home and use only the Internet for work, recreation and social contact outside of the officially cohabiting family. The "pandemic," a label with terrorizing effects out of proportion with the effects of the COVID-19 contagion, was so declared by the World Health Organization (WHO). The WHO is part of the UN, but it is also financed by private entities, such as the Bill and Melinda Gates Foundation, which is at the top of its voluntary contributors, conferring 14.8 percent of its financial flow,[13] and giving more than 450 million USD to the WHO budget of 3.4 billion USD for 2018–19.[14] For the WHO to declare a pandemic, the actual mortality of the illness does not matter, but only its international spreading. Influenza waves are also pandemics, but states never before reacted in the way they did, allegedly to reduce or stop the contagion, when the WHO declared COVID-19 a pandemic in 2020. This sudden preoccupation for public health by neoliberal states that for decades have cut public spending in this sector seems rather a gigantic push by entrepreneurial states in favor of the digital technology sold by giant corporations (Danna 2020a). The Internet of Things, to be implemented with 5G transmission technology, promises to entrepreneurs to curtail the workforce (who is interested in self-driving cars if not taxi companies?) and promises to politicians the complete surveillance of what people do and think—entrepreneurs will also benefit from this possibility. But the Internet of Things is energy-consuming, massively so. Will this next wave of technology have enough power to function? Will it be implemented by cutting down on other energy uses (like private travel on airplanes for tourism, as it is still done as I am writing) because of its possibility of controlling the masses' every movement? One of the effects of the lockdown in fact has been the lowering of the price of oil worldwide.

Energy questions apart, the total control promised by 5G technology is illusory. A part cannot control its whole (Bateson 1972): "Se l'uomo dominasse la Natura/La parte sopra il tutto prevarrebbe" (If man dominated Nature/A part would prevail on its whole) (Ghetilieri 2021, Canto VII). This general principle of system theory can be applied to the particular case of 5G/Internet of Things: the intensified use of electromagnetism can transmit enormous quantities of information, but its downside is to put at risk, precisely with the electromagnetic fields generated

13 http://open.who.int/2020-21/contributors/contributor.

14 WHO, *Programme Budget 2020 –2021*, p. 20. https://www.who.int/about/finances-accountability/budget/WHOPB-PRP-19.pdf?ua=1. The table of the top 10 contributors in 2018–19 is here: https://www.who.int/about/planning-finance-and-accountability/how-who-is-funded.

in the transmission of data, all biological activity, including the capacity to reproduce (Pall 2020), which is already diminishing, especially due to chemical pollution. Will humanity, led by a dominant class selected by greed and aggression in the current capitalist world-economy, follow the transhumanist promise of a paradise of technological hybridization, or will it rebel to come back to Nature, ceasing to combat Her and abiding instead by Her rules—at least to more of them?

## 8.5 Conclusion: Population in the Post-Fossil Fuels Era

The biologist David Pimentel and the nutritionist Marcia Pimentel (1996) believe that a population of only two billion humans is sustainable in the long term, when the depletion of fossil fuels will force the human species to return to organic farming without machines for its subsistence. Lloyd T. Evans (1998, 226) and Edward Anthony Wrigley (2004) make analogous estimates, affirming that organic agriculture would have been insufficient to sustain the world's human population beyond its second billion. Indeed, the application of machines to agriculture is energetically inefficient, but it permits the attainment of more food, though at high energetic costs. For example, in Denmark in 2004–7 the Food Energy Returned on Fossil Energy Invested, or Food-EROI was much less than 1. As Bellanca and Pardi (2021, 24) succinctly write: "The so-called 'green revolution' is nothing other than a way to turn oil into food." Agro-industry played a role in population growth by supplying food obtained with the use of fertilizers, herbicides and agricultural machines, thereby increasing short-term yields at the expense of the fertility of the land. Warning signs that the chickens are coming home to roost are multiplying, with soil erosion and the decrease of other resources, such as water and fertilizers, nearing depletion. In fact, since 1984 per capita food production, in particular grain production, has been decreasing mainly due to the scarcity of water:

> Approximately 17 percent of all crops are irrigated and this irrigation provides the world with 40 percent of its food. World agriculture consumes from 70 to 80 percent of the freshwater and currently serious shortages exist in many regions. This is one of the major limits to world food production. (Pimentel and Pimentel 1996, 18)[15]

15 The Pimentels, biologists, however, have a very crude vision of human society. They ignore social structures and limit their reasoning to people's numbers (Hartmann 1995; Bashford 2014). The ecologist Howard Odum (2007) does the same.

Nevertheless, Alf Hornborg (2012) disagrees with the proposition that "fossil fuels feed the population" because only about one half of the 1.5 billion hectares cultivated today are used for the production of basic food for humans. The rest is for fiber, lubricants, biofuels, animal feed, tobacco and colonial drinks. Furthermore, half of the food produced is wasted. In fact another problem reported by biologists is that our species is appropriating about half of the biomass of the planet for food supplies, medicines or as raw material to be processed into other products (Pimentel 2002). Cultivated fields, pastures and cities covered 5 percent of Earth's surface in 1750, while now they cover one-third of it (Bonneuil and Fressoz 2016). Limiting and confining wildlife affects long ecological cycles, especially those of forests, which are necessary to make the minerals of the subsoil available for the food chain. But we cannot eliminate wildlife, because we depend on it. For example, agriculture depends on bees (wild and kept) and other pollinating insects (wild), which are not technically replaceable—though in China fruit trees are sometimes pollinated by hand, as work is cheap. The suggested pollinating drones would make the energy consumption of agriculture even more unsustainable.

It is clear that the changes in our social organization necessary for the survival of life on the planet, especially human life, imply a necessary change in the structures and objectives of the capitalist world-economy, that is, its demise, because the actions that support a system based on free-market initiative and waged labor are intrinsically harmful:

> Poll after poll shows that ordinary citizens want to see the environment cleaned up, want to see a stop to the pillage of the planet, the threat of destruction of their children's future. But as workers in a capitalist economy, "no growth" just means no jobs. [...] As a recent headline in the satirical weekly The Onion ran: "Masses Clamor for New Bubble." (Smith 2010, 35)

Ugo Bardi (2020, 213) puts his critique to growth-chasing governments as follows:

> But what should a government exactly do? Financial matters are the most debated area of government action and they can be seen as attempts to control the system by acting, for instance, on the interest rate. The problem is that, here as in other sectors, the government is not normally trying to control the economy in the sense of stabilizing it. Rather, it tries its best to make it grow at the fastest possible speed. For most people, this is supposed to be the obvious thing to do but it may not be such a smart idea. It is as if the governor of a steam engine were

> to be operated to open the valve as much as possible, all the time. That could lead the machine to rev up over its limits and maybe even explode.

What is needed is redistribution, reorganization, changes in our attitude toward Nature (Danna 2018), the end to all social and economic incentives for procreation, and a return to the land.[16] The dire situation is hidden by the illusions propagated by the ruling classes, thriving on increasing inequalities:

> We are cajoled and forced to give up rights, wages, conditions and sovereignty for an illusion. The illusion is that things will go back to the way they were when fossil fuel was plentiful and humans were not so multitudinous, but no official authority is given to the reality that fossil fuel is not being replenished and we are running down supply at an accelerating rate. (Newman 2013, 47)

The current commitment must be to contrast capitalism and the market in all its forms and then, if (or rather: when) the collapse comes, the future commitment should be to prevent its reconstitution, particularly the growing spiral of money, that, as Hornborg said, permits to exchange the Amazon forest for cans of carbonated drinks.

---

16 According to others, in order to prevent the end of capitalism from being the destruction of life on Earth, energy consumption and "civilization" in general must be countered. A text that reflects on the actions and political organization necessary to save the planet from ecocide is *Deep Green Resistance: A Strategy to Save the Planet* by Jensen, McBay and Keith (2011), who nevertheless do not seem to worry that the transition is not marked by chaos and barbarism.

# REFERENCES AND DATASETS


Abernethy, Virginia Deane. 2000. *Population Politics*. 2nd ed. New Brunswick, NJ: Transaction.

———. 2005. *Population Pressure and Cultural Adjustment: With a New Introduction by the Author*. New Brunswick, NJ: Transaction.

ACOG (The American Congress of Obstetricians and Gynecologists). 2005. "ACOG Committee Opinion 324: Perinatal Risks Associated with Assisted Reproductive Technology." *Obstetrics and Gynecology* 106: 1143–46 (revised in 2007). http://www.acog.org/ Resources-And-Publications/Committee-Opinions/Committee-on-Obstetric-Practice/Perinatal-Risks-Associated-With-Assisted-Reproductive-Technology.

Akhter, Farida. 1995. *Resisting Norplant: Women's Struggle in Bangladesh against Coercion and Violence*. Dhaka: Narigrantha Prabartana.

———. 2005. *Depopulating Bangladesh: Essays on the Politics of Fertility*. 3rd ed. Dhaka: Narigrantha Prabartana.

Alam, Fakhre. 2012. *Poverty and Environmental Sustainability*. New Delhi: Deep & Deep.

Alexander, Paul. 1986. "Labor Expropriation and Fertility: Population Growth in Nineteenth Century Java." In *Culture and Reproduction. An Anthropological Critique of Demographic Transition Theory*, edited by W. Penn Handwerker, 249–62. Boulder, CO: Westview Press.

Amin, Samir. 1971. *Under-Populated Africa*. Dakar: UN; IDEP. https://repository.uneca.org/handle/10855/42261.

Anderson, Michael. 1988. *Population Change in North-Western Europe, 1750-1850*. Houndmills: Macmillan Education.

Andorka, Rudolf. 1978. *Determinants of Fertility in Advanced Societies*. London: Methuen.

Angel, J. Lawrence. 1975. "Paleoecology, Paleodemography, and Health." In *Population, Ecology, and Social Evolution*, edited by Steven Polgar, 167–90. Paris: de Gruyter Mouton.

Angus, Ian, and Simon Butler. 2011. *Too Many People?: Population, Immigration, and the Environmental Crisis*. Chicago: Haymarket Books.

Anker, Richard, Mayra Buvinic and Nadia H. Youssef, eds. 1982. *Women's Roles and Population Trends in the Third World*. London: Croom Helm.

Ariès, Philippe. 1960. *L'enfant et la vie familiale sous l'ancien régime*. Paris: Seuil.

Arrighi, Giovanni. 1996. *Il lungo XX secolo: denaro, potere and le origini del nostro tempo*. Milano: Il Saggiatore.

———, and Beverly J. Silver. 2003. *Caos and governo del mondo*. Milano: B. Mondadori.

Aston, Trevor Henry, and C. H. E. Philpin, eds. 1989. *Il dibattito Brenner: agricoltura e sviluppo economico nell'Europa preindustriale*. Torino: Einaudi.

Axelsson, Per, and Peter Sköld, eds. 2011. *Indigenous Peoples and Demography: The Complex Relation between Identity and Statistics*. New York: Berghahn.

Babones, Salvatore J. 2014. *Methods for Quantitative Macro-Comparative Research.* Los Angeles, CA: Sage.

Bagchi, Amiya Kumar. 2010. *Colonialism and Indian Economy.* New Delhi: Oxford University Press.

Bakan, Joel. 2004. *The corporation: la patologica ricerca del profitto and del potere.* Roma: Fandango libri.

Bakker, Isabella, and Rachel Silvey. 2008. *Beyond States and Markets. The Challenges of Social Reproduction.* London: Routledge.

Bandarage, Asoka. 1997. *Women, Population and Global Crisis: A Political-Economic Analysis.* London: Zed Books.

Banerji, Debabar. 1980. "The Political Economy of Population Control in India." In *Poverty and Population Control*, edited by Lars Bondestam and Staffan Bergström, 83–102. London: Academic Press.

Baran, Paul A. 1975. *Il surplus economico and la teoria marxista dello sviluppo.* 2nd ed. Milano: Feltrinelli (original edition *The Political Economy of Growth*, 1957).

Barbagli, Marzio, Gianpiero Dalla Zuanna and Franco Garelli. 2010. *La sessualità degli italiani.* Bologna: Il Mulino.

Bardi, Ugo. 2020. *Before the Collapse: A Guide to the Other Side of Growth.* Heidelberg: Springer.

Barrett, Ruth, ed. 2016. *Female Erasure: What You Need To Know about Gender Politics' War on Women, the Female Sex and Human Rights.* Tidal Time.

Bashford, Alison. 2014. *Global Population: History, Geopolitics, and Life on Earth.* New York: Columbia University Press.

Basu, Alaka Malwade. 1992. *Culture, the Status of Women, and Demographic Behaviour: Illustrated with the Case of India.* Oxford: Clarendon Press; Oxford: Oxford University Press.

Bateson, Gregory. 1972. *Steps to an Ecology of Mind.* New York: Ballatine Books.

Bebel, August. 1910. *Woman and Socialism.* New York: Socialist Literature (original edition *Die Frau und der Sozialismus*, 1879).

Becker, Gary. 1981. *A Treatise on the Family.* Cambridge: Harvard University Press.

Behrman, Jere R., Hans-Peter Kohler and Susan Cotts Watkins. 2002. "Social Networks and Changes in Contraceptive Use over Time: Evidence from a Longitudinal Study in Rural Kenya." *Demography* 39, no. 4: 713–38.

Belich, James. 2009. *Replenishing the Earth: The Settler Revolution and the Rise of the Anglo-World, 1783—1939.* New York: Oxford University Press.

Bellanca, Niccolò, and Luca Pardi. 2021. *O la capra o i cavoli. La biosfera, l'economia e il futuro da inventare.* Firenze: Firenze University Press. https://fupress.com/catalogo/o-la-capra-o-i-cavoli/4387.

Bellettini, Athos. 1987. *La popolazione italiana: un profilo storico.* Torino: Einaudi.

Beloch, Karl Julius. 1994. *Storia della popolazione d'Italia.* Firenze: Le lettere.

Bengtsson, Tommy, and Geraldine P. Mineau, eds. 2009. *Kinship and Demographic Behavior in the Past.* Berlin: Springer.

Bengtsson, Tommy, and Saito, Osamu, eds. 2000. *Population and Economy: From Hunger to Modern Economic Growth.* Oxford: Oxford University Press.

Berkes, Fikret, and Carl Folke, eds. 1998. *Linking Social and Ecological Systems. Management Practices and Social Mechanisms for Building Resilience.* New York: Cambridge University Press.

Berry, Brian J. L. 2010. "Secular Cycles" (review). *American Journal of Sociology* 116, no. 2: 707–9.

Bestetti, Giovanna, Anita Regalia and Grazia Colombo. 2005. *Mani sul parto, mani nel parto: Mantenere normale la nascita.* Roma: Carocci.

Bhatia, Balmokand. 1967. *Famines in India: A Study in Some Aspects of the Economic History of India, 1860-1965.* London: Asia Publishing House.

Bhattacharya, Prabir C. 2006. "Economic Development, Gender Inequality, and Demographic Outcomes: Evidence from India." *Population and Development Review* 32, no. 2: 263–91.

Binswanger, Hans Christoph. 2013. *The Growth Spiral. Money, Energy, and Imagination in the Dynamics of the Market Process.* Heidelberg: Springer.

Birdsall, Nancy. 1976. "Women and Population Studies." *Signs: Journal of Women in Culture and Society* 1, no. 3, part 1: 699–712.

Birdsall, Nancy, Allen C. Kelley and Steven W. Sinding, eds. 2001. *Population Matters: Demographic Change, Economic Growth, and Poverty in the Developing World.* New York: Oxford University Press.

Blank, Martin. 2014. *Overpowered: The Dangers of Electromagnetic Radiation and What You Can Do about It.* New York: Seven Stories Press.

Bolt, Jutta, Robert Inklaar, Herman de Jong and Jan Luiten van Zanden. 2018. *Maddison Project Database, Version 2018.* ("Rebasing 'Maddison': New Income Comparisons and the Shape of Long-Run Economic Development." Maddison Project Working paper 10).

Bonneuil, Christophe, and Jean-Baptiste Fressoz. 2016. *The Shock of the Anthropocene: The Earth, History and Us.* London: Verso (original edition *L'Evénement Anthropocene*, 2016).

Boserup, Ester. 1970. *Women's Role in Economic Development.* London: Earthscan.

———. 1981. *Population and Technological Change: A Study of Long-Term Trends.* Chicago: University of Chicago Press.

———. [1965] 2005. *The Conditions of Agricultural Growth: The Economics of Agrarian Change under Population Pressure.* New Brunswick, NJ: Aldine Transaction.

Bosworth, Andrew. 2000. "The Evolution of the World-City System, 3000 BCE to AD 2000." In *World System History: The Social Science of Long-Term Change*, edited by Robert A. Denemark, Jonathan Friedman, Barry K. Gills and George Modelski, 273–84. London: Routledge.

Bourguignon, François, and Morrisson, Christian. 2002. "Inequality among World Citizens: 1820–1992." *American Economic Review* 92, no. 4: 727–44.

Bowles, Samuel, and Richard Edwards. 1993. *Understanding Capitalism: Competition, Command, and Change.* 2nd ed. New York: HarperCollins College.

Bowles, Samuel, Richard Edwards and Frank Roosevelt. 2011. *Introduzione all'economia politica: Le dinamiche del capitalismo.* Milano: Springer.

Braudel, Fernand. 1977. *La dinamica del capitalismo.* Bologna: Il Mulino.

———. 1982. *Civiltà materiale, economia and capitalismo: secoli 15.-18.* Vol. 1: *Le strutture del quotidiano.* Torino: Einaudi.

———. [1958] 2012. "History and the Social Science: The *Longue Durée.*" In *The Longue Durée and World-Systems Analysis*, edited by Richard E. Lee, 241–77. Albany: SUNY Press.

Braun, Rudolf. 1966. "The Impact of Cottage Industry on an Agricultural Population." In *The Rise of Capitalism*, edited by David S. Landes, 53–64. New York: Macmillan.

Brenner, Robert. 1977. "The Origins of Capitalist Development: A Critique of Neo-Smithian Marxism." *New Left Review* 104: 25–92.

Bronson, Bennet. 1975. "The Earliest Farming: Demography as Cause and Consequence." In *Population, Ecology, and Social Evolution*, edited by Steven Polgar, 53–78. Paris: de Gruyter Mouton.

Bryant, John. 2007. "Theories of Fertility Decline and the Evidence from Development Indicators." *Population and Development Review* 33, no. 1: 101–27.

Bulatao, Rodolfo A., and John B. Casterline, eds. 2001. *Global Fertility Transition.* New York: Population Council.

Burch, Thomas K. 2003. "Data, Models, Theory, and Reality: The Structure of Demographic Knowledge." In *Agent-Based Computational Demography*, edited by Francesco C. Billari, 19–40. Heidelberg: Springer.

Cai, Yong. 2014. "Looking at the Future of China's Population from the Sixth Nationa Population Census and the United Nations Population Projections". In *Chinese Research Perspectives on Population and Labor*, edited by Fang Cai, Volume 1, 1–19. Leiden-Boston: Brill.

Cain, Mead.1983. "Perspectives on Family and Fertility in Developing Countries." *Population Studies* 36, no. 2: 159–60.

Čajanov, Aleksandr Vasil'evič. [1923] 1991. *The Theory of Peasant Co-operatives.* London; New York: I.B. Tauris.

Caldwell, John C. 2006. *Demographic Transition Theory*. Dordrecht: Springer (contributing co-authors: Bruce K. Caldwell, Pat Caldwell, Peter F. McDonald, Thomas Schindlmayr).

———. 1982. *Theory of Fertility Decline.* New York: Academic Press.

Caldwell, John C., and Bruce K. Caldwell. 2003. "Pretransitional Population Control and Equilibrium." *Population Studies* 57, no. 2: 199–215.

Cappuccino, Naomi, and Peter W. Price, eds. 1995. *Population Dynamics: New Approaches and Synthesis.* San Diego, CA: Academic Press.

Carchedi, Guglielmo. 1991. *Frontiers of Political Economy*. London: Verso.

Carneiro, Robert L. 1970. "A Theory of the Origin of the State." *Science* 169: 733–38.

Carr-Saunders, Alexander M. 1922. *The Population Problem: A Study in Human Evolution.* London: Oxford University Press.

Chase-Dunn, Christopher K., and Thomas Hall. 1997. *Rise and Demise: Comparing World-Systems*. Boulder, CO: Westview Press.

———. 2000. "Comparing World-Systems to Explain Social Evolution." In *World System History: The Social Science of Long-Term Change*, edited by Robert A. Denemark, Jonathan Friedman, Barry K. Gills and George Modelski, 85–112. London: Routledge.

Chase-Dunn, Christopher, Thomas Hall and Peter Turchin. 2007. "World-Systems in the Biogeosphere: Urbanization, State Formation, and Climate Change Since the Iron Age." In *The World System and the Earth System: Global Socioenvironmental Change and Sustainability Since the Neolithic*, edited by Alf Hornborg and Carole L. Crumley, 132–48. Walnut Creek, CA: Left Coast Books.

Chazan, Michael. 2017. "Toward a Long Prehistory of Fire." *Current Anthropology* 58, suppl. 16: S351–S359.

Chesnais, Jean Claude. 1991. *La population du monde: de l'antiquité a 2050*. Paris: Bordas.

Childs, Geoff H. 2008. *Tibetan Transitions: Historical and Contemporary Perspectives on Fertility, Family Planning, and Demographic Change*. Leiden: Brill.

Chirot, Daniel, and Thomas D. Hall. 1982. "World-System Theory." *Annual Review of Sociology* 8: 81–106.

Cipolla, Carlo M. 1962. *The Economic History of Word Population.* Baltimore, MD: Penguin Books.

———. 1999. *Vele e cannoni*. Bologna, Il Mulino.

Cipolletta, Sabrina, and Angela Sperotto. 2012. "From the Hospital Organisation to the Childbirth Practice: Italian Women's Experiences." *Journal of Reproductive and Infant Psychology*, 30, no. 3: 326–36.

Cleland, John. 2001. "The Effects of Improved Survival on Fertility: A Reassessment." *Population and Development Review* 27 (Supplement: *Global Fertility Transition*): 60–92.

Cleland, John, and John Hobcraft, eds. 1985. *Reproductive Change in Developing Countries: Insights from the World Fertility Survey.* Oxford: Oxford University Press.

Cleveland, David A. 1986. "The Political Economy of Fertility Regulation: The Kusasi of Savanna West Africa (Ghana)." In *Culture and Reproduction. An Anthropological Critique of Demographic Transition Theory*, edited by W. Penn Handwerker, 249–62. Boulder, CO: Westview Press.

Coale, Ansley J., and Edgard M. Hoover. 1958. *Population Growth and Economic Development in Low-Income Countries: A Case Study of India's Prospects.* Princeton, NJ: Princeton University Press.

Coale, Ansley J., and Susan Cotts Watkins, eds. 1986. *The Decline of Fertility in Europe: The Revised Proceedings of a Conference on the Princeton European Fertility Project.* Princeton, NJ: Princeton University Press.

Cohen, Mark Nathan. 1977. *The Food Crisis in Prehistory: Overpopulation and the Origins of Agriculture.* New Haven, CT: Yale University.

Commoner, Barry. 1977. *Il cerchio da chiudere: la natura, l'uomo e la tecnologia.* Milano: Garzanti.

Coontz, Sidney H. 1957. *Population Theories and the Economic Interpretation.* London: Routledge & Kegan Paul.

Coquery-Vidrovitch, Catherine, and Henri Moniot. 1977. *L'Africa nera dal 1800 ai nostri giorni.* Milano: Mursia.

Cordell, Dennis D., ed. 1993. *Population, reproduction, sociétés: perspectives et enjeux de démographie sociale; mélanges en l'honneur de Joel W. Gregory.* Montréal: Presses de l'Universitéde Montréal.

Cordell, Dennis D., and Joel W. Gregory, eds. 1987. *African Population and Capitalism: Historical Perspectives.* Boulder, CO: Westview Press.

Crédit Suisse Research Institute. 2019. *Global Wealth Databook.* https://www.credit-suisse.com/media/assets/corporate/docs/about-us/research/publications/global-wealth-databook-2019.pdf.

Crosby, Alfred W. 1988. *Imperialismo ecologico: l'espansione biologica dell'Europa, 900-1900.* Roma: Laterza.

Dall'Orto, Giovanni. 2017. "I vincitori scrivono la storia, non la verità." https://sinistrainrete.info/societa/10460-giovanni-dall-orto-i-vincitori-scrivono-la-storia-non-la-verita.html.

Dalla Costa, Mariarosa, and Selma James. 1972. *The Power of Women and the Subversion of the Community.* Bristol: Falling Wall Press.

Daly, Mary. 1979. *Gyn/ecology: The Metaethics of Radical Feminism.* London: Women's Press.

Danna, Daniela. 1991. *La teoria della transizione demografica di John Caldwell e il caso della Danimarca.* Universitàdegli Studi di Milano (MA thesis).

———. 2007. *Ginocidio. La violenza contro le donne nell'era globale.* Milano: Eleuthera.

———. 2012. "The Debate about the Falling Birth Rate in Italy." Paper presented to the 3rd Conference on Degrowth, Venezia, 19–23 September. http://www.danieladanna.it/wordpress/venezia-3a-conferenza-sulla-decrescita/.

———. 2014. "Population Dynamics and World-Systems Analysis." *Journal of World Systems Research* 20, no. 2: 207–28.

———. 2017a. *"Fare un figlio* per altri è *giusto" (Falso!).* Roma-Bari: Laterza.

———. 2017b. *Maternità. Surrogata?.* Trieste: Asterios.

———. 2018. *Dalla parte della Natura. L'ecologia spiegata agli esseri umani.* Milano, Morellini-VandA epublishing.

———. 2019. "La legge del valore: da Marx a Hornborg passando per Wallerstein." In *Capitalismo e Teoria Sociologica*, edited by Massimo Pendenza, Vincenzo Romania, Giuseppe Ricotta, Roberta Iannone and Emanuela Susca, 47–62. Milano: FrancoAngeli. http://ojs.francoangeli.it/_omp/index.php/oa/catalog/book/428.

———. 2020a. *Il modo di produzione informatico*. www.danieladanna.it.

———, ed. 2020b. *Mater Iuris. Uscire dalla simmetria giuridica dei sessi nella procreazione*. Milano. Editrice XXD. www.danieladanna.it.

———. 2020c. *Sesso e genere*. Trieste: Asterios.

Das Gupta, Monica, Woojin Chung and Li Shuzhuo. 2009. "Evidence for an Incipient Decline in Numbers of Girls in China and India." *Population Development Review* 35: 401–16.

Davis, Donagh, and Kevin C. Feeney. 2017. "Explaining British Political Stability after 1832". *Cliodynamics* 8: 182–228.

Davis, Kingsley, ed. 1945. "World Population in Transition." *Annals of the American Academy of Political and Social Science* 237: 1–11.

Davis, Kingsley, and Judith Blake. 1956. "Social Structure and Fertility: An Analytic Framework." *Economic Development and Cultural Change* 4, no. 3: 211–35.

Davis, Mike. 2002. *Olocausti tardovittoriani: el niño, le carestie e la nascita del Terzo mondo*. Milano: Feltrinelli.

Dawson, Marc H. 1987. "Health, Nutrition, and Population in Central Kenya, 1890-1945." In *African Population and Capitalism: Historical Perspectives*, edited by Dennis D. Cordell and Joel W. Gregory, 201–19. Boulder, CO: Westview Press.

Deevey, E. S. 1960. "The Human Population," *Scientific American* 203: 49–55.

de Vries, Jan. 1976. *Europe in an Age of Crisis, 1650-1750*. Cambridge: Cambridge University Press.

———. 1984. *European Urbanization, 1500-1800*. Cambridge, MA: Harvard University Press.

———. 1986. "The Population and Economy of Preindustrial Netherlands." In *Population and Economy. Population and History from the Traditional to the Modern World*, edited by Roger S. Schofield and E. Anthony Wrigley, 101–22. Cambridge: Cambridge University Press.

de Zeeuw, J. W. 1978. "Peat and the Dutch Golden Age: The Historical Meaning of Energy-Attainability." *A.A.G. Bijdragen* 25: 3–31. http://peatsociety.nl/documenten/Zeeuw.pdf.

Del Panta, Lorenzo, Massimo Livi Bacci, Giuliano Pinto and Eugenio Sonnino. 1996. *La popolazione italiana dal Medioevo a oggi*. Roma: Laterza.

Demeny, Paul. 1987. "Pronatalist Policies in Low-Fertility Countries: Patterns, Performance, and Prospects." In *Below-Replacement Fertility in Industrial Societies: Causes, Consequences, Policies*, edited by Kingsley Davis, Mikhail S. Bernstam and Rita Ricardo-Campbell, 225–58, New York: Population Council (also in *Population and Development Review* 12, 1986, Supplement: 335–58).

Denemark, Robert A., and Kenneth P. Thomas. 1988. "The Brenner-Wallerstein Debate." *International Studies Quarterly* 32, no. 1: 47–65.

Denemark, Robert A., Jonathan Friedman, Barry K. Gills and George Modelski, eds. 2000. *World System History: The Social Science of Long-Term Change*. London: Routledge. https://www.eolss.net/outlinecomponents/World-System-History.aspx.

Diamond, Jared. 1998. *Armi, acciaio e malattie: breve storia del mondo negli ultimi tredicimila anni*. Torino: Einaudi (original edition *Guns, Germs, and Steel*, 1997).

Diamond-Smith, Nadia, and Malcolm Potts. 2010. "Are the Population Policies of India and China Responsible for the Fertility Decline?." *International Journal of Environmental Studies* 67, no. 3: 291–301.

Diehl, Sarah. 2014. *Die Uhr, die nicht tickt: Kinderlos glücklich. Eine Streitschrift.* Hamburg: Arche Literatur Verlag.

Doepke, Matthias. 2004. "Accounting for Fertility Decline during the Transition to Growth." *Journal of Economic Growth* 9, no. 3: 347–83.

Doepke, Matthias, and Fabrizio Zilibotti. 2005. "The Macroeconomics of Child Labor Regulation." *American Economic Review* 95, no. 5: 1492–524.

Donath, Orna. 2016. *Regretting Motherhood. A Study.* London: Penguin Random House.

Duden, Barbara. 1993. "Population." In *The Development Dictionary. A Guide to Knowledge as Power*, edited by Wolfgang Sachs, 161–73. London: Zed Books.

———. 1994. *Il corpo della donna come luogo pubblico: sull'abuso del concetto di vita.* Torino: Bollati Boringhieri.

Dull, Robert A., Richard J. Nevle, William I. Woods, Dennis K. Bird, Shiri Avnery and William M. Denevan. 2010. "The Columbian Encounter and the Little Ice Age: Abrupt Land Use Change, Fire, and Greenhouse Forcing." *Annals of the Association of American Geographers*, 100, no. 4: 755–71.

Dumond, Don. 1975. "The Limitations of Human Population: A Natural History." *Science*, 187: 713–21.

Dupaquier, Jacques, ed. 1991. *Histoire de la population francaise*, vol. 2: *De la Renaissance a 1789.* Paris: PUF.

Durand, John D. 1977. "Historical Estimates of World Population: An Evaluation." *Population and Development Review* 3, 253–96.

Dyson, Tim. 2010. *Population and Development: The Demographic Transition.* London: Zed Books.

Easterlin, Richard. 1978. "The Economics and Sociology of Fertility." In *Historical Studies of Changing Fertility*, edited by Charles Tilly, 57–133. Princeton, NJ: Princeton University Press.

———. 2009. *Growth Triumphant: The Twenty-First Century in Historical Perspective.* Ann Arbor: University of Michigan Press.

Eckl, Andreas. 2004. *Herrschaft, Macht und Einfluß. Koloniale Interaktionen am Kavango (Nord-Namibia) von 1891 bis 1921.* Köln

Egerö, Bertil, and Mikael Hammarskjöld, eds. 1994. *Understanding Reproductive Change: Kenya, Tamil Nadu, Punjab, Costa Rica.* Lund: Lund University Press; Bromley: Chartwell-Bratt.

Ehrlich, Paul R. 1968. *The Population Bomb.* New York: Sierra Club/Ballantine Books.

Elwert, Georg. 1984. "Conflict Inside and Outside the Household: A West African Case Study." In *Households and the World Economy*, edited by Joan Smith, Immanuel Wallestein and Hans-Dieter Evers, 272–96. Beverly Hills, CA: Sage.

Emmanuel, Arghiri. 1972. *Lo scambio ineguale: gli antagonismi nei rapporti economici internazionali.* Torino: Einaudi.

Eng, Robert Y., and Thomas C. Smith. 1976. "Peasant Families and Population Control in Eighteenth-Century Japan." *Journal of Interdisciplinary History* 6: 417–45.

Engels, Friedrich. [1884] 1942. *Origins of the Family. Private Property and the State.* translated by Alick West published in 1942, and revised against the *MEW* [*Marx-Engels Werke*] Volume 21. Berlin: Dietz Verlag, 1962. https://www.marxists.org/archive/marx/works/1884/origin-family/index.htm).

———. [1844] 1972. *La condizione della classe operaia in Inghilterra.* Roma: La nuovasinistra reprint.

Escudero, Alexis. 2016. *La riproduzione artificiale dell'umano.* Aprilia: Edizioni Ortica (original edition *La reproduction artificielle de l'humain*, 2014).

Esping-Andersen, Gøsta, and Francesco C. Billari. 2015. "Re-Theorizing Family Demographics." *Population and Development Review* 41, no. 1: 1–31.

Evans, Lloyd T. 1998. *Feeding the Ten Billion: Plants and Population Growth.* Cambridge: Cambridge University Press.

Eversley, David E. C. 1959. *Social Theories of Fertility and the Malthusian Debate.* Oxford: Clarendon Press.

Faris, James. 1975. "Social Evolution, Population, and Production." In *Population, Ecology, and Social Evolution*, edited by Steven Polgar, 235–72. The Hague-Paris: Mouton.

Federici, Nora, Karen Oppenheim Mason and Solvi Sogner, eds. 1988. *Women's Position and Demographic Change.* Oxford: Clarendon Press; New York: Oxford University Press.

Federici, Silvia. 2004. *Caliban and the Witch.* New York: Autonomedia.

———. 2014. *Il punto zero della rivoluzione: lavoro domestico, riproduzione and lotta femminista.* Verona: Ombre corte.

Federici, Silvia, and Leopoldina Fortunati. 1984. *Il grande Calibano. Storia del corpo sociale ribelle nella prima fase del capitale.* Milano: Franco Angeli.

Ferrero, Guglielmo. 1994. "An Historian's View of Population." *Population and Development Review* 20, no. 4: 893–97 (original edition 1922).

Filippini, Nadia Maria. 2020. *Pregnancy, Delivery, Childbirth. A Gender and Cultural History from Antiquity to Test Tube.* London: Routledge.

———. 2021. "Parto e nascita: i molteplici scenari di una storia complessa." In *Nascere e mettere al mondo: sguardi sociali e filosofico politici. Atti della Summer School (23-26.9.2020)*, edited by Daniela Danna, Lecce: ESE Salento University Publishing. http://www.danieladanna.it/wordpress/wp-content/uploads/2021/03/volume_ESE_nascere_definitivo.pdf.

Finley, Moses I., and Lepore, Ettore. 2000. *Le colonie degli antichi e dei moderni.* Roma: Donzelli.

Firstenberg, Arthur. 2020. *The Invisible Rainbow: A History of Electricity and Life.* White River Junction, VT: Chelsea Green.

Firth, Raymond. [1929] 2011. *Primitive Economics of the New Zealand Maori.* London: Routledge.

———. 1939. *Primitive Polynesian Economy.* London: George Routledge.

———. 1959. *Social Change in Tikopia*, London: Allen and Unwin.

Fisher, F. J. 1965. "Influenza and Inflation in Tudor England." *Economic History Review*, New Series 18, no. 1 (Essays in Economic History Presented to Professor M. M. Postan): 120–29.

Fletcher, Jesse B., Jacob Apkarian, Robert A. Hanneman, Hiroko Inoue, Kirk Lawrence, Christopher Chase-Dunn. 2011. "Demographic Regulators in Small-Scale World-Systems." *Structure and Dynamics* 5, no. 1. https://escholarship.org/uc/imbs_socdyn_sdeas/5/1.

Flinn, Michael W. 1981. *The European Demographic System, 1500-1820.* Baltimore, MD: John Hopkins University Press.

Folbre, Nancy. 1977. "Population Growth and Capitalist Development in Zongolica, Veracruz." *Latin American Perspectives* 4, no. 4: 41–55.

———. 1986. "Hearts and Spades: Paradigms of Household Economics." *World Development* 14, no. 2: 245–55.

———. 1990. "Of Patriarchy Born: The Political Economy of Fertility Decisions." In *Radical Political Economy*, edited by Samuel Bowles and Richard Edwards, 390–413. Aldershot: E. Elgar.

———. 1994. *Who Pays for the Kids?: Gender and the Structures of Constraint.* London: Routledge.
———. 2001. *The Invisible Heart: Economics and Family Values.* New York: New Press.
———. 2009. *Greed, Lust and Gender: A History of Economic Ideas.* Oxford: Oxford University Press.
Foster, John Bellamy. 1998. "Malthus' Essay on Population at Age 200. A Marxian View." *Monthly Review* 50, no. 7. https://monthlyreview.org/1998/12/01/malthus-essay-on-population-at-age-200/.
———. 2000. *Marx's Ecology: Materialism and Nature.* New York: Monthly Review Press.
Foucrier, Annick. 2007. "Populations coloniales." *Annales de démographie historique: ADH* 1, no. 113: 5–11.
Frank, Andre Gunder. 1969. *Capitalismo e sottosviluppo in America Latina.* Torino: Einaudi.
———. 1998. *ReOrient: Global Economy in the Asian Age.* Berkeley: University of California Press.
———. 2007. "Entropy Generation and Displacement: The Nineteenth Century Multilateral Network of World Trade." In *The World System and the Earth System: Global Socioenvironmental Change and Sustainability since the Neolithic*, edited by Alf Hornborg and Carole Crumley, 303–16. Walnut Creek: Left Coast Press.
Frank, Andre Gunder, and Barry K. Gills, eds. 1993. *The World System: Five Hundred Years or Five Thousand?.* London: Routledge.
Frank, Odile, and Geoffrey McNicoll. 1987. "An Interpretation of Fertility and Population Policy in Kenya." *Population and Development Review* 13, no. 2: 209–43.
Franke, Richard W. 1981. "Mode of Production and Population Patterns: Policy Implications for West African Development." *International Journal of Health Services* 11, no. 3: 361–87.
Freeman, Richard. 2005. "What Really Ails Europe and America: The Doubling of the Global Workforce." *The Globalist*, June 3. http://www.theglobalist.com/StoryId.aspx?StoryId=4542.
Frye, Marilyn. 1988. "Lesbian 'Sex'". *Sinister Wisdom* 35: 46–54.
Galloway, Patrick R. 1986. "Long Term Fluctuations in Climate and Population in the Preindustrial Era." *Population and Development Review* 12, no. 1: 1–24.
Galor, Oded. 2011. *Unified Growth Theory.* Princeton, NJ: Princeton University Press.
Garcia, Renaud. 2016. *Il deserto della critica.* Milano: Elèuthera (original edition *Le désert de la critique: Déconstruction et politique*, 2015).
Garrett, Eilidh, Alice Reid, Kevin Schürer and Simon Szreter. 2001. *Changing Family Size in England and Wales: Place, Class and Demography, 1891–1911.* Cambridge: Cambridge University Press.
Gauthier, Anne H. 1996. *The State and the Family: A Comparative Analysis of Family Policies in Industrialized Countries.* Oxford: Clarendon.
Geertz, Clifford. 1963. *Agricultural Involution: The Process of Ecological Change in Indonesia.* Berkeley: University of California Press.
Georgescu-Roegen, Nicholas. 1970. *The Entropy Law and the Economic Problem.* Tuscaloosa: University of Alabama.
Ghetilieri, Dana. 2021. *L'Infernale Tragedia.* Bolsena: Massari.
Gillis, John R., Louise A. Tilly and David Levine, eds. 1992. *The European Experience of Declining Fertility 1850-1970: The Quiet Revolution.* Cambridge, MA: Blackwell.
Gimbutas, Marija. 1990. *Il linguaggio della dea: mito e culto della dea madre nell'Europa neolitica.* Milano: Longanesi.
Gimenez, Martha E. 1977. "Population and Capitalism." *Latin American Perspectives* 4, no. 4: 5–40.

Glass, D. V., and D. E. C. Eversley, eds. 1965. *Population in History: Essays in Historical Demography*. London: Arnold.

Global Justice Now. 2016. *Controlling Corporations: The Case for a UN Treaty on Transnational Corporations and Human Rights*. http://www.globaljustice.org.uk/sites/default/files/files/resources/controlling_corporations_briefing.pdf.

Goldberg, Michelle. 2009. *The Means of Reproduction: Sex, Power, and the Future of the World*. New York: Penguin Press.

Goldstone, Jack A. 1986. "The Demographic Revolution in England: A Reexamination." *Population Studies* 40: 15–33.

———. 1991. *Revolution and Rebellion in the Early Modern World*. Berkeley: University of California Press.

———. 1996. "Gender, Work, and Culture: Why the Industrial Revolution Came Early to England but Late to China." *Sociological Perspectives* 39, no. 1: 1–21.

———. 2010. "The New Population Bomb: Four Population Megatrends That Will Shape the Global Future." *Foreign Affairs*, Jan/Feb: 31–43.

———. 2011. "Understanding the Revolutions of 2011: Weakness and Resilience in Middle Eastern Autocracies." *Foreign Affairs* 90: 8–16.

Graeber, David. 2010. *Debt: The First 5000 Years*. New York: Melville House.

Green, Andy. 1990. *Education and State Formation: The Rise of Education Systems in England, France and the USA*. New York: St. Martin's Press.

Greenhalgh, Susan, and Edwin A. Winckler. 2005. *Governing China's Population: From Leninist to Neoliberal Biopolitics*. Stanford, CA: Stanford University Press.

Gregory, Joel W., and Victor Piché. 1981. *The Demographic Process of Peripheral Capitalism Illustrated with African Examples*. Montreal, Canada: Centre for Developing-Area Studies, McGill University.

Grigg, David B. 1980. *Population Growth and Agrarian Change*. Cambridge: Cambridge University Press.

Grimes, Peter. 1981. *Poverty, Exploitation, and Population Growth: Marxist and Malthusian Views on the Political Economy of Childbearing in the Third World*. Michigan State University, East Lansing, Michigan (MA thesis).

———. 1999. "The Horsemen and the Killing Fields: the Final Contradiction of Capitalism." In *Ecology and the World-System*, edited by Goldfrank, Walter L., David Goodman and Andrew Szasz, 13–42. Westport, CT: Greenwood Press.

Guérin, Mathieu. 2008. *Paysans de la forêt àl'époque coloniale. La pacification des aborigènes des hautes terres du Cambodge (1863-1940)*. Rennes: Presses universitaires de Rennes/HSR.

Habakkuk, Hrothgar J. 1974. *Population Growth and Economic Development since 1750*. Leicester: Leicester University Press.

Hall, Charles A. S. 2000. *Quantifying Sustainable Development: The Future of Tropical Economies*. San Diego, CA: Academic Press.

———. 2017. *Energy Return on Investment. A Unifying Principle for Biology, Economics, and Sustainability*. Cham: Springer.

Hall, Charles A. S., and Carey W. King. 2011. "Relating Financial and Energy Return on Investment." *Sustainability: Special Issue on EROI*: 1810–1832.

Hall, Charles A. S., and Kent Klitgaard. 2018. *Energy and the Wealth of Nations. An Introduction to Biophysical Economics*. 2nd ed. Cham, Switzerland: Springer International.

Hall, Thomas D., and Turchin, Peter. 2007. "Lessons from Population Ecology for World-Systems Analysis of Long-Distance Syncrony." In *The World System and the Earth*

*System: Global Socioenvironmental Change and Sustainability since the Neolithic*, edited by Alf Hornborg and Carole L. Crumley, 74–90. Walnut Creek, CA: Left Coast Books.

Handwerker, W. Penn, ed. 1986a. *Culture and Reproduction: An Anthropological Critique of Demographic Transition Theory*. Boulder, CO: Westview Press.

———. 1986b. "The Modern Demographic Transition: An Analysis of Subsistence Choices and Reproductive." *American Anthropologist*, New Series. 88, no. 2: 400–17.

———, ed. 1990. *Births and Power: Social Change and the Politics of Reproduction*. Boulder, CO: Westview Press.

Harris, Marvin. 1974. *Cows, Pigs, Wars and Witches: The Riddles of Culture*. London: Hutchinson.

———. 1979. *Cultural Materialism: The Struggle for a Science of Culture*. New York: Random House.

Harris, Marvin, and Eric B. Ross. 1987. *Death, Sex, and Fertility: Population Regulation in Preindustrial and Developing Societies*. New York: Columbia University.

Hartmann, Betsy. 1995. *Reproductive Rights and Wrongs: The Global Politics of Population Control*. Boston, MA: South End Press.

Harvey, David. 1993. *La crisi della modernità*. Milano: Il saggiatore.

———. 2007. *A Brief History of Neoliberalism*. Oxford: Oxford University Press.

Hayden, Brian. 1986. "Resources, Rivalry, and Reproduction: The Influence of Basic Resource Characteristics on Reproductive Behavior." In *Culture and Reproduction. An Anthropological Critique of Demographic Transition Theory*, edited by W. Penn Handwerker, 176–95. Boulder, CO: Westview Press.

Heath, John, and Binswanger, Hans. 1996. "Natural Resource Degradation Effects of Poverty and Population Growth Are Largely Policy-Induced: The case of Colombia." *Environment and Development Economics* 1: 65–84.

Helleiner, K. F. 1965. "The Vital Revolution Reconsidered." In *Population in history. Essays in Historical Demography*, edited by D. V. Glass and D. E. C. Eversley, 79–86. London: Arnold.

Heller, Henry. 2011. *The Birth of Capitalism: A Twenty-First Century Perspective*. London: Pluto Press.

Henry, Louis. 1953. *Féconditédes mariages: nouvelle méthode de mesure*. Institut national d'études démographiques.

Hirschman, Charles. 1994. "Why Fertility Changes." *Annual Review of Sociology* 20: 203–33.

Hite, Shere. 1997. *Il primo rapporto Hite*. Milano: Bompiani.

Hobsbawm, Eric John. 1999. *Industry and Empire: From 1750 to the Present Day*, 2nd ed. London : Penguin Group.

Hochschild, Arlie R. 2012. *The Outsourced Self: Intimate life in market times*. New York: Metropolitan Books.

Hodgson, Dennis, and Susan Cotts Watkins. 1997. "Feminists and Neo-Malthusians: Past and Present Alliances." *Population and Development Review* 23, no. 3: 469–523.

Hornborg, Alf. 2001. *The Power of the Machine: Global Inequalities of Economy, Technology, and Environment*. Walnut Creek, CA: AltaMira Press.

———. 2011. *Global Ecology and Unequal Exchange: Fetishism in a Zero-Sum World*. London: Routledge.

———. 2012. "Accumulation." In *Ecology and Power: Struggles over Land and Material Resources in the Past, Present, and Future*, edited by Alf Hornborg, Brett Clark, and Kenneth Hermele, 13–22. London: Routledge.

———. 2015. "The Political Ecology of the Technocene." In *The Anthropocene and the Global Environmental Crisis: Rethinking Modernity in a New Epoch*, edited by Clive Hamilton, François Gemenne and Christophe Bonneuil, 57–69. London: Routledge.

———. 2016. *Global Magic: Technologies of Appropriation from Ancient Rome to Wall Street.* Houndmills: Palgrave Macmillan.

———. 2019. *Nature, Society, and Justice in the Anthropocene.* Cambridge: Cambridge University Press.

Hout, Michael. 1980. "Trade Dependence and Fertility in Hispanic America: 1900–1975." In *Studies of the Modern World System*, edited by Albert Bergesen, 159–88. New York: Academic Press.

Howell, Nancy. 1986. "Feedbacks and Buffers in Relation to Scarcity and Abundance: Studies of Hunter-Gatherers Populations." In *The State of Population Theory: Forward from Malthus*, edited by David Coleman and Roger Schofield, 156–87. Oxford: Blackwell.

Howitt, Alfred William. 1904. *The Native Tribes of South-East Australia.* New York: MacMillan.

Hull, Terence H., and Valerie J. Hull. 1977. "The Relation of Economic Class and Fertility: An Analysis of Some Indonesian Data." *Population Studies*, 31, no. 1, 43–57.

Hymer, Stephen. 1979. "Politica ed economia internazionale: un approccio radicale." In *Imperialismo and sistema capitalista mondiale*, edited by Giovanni Arrighi, 217–33. Napoli: Liguori (original edition Hymer, S. H. 1975. "International Politics and International Economics: A Radical Approach." In *Stress and Contradiction in Modern Capitalism*, edited by L. Lindberg, R. Alford, C. Crouch and C. Offe. Lexington, MA: Lexington Books).

Ingerson, Alice. 1984. "The Textile Industry and Working Class Culture." In *Labor in The Capitalist World-Economy*, edited by Charles Bergquist, 217–42. Beverly Hills, CA: Sage.

Inglehart, Ronald. 1998. *La societàpostmoderna: mutamento, valori and ideologie in 43 paesi*, Roma: Editori riuniti.

Inman, Phillip. 2016. "Study: Big Corporations Dominate List of World's Top Economic Entities." *The Guardian*, September 12. https://www.theguardian.com/business/2016/sep/12/global-justice-now-study-multinational-businesses-walmart-apple-shell.

International Energy Agency. 2018. *World Energy Outlook 2018.* OECD/IEA, https://www.iea.org/reports/world-energy-outlook-2018.

Ittmann, Karl, Dennis D. Cordell and Gregory H. Maddox, eds. 2010. *The Demographics of Empire: The Colonial Order and the Creation of Knowledge.* Athens: Ohio University Press.

Jackson, Richard, and Howe, Neil. 2008. *The Graying of the Great Powers: Demography and Geopolitics in the 21st Century* (with Rebecca Strauss and Keisuke Nakashima). Washington, DC: Center for Strategic and International Studies.

Jensen, Derrick, Aric McBay and Lierre Keith. 2011. *Deep Green Resistance: Strategy to Save the Planet.* Seven Stories Press.

Jones, Eric. [1981] 2003. *The European Miracle: Environments, Economies, and Geopolitics in the History of Europe and Asia.* Cambridge: Cambridge University Press.

Jones, Gavin, Tay Straughan, Paulin and Chan, Angelique. 2009. *Ultra-Low Fertility in Pacific Asia: Trends, Causes and Policy Issues.* New York: Routledge, Taylor & Francis Group.

Jorgenson, Andrew K., and Brett Clark. 2012. "Footprints: The Division of Nations and Nature." In *Ecology and Power: Struggles over Land and Material Resources in the Past, Present, and Future*, edited by Alf Hornborg, Brett Clark, and Kenneth Hermele, 155–67. London: Routledge.

Kaiser, Elke; Joachim Burger and Wolfram Schier, eds. 2012. *Population Dynamics in Prehistory and Early History: New Approaches Using Stable Isotopes and Genetics.* Berlin: de Gruyter.

Kander, Astrid, Paolo Malanima and Paul Warde. 2014. *Power to the People: Energy in Europe over the Last Five Centuries.* Princeton, NJ: Princeton University Press.

Kaplan, Hillard. 1994. "Evolutionary and Wealth Flows Theories of Fertility: Empirical Tests and New Models." *Population and Development Review* 20, no. 4: 753–91.

Kapp, Karl William. 1950. *The Social Costs of Private Enterprise.* Cambridge, MA: Harvard University Press.

Kennedy, Margrit. 2006. *La moneta libera da inflazione and da interesse. Un libro che spiega in modo semplice come funziona and quanto puònuocere la moneta.* Bologna: Arianna Remainder.

Kennedy, Paul. 1988. *The Rise and Fall of the Great Powers: Economic Change and Military Conflict from 1500 to 2000.* London; Sydney; Wellington: Uniwin and Hyman (Italian edition *Ascesa e decline delle grandi potenze*, 2006).

Kertzer, David I., and Dennis P. Hogan. 1989. *Family, Political Economy, and Demographic Change: The Transformation of Life in Casalecchio, Italy, 1861-1921.* Madison, WI: University of Wisconsin Press.

Kertzer, David I., and Tom Fricke, eds. 1997. *Anthropological Demography: Toward a New Synthesis.* Chicago: University of Chicago Press.

Kesper-Biermann, Sylvia. 2012. *Bevölkerung in Wissenschaft und Politik des 19. und 20. Jahrhunderts.* München: Dreesbach.

Kirk, Dudley. 1996. "Demographic Transition Theory." *Population Studies* 50: 361–87.

Kleinman, David S. 1980. *Human Adaptation and Population Growth: A Non-Malthusian Perspective.* Montclair, NJ: Allanheld, Osmun.

Knieper, Barbara M. C. 2000. *Zur Kritik einer westlicher Familienplanung in Afrika.* Münster: Westfälisches Dampfboot.

Kohler, Hans-Peter. 2001. *Fertility and Social Interaction: An Economic Perspective.* New York: Oxford University Press.

Korotayev, Andrey, and Julia Zinkina. 2011. "The Egyptian Revolution: A Demographic-Structural Analysis." *Middle East Studies Online Journal* 2, no. 5: 57–95.

Korotayev, Andrey, and Sergey Malkov. 2012. "Mathematical Models of World-Systems Development." In *Routledge Handbook of World-Systems Analysis*, edited by Salvatore J. Babones and Christopher Chase-Dunn, 158–60. London: Routledge.

Korzeniewicz, Roberto Patricio, ed. 2018. *The World-System as Unit of Analysis: Past Contributions and Future Advances.* New York: Routledge.

Kostoff, Ronald N. 2020. *Largest Unethical Medical Experiment in Human History.* https://smartech.gatech.edu/bitstream/handle/1853/62452/LARGEST_UNETHICAL_MEDICAL_EXPERIMENT_FINAL.pdf?sequence=4&isAllowed=y.

Kravdal, Øystein. 2002. "Education and Fertility in Sub-Saharan Africa: Individual and Community Effects." *Demography* 39, no. 2: 233–50.

Kriedte, Peter, Hans Medick and Jürgen Schlumbohm. 1988. *L' industrializzazione prima dell'industrializzazione.* Bologna: Il Mulino.

Kumar, Arun, ed. 2000. *Dimensions of Population Growth and Its Social Implications.* Lucknow: Institute for Sustainable Development; New Delhi: Anmol.

Kuznets, Simon. 1990. *Popolazione, tecnologia, sviluppo.* Bologna: Il Mulino.

Lam, David. 2011. "How the World Survived the Population Bomb: Lessons From 50 Years of Extraordinary Demographic History." *Demography* 48: 1231–62.

Landes, David Saul. 1966. "Introduction." In *The Rise of Capitalism*, 1–25. New York: Macmillan; London: Collier-Macmillan.

Langer, William. 1975. "Infanticidio, una rassegna storica." In McKeown, Thomas. *L' aumento della popolazione nell'era moderna*, 225–38. Milano: Feltrinelli.

Lappé, Frances Moore, and Rachel Schurman. 1990. *Taking Population Seriously.* San Francisco, CA: Institute for Food and Development Policy.

LeClerc, Grégoire, and Charles A.S. Hall, eds. 2008. *Making Development Work: A New Role for Science*. Albuquerque: University of New Mexico Press.
Lee, Richard B. 1975. "What Hunters Do for a Living?." In *Man the Hunter*, edited by Richard B. Lee and Irven DeVore, 30–48. Chicago: Aldine.
Lee, Richard E. ed. 2012. *The* Longue *Durée and World-Systems Analysis*. Albany: SUNY Press.
Lee, Ronald Demos. 1986. "Malthus and Boserup: A Dynamic Synthesis." In *The State of Population Theory: Forward from Malthus*, edited by David Coleman and Roger Schofield, 96–130. Oxford: Blackwell.
Lenski, Gerhard Emmanuel. 2005. *The Ecological-Evolutionary Theory: Principles and Applications*. Boulder, CO: Paradigm.
Leonardi, Paola, and Ferdinanda Vigliani. 2009. *Perchénon abbiamo avuto figli: donne speciali si raccontano*. Milano: FrancoAngeli.
Lesthaeghe, Ron. 2010. "The Unfolding Story of the Second Demographic Transition." *Population and Development Review* 36, no. 2: 211–51.
Levine, David. 1977. *Family Formation in an Age of Nascent Capitalism*. New York: Academic Press.
———. 1984. *Proletarianization and Family History*. Orlando, FL: Academic Press.
Levy, Gertrude Rachel. 1963. *The Gate of Horn: A Study of the Religious Conceptions of the Stone Age, and Their Influence upon European Thought*. London: Faber and Faber.
Lindahl-Kiessling, Kerstin, and Hans Landberg, eds. 1994. *Population, Economic Development, and the Environment*. New York: Oxford University Press.
Littlewood, Thomas B. 1977. *The Politics of Population Control*, Notre Dame: University of Notre Dame Press.
Livi Bacci, Massimo. 1971. *A Century of Portuguese Fertility*. Princeton, NJ: Princeton University Press.
———. 1989. *Popolazione and alimentazione. Saggio sulla storia demografica europea*. 2nd ed. Bologna: Il Mulino.
———. 2012. *A Concise History of World Population*. Chichester, West Sussex: Wiley-Blackwell.
———. 2016. *Il lungo viaggio dell'umanità: dalle savane dell'Africa alle migrazioni globali*. Bologna: Zanichelli,
Livi Bacci, Massimo, Gian Carlo Blangiardo and Antonio Golini, eds. 1994. *Demografia*. Torino: Edizioni della Fondazione Giovanni Agnelli.
Lockwood, Matthew. 1998. *Fertility and Household Labour in Tanzania: Demography, Economy, and Society in Rufiji District, c.1870-1986*. Oxford: Clarendon Press.
Lombardi, Daniela. 2008. *Storia del matrimonio: dal Medioevo a oggi*. Bologna: Il Mulino.
London, Bruce. 1988. "Dependence, Distorted Development, and Fertility Trends in Noncore Nations: A Structural Analysis of Cross-National Data." *American Sociological Review* 53, no. 4: 606–18.
Luke, Nancy, and Susan Cotts Watkins. 2002. "Reactions of Developing-Country Elites to International Population Policy." *Population and Development Review* 28, no. 4: 707–33.
Luxemburg, Rosa. 2012. *L' accumulazione del capitale*. Milano: PGreco (original edition *Die Akkumulation des Kapitals*, 1913).
Malm, Andreas. 2016. *Fossil Capital: The Rise of Steam Power and the Roots of Global Warming*. London: Verso.
Malm, Andreas, and Alf Hornborg. 2014. "The Geology of Mankind? A Critique of the Anthropocene Narrative." *Anthropocene Review* 1, no.1: 62–69.
Malthus, Thomas Robert. 1798. *An Essay on the Principle of Population As It Affects the Future Improvement of Society, with Remarks on the Speculations of Mr. Godwin, M. Condorcet, and Other Writers*. London: J. Johnson, St. Paul's Church-yard.

———. 1821. *Principles of Political Economy: Considered with a View to Their Practical Application.* Boston, MA: Wells and Lilly.
———. 1868. *Saggio sul principio di popolazione* (ed. 1798). Torino: stamperia dell'Unione-tipografico editrice.
———. 1965. *Saggio sul principio di popolazione.* Torino: Unionetipografico-editrice torinese.
———. 1992. *An Essay on the Principle of Population.* Cambridge: Cambridge University Press (original edition 1803).
Mamdani, Mahmood. 1972. *The Myth of Population Control: Family, Caste and Class in an Indian Village.* New York: Monthly Review Press.
Mann, Michael. 1986. *The Sources of Social Power.* Vol. 1: *A History of Power from the Beginning to A.D. 1760.* Cambridge: Cambridge University Press.
Mareen Spranz, Nina. 2008. "Warum viele deutsche Männer keine Kinder wollen." *WeltN24.* https://www.welt.de/welt_print/article1729121/Warum-viele-deutsche-Maenner-keine-Kinder-wollen.html.
Markussen, Mads, and Østergård, Hanne. 2013. "Energy Analysis of the Danish Food Production System: Food-EROI and Fossil Fuel Dependency." *Energies* 6, no. 8: 4170–86.
Marshall, T. H. 1965. "The Population Problem during the Industrial Revolution." In *Population in History: Essays in Historical Demography*, edited by D. V. Glass and D. E. C. Eversley, 247–68. London: Arnold. Reprinted in *Economic History* (supplement to *Economic Journal*) 1, no. 4, 1929.
Martinez-Alier, Juan. 1987. *Ecological Economics: Energy, Environment and Society.* Oxford: Basil Blackwell.
Marx, Karl. [1867] 1992. *Capital. Volume 1: A Critique of Political Economy.* London: Penguin (in association with *New Left Review*).
Mason, Karen Oppenheim. 1987. "The Impact of Women's Social Position on Fertility in Developing Countries." *Sociological Forum* 2, no. 4: 718–45.
———. 1997. "Explaining Fertility Transitions." *Demography* 34: 443–54.
Massa, Ilmo. 1999. "The Development of the Risk Economy in the Circumpolar North." In *Ecology and the World-System*, edited by Walter L. Goldfrank, David Goodman and Andrew Szasz, 123–46. Westport: Greenwood Press.
Masters, William H., and Virginia E. Johnson. 1972. *L' atto sessuale nell'uomo e nella donna.* Milano: Feltrinelli.
Mathew, John. [1910] 2010. *Two Representative Tribes of Queensland: With an Inquiry Concerning the Origin of the Australian Race.* Cambridge: Cambridge University Press.
Matysiak, Anna. 2011. *Interdependencies between Fertility and Women's Labour Supply.* Dordrecht: Springer.
May, John F. 2012. *World Population Policies: Their Origin, Evolution and Impact.* Heidelberg: Springer.
Mazzetti, Giovanni. 2013. *Dare di piùai Padri per far avere di piùai Figli: perché i tagli alle pensioni e l'allungamento della vita lavorativa aggravano la crisi.* Trieste: Asterios.
McCann, James C. 1995. *People of the Plow: An Agricultural History of Ethiopia, 1800-1990.* Madison: University of Wisconsin Press.
McEvedy, Colin, and Richard Jones. 1978. *Atlas of World Population History.* London: Penguin.
McIntosh, C. Alison. 1981. "Low Fertility and Liberal Democracy in Western Europe." *Population and Development Review* 7, no. 2: 181–207.
McKeown, Thomas. 1976. *The Modern Rise of Population,* London: Arnold.

McNeill, John Robert. 2012. "Global Environmental History: The First 150,000 Years." In *A Companion to Global Environmental History*, edited by John Robert McNeill and Erin Stewart Mauldin, 3–17. Chichester: Wiley Blackwell.

McNeill, William H. 1982. *The Pursuit of Power: Technology, Armed Force, and Society since A.D. 1000*. Chicago: University of Chicago Press.

Meek, Ronald L. 1971. *Marx and Engels on the Population Bomb*. Berkeley: Rampart Press.

———, ed. 1953. *Marx and Engels on Malthus*. London: Lawrence & Wishart.

Meillassoux, Claude. 1975. *Femmes, greniers et capitaux*. Paris: F. Maspero.

Menard, Scott. 1986. "Fertility, Family Planning, and Development: Indirect Influences." *Studies in Comparative International Development* 21: 32–50.

Mies, Maria. 1999. *Patriarchy and Accumulation on a World Scale: Women in the International Division of Labour*. London: Zed Books.

Mies, Maria, and Veronika Bennholdt-Thomsen. 2000. *The Subsistence Perspective: Beyond the Globalised Economy*. London: Zed Books.

Mies, Maria, Veronika Bennholdt-Thomsen and Claudia von Werlhof. 1988. *Women: The Last Colony*. New Delhi: Kali for Women.

Mill, John Stuart. [1869] 2017. *The Subjection of Women*. Jonathan Bennett. http://www.earlymoderntexts.com/assets/pdfs/mill1869.pdf.

Mitchell, Brian Redman. [various years]. *International Historical Statistics*. London: PalgraveMacmillan.

Modelski, George. 2000. "World System Evolution." In *World System History: The Social Science of Long-Term Change*, edited by Robert A. Denemark, Jonathan Friedman, Barry K. Gills and George Modelski, 24–53. London: Routledge.

Moore, Jason W. 2017. *Antropocene o Capitalocene? Scenari di ecologia mondo nell'era della crisi planetaria*. Verona: Ombre corte (original edition *Anthropocene or Capitalocene? Nature, History, and the Crisis of Capitalism*, 2015).

Moran, Rachel. 2017. *Stupro a pagamento: la veritàsulla prostituzione*. Roma: Round Robin.

Morgan, Elaine. 1972. *The Descent of Woman*. New York: Stein and Day.

Moulier-Boutang, Yann. 2002. *Dalla schiavitùal lavoro salariato*, Roma: Manifestolibri.

Mueller, Eva. 1976. "The Economic Value of Children in Peasant Agriculture." In *Population and Development: The Search for Selective Interventions*, edited by Ronald G. Ridker, 98–153. Baltimore, MD: Johns Hopkins University Press.

Murdoch, William W. 1980. *The Poverty of Nations: The Political Economy of Hunger and Population*. Baltimore, MD: Johns Hopkins University Press.

Nag, Moni. 1980. "How Modernization Can Also Increase Fertility." *Current Anthropology* 21, no. 5: 571–87.

Nag, Moni, and Kak Neeraj. 1984. "Demographic Transition in a Punjab Village." *Population and Development Review* 10, no. 4: 661–78.

Nardi, Bonnie Anna. 1981. "Modes of Explanation in Anthropological Population Theory: Biological Determinism vs. Self-Regulation in Studies of Population Growth in Third World Countries." *American Anthropologist*, New Series, 83, no. 1: 28–56.

Newman, Sheila M. 2013. *Demography, Territory and Law: Rules of Animal and Human Populations*, Frankstone: Countershock Press.

Nolan, Patrick, and Gerhard Lenski. 2004. *Human Societies: An Introduction to Macrosociology*. 11th ed. Boulder, CO: Paradigm.

Notestein, Farnk W. 1953. "Economic Problems of Population Change." In *Proceedings of the Eighth International Conference of Agricultural Economists* held at Kellogg Center Michigan State College, U.S.A., 15–22 August 13–31. London: Oxford University Press.

Nukunya, Godwin Kwaku. 1975. "Population Pressure, Land Tenure and Agricultural Development." In *Population, Ecology, and Social Evolution*, edited by Steven Polgar, 191–217. Paris: de Gruyter Mouton.

Odum, Eugene P. 1966. *Ecologia*, Bologna: Zanichelli.

———. 1971. "The Strategy of Ecosystem Development." *Science* 164: 262–70.

Odum, Howard T. 2007. *Environment, Power, and Society for the Twenty-First Century: The Hierarchy of Energy*. New York: Columbia University Press.

Owino, Meshack. 2010. "The Discourse of Overpopulation in Western Kenya and the Creation of the Pioneer Corps." In *The Demographics of Empire: The Colonial Order and the Creation of Knowledge*, edited by Karl Ittmann, Dennis D. Cordell and Gregory H. Maddox, 157–73. Athens: Ohio University Press.

Pall, Martin L. 2013. "Electromagnetic Fields Act *via* Activation of Voltage-Gated Calcium Channels to Produce Beneficial or Adverse Effects." *Journal of Cellular and Molecular Medicine* 17, no. 8: 958–65.

———. 2020. *Massive Predicted Effects of 5G. Very High Level VGCC Sensitivity to Low Intensity EMFs and Especially to Pulsations.* 25.2.2020 (version 17.2.2020: http://coeursdehs.fr/pr-martin-pall-massive-predicted-effects-of-5g-in-the-context-of-safety-guideline-failures/).

Parrique, Timothée, Jonathan Barth, François Briens, Christian Kerschner, Alejo Kraus-Polk, Anna Kuokkanen and Joachim H. Spangenberg. 2019. *Decoupling Debunked: Evidence and Arguments against Green Growth as a Sole Strategy for Sustainability*, July 8. https://eeb.org/library/decoupling-debunked/.

Patterson, John G., and Nanda R. Shrestha. 1988. "Population Growth and Development in the Third World: The Neocolonial Context." *Studies in Comparative International Development* 23, no. 2: 3–32.

Petersen, William. 1988. "Marxism and the Population Question: Theory and Practice." *Population and Development Review* 14, Supplement: *Population and Resources in Western Intellectual Traditions*: 77–101.

Phelps Brown, E. H., and Sheila V. Hopkins. 1957. "Wage-Rates and Prices: Evidence for Population Pressure in the Sixteenth Century." *Economica,* New Series 24, no. 96: 289–306.

Pimentel, David. 2002. "Biomass Utilization, Limits of." *Encyclopedia of Physical Science and Technology*. 3rd ed. vol. 2, 1–13. Cambridge, MA: Academic Press.

Pimentel, David, and Marcia Pimentel, eds. 1996. *Food, Energy and Society*. Niwot: University Press of Colorado.

Prabhu, Pingali, and Hans P. Binswanger. 1988. "Population Density and Farming Systems: The Changing Locus of Innovations and Technical Change." In *World Population Trends and Their Impact on Economic Development*, ed. Dominick Salvatore, 165–86. New York: Greenwood Press.

Piotrow, Phyllis Tilson, and Jose G. Rimon II. 1999. "Asia's Population and Family Planning Programs: Leaders in Strategic Communication." *Asia-Pacific Population Journal* 14, no. 4: 73–90.

Pirie, Peter. 2000. "Untangling the Myths and Realities of Fertility and Mortality in Pacific Islands." *Asia-Pacific Population Journal* 15, no. 2: 5–20.

Pizzuti, Felice Roberto, ed. 2017. *Stagnazione secolare, produttivitàcontrattazione salariale e benessere sociale: rapporto sullo stato sociale 2017.* Roma: Sapienza Universitàeditrice.

Polgar, Steven. 1972. "Population History and Population Policies from an Anthropological Perspective." *Current Anthropology* 13, no. 2: 203–11.

———. 1975. "Population, Evolution, and Theoretical Paradigms." In *Population, Ecology, and Social Evolution*, edited by Steven Polgar, 1–26. The Hague-Paris: Mouton.

Pomeranz, Kenneth. 2000. *The Great Divergence: China, Europe, and the Making of the Modern World Economy*. Princeton, NJ: Princeton University Press.

Poston, Dudley L., Che-Fu Lee, Chiung Fang Chang, Sherry L. McKibben and Walther Carol S., eds. 2006. *Fertility, Family Planning, and Population Policy in China*. London: Routledge.

Potts, Malcolm. 1997. "Sex and the Birth Rate: Human Biology, Demographic Change and Access to Fertility Regulation Methods." *Population and Development Review*, 23, 1–39.

Presser, Harriet B. 2001. "Comment: A Gender Perspective for Understanding Low Fertility in Post-Transitional Societies." In *Global Fertility Transition*, edited by Rodolfo A. Bulatao and John B. Casterline, 177–83. New York: Population Council.

Pritchett, Lant H. 1994. "Desired Fertility and the Impact of Population Policies." *Population and Development Review* 20, no. 1: 1–55.

Rajkai, Zsombor, ed. 2015. *Family and Social Change in Socialist and Post-Socialist Societies: Change and continuity in Eastern Europe and East Asia*. Leiden: Brill.

Reed, James. 1983. *The Birth Control Movement and American Society: From Private Vice to Public Virtue*. Princeton, NJ: Princeton University Press.

Regalia, Anita, Grazia Colombo, Franca Pizzini.1984. *Mettere al mondo: la produzione sociale del parto*. Milano: Franco Angeli.

Reinhard, Marcel, André Armengaud and Jacques Dupaquier. 1971. *Storia della popolazione mondiale*. Bari, Laterza (original edition *Histoire generale de la population mondiale*, 1968).

Repetto, Robert. 1979. *Economic Equality and Fertility in Developing Countries*. Baltimore, MD: Johns Hopkins University Press.

Rodgers, Gerry. 1989. "An Overview." In *Population Growth and Poverty in Rural South Asia*, edited by Gerry Rodgers, 9–26. New Delhi: Sage.

Rosati Freeman, Francesca. 2010. *Benvenuti nel paese delle donne: un viaggio straordinario alla scoperta dei Moso una societàmatriarcale senza violenze négelosie*. Roma: XL.

Rubin, Marcus, and Harald Westergaard. 1890. *Statistik der Ehen auf Grund der socialen Gliederung der Bewölkerung, nach Volkszählungen und Kirchenbüchern in Dänemark*. Kopenhagen: Jena.

Sacchetti, Aldo. *L'uomo antibiologico. Riconciliare societàe natura*. Milano: Feltrinelli.

Safilios-Rothschild, Constantina. 1982. "Female Power, Autonomy and Demographic Change." In *Women's Roles and Population Trends in the Third World*, edited by Richard Anker, Mayra Buvinic and Nadia H. Youssef, 117–32. London: Croom Helm.

Sahlins, Marshall D. 1980. *Stone Age Economics*. Chicago: Aldine-Atherton (original edition 1972).

Satterthwaite, David. 2009. "The Implications of Population Growth and Urbanization for Climate Change." *Environment & Urbanization* 21: 545–67.

Schäfer, Julia. 2012. "'Menschenökonomie' und Kolonialmedizin: ein symbiotisches Verhältnis?." In *Bevölkerung in Wissenschaft und Politik des 19. und 20. Jahrhunderts*, edited by Sylvia Kesper-Biermann, 201–39. München: Dreesbach.

Scheper Hughes, Nancy. 1992. *Death without Weeping: The Violence of Everyday Life in Brazil*. Berkeley: University of California Press.

Schiel, Tilman. 1984. "Development and Underdevelopment of Household-Based Production in Europe." In *Households and the World Economy*, edited by Joan Smith, Immanuel Wallestein and Hans-Dieter Evers, 101–30. Beverly Hills, CA: Sage.

Schneider, Jane. 1977. "Was There a Pre-Capitalist World-System?." *Peasant Studies* 6, no. 1: 20–29.

Schneider, Jane, and Peter T. Schneider. 1992. "Going Forward in Reverse Gear: Culture, Economy, and Political Economy in the Demographic Transitions of a Rural Sicilian Town." In *The European Experience of Declining Fertility, 1850–1970. The Quiet Revolution*, edited by John R. Gillis, Louise A. Tilly, and David Levine, 146–74. Cambridge, MA: Blackwell.

Schumann, Debra A. 1986. "Fertility and Historical Variation in Economic Strategy among Migrants to the Lacandon Forest, Mexico." In *Culture and Reproduction. An Anthropological Critique of Demographic Transition Theory*, edited by W. Penn Handwerker, 144–58. Boulder, CO: Westview Press.

Seccombe, Wally. 1978. *The Housewife and Her Labour under Capitalism*. London: Red Books.

Seccombe, Wally. 1983. "Marxism and Demography." *New Left Review* 137: 22–47.

———. 1992. *A Millennium of Family Change: Feudalism to Capitalism in Northwestern Europe*. London: Verso.

———. 1995. *Weathering the Storm: Working-Class Families from the Industrial Revolution to the Fertility Decline*. London: Verso (1st edition 1993).

Sharif, Mohammed. 2007. *Poverty Reduction – An Effective Means of Population Control: Theory, Evidence and Policy*. Aldershot: Ashgate.

Simmons, Ozzie G. 1988. *Perspectives on Development and Population Growth in the Third World*. New York: Plenum.

Simon, Julian Lincoln. 1977. *The Economics of Population Growth*. Princeton, NJ: Princeton University Press.

Skocpol, Theda. 1979. *States and Social Revolutions: A Comparative Analysis of France, Russia and China*. Cambridge: Cambridge University Press.

Smil, Vaclav. 2008. *Energy in Nature and Society: General Energetics of Complex Systems*. Cambridge: MIT Press.

Smith Oboler, Regina 1985. *Women, Power, and Economic Change: The Nandi of Kenya*. Stanford, CA: Stanford University Press.

Smith, Adam. [1776] 1995. *La ricchezza delle nazioni*. Roma: Newton Compton (original edition *An Inquiry into the Nature and Causes of the Wealth of Nations*).

Smith, Joan, and Immanuel Wallestein, eds. 1992. *Creating and Transforming Households: The Constraints of the World-Economy*. Cambridge: Cambridge University Press.

Smith, Richard. 2002. "Social Institutions and Demographic Regimes in Non-Industrial Societies: A Comparative Approach." In *Human Population Dynamics: Cross-Disciplinary Perspectives*, edited by Helen Macbeth and Paul Collinson, 103–23. Cambridge: Cambridge University Press.

———. 2010. "Beyond Growth or beyond Capitalism?." *Real-World Economics Review* 53: 28–42. http://www.paecon.net/PAEReview/issue53/Smith53.pdf.

Sokal, Alan, and Bricmont, Jean. 1999. *Imposture intellettuali*. Milano: Garzanti.

Stein, Dorothy. 1995. *People Who Count: Population and Politics, Women and Children*. London: Earthscan.

Sweezy, Paul. 1956. *The Theory of Capitalist Development*. New York: Monthly Review.

Szreter, Simon. 1993. "The Idea of Demographic Transition and the Study of Fertility Change: A Critical Intellectual History." *Population and Development Review* 19, no. 4: 659–701.

Tabet, Paola. 2014. *Le dita tagliate*. Roma: Ediesse.

Tainter, Joseph A. 1989. *The Collapse of Complex Societies*. Cambridge: Cambridge University Press.

Teeple, Gary. 1995. *Globalization and the Decline of Social Reform*. Atlantic Highlands, NJ: Humanities Press; Toronto: Garamond Press.

Teitelbaum, Michael S., and Jay M. Winter.1985. *The Fear of Population Decline*. Orlando, FL: Academic Press.

Testart, Jacques. 2014. *Faire des enfants demain*. Paris: Seuil.

Therborn, Göran. 2004. *Between Sex and Power: Family in the World, 1900-2000*. London: Routledge.

Thomlinson, Ralph. 1965. *Population Dynamics: Causes and Consequences of World Demographic Change*. New York: Randon House.

Tilly, Charles. 1978. "The Historical Study of Vital Processes." In *Historical Studies of Changing Fertility*, edited by Charles Tilly, 3–56. Princeton, NJ: Princeton University Press.

———. 1984. "Demographic Origins of the European Proletariat." In *Proletarianization and Family History*, edited by Charles Tilly, 1–86. Orlando, FL: Academic Press.

Turchin, Peter. 1995. "'Population Regulation' Old Arguments and a New Synthesis." In *Population Dynamics: New Approaches and Synthesis*, edited by Naomi Cappuccino and Peter W. Price, 19–40. San Diego, CA: Academic Press.

———. 2003. *Complex Population Dynamics: A Theoretical/Empirical Synthesis*. Princeton, NJ: Princeton University Press.

———. 2016. *Ages of Discord: A Structural-Demographic Analysis of American History*. Chaplin, CT: Beresta Books.

Turchin, Peter, and Thomas D. Hall. 2003. "Spatial Synchrony among and within World-Systems: Insights from Theoretical Ecology." *Journal of World-Systems Research* 9, no. 1: 37–64.

Turchin, Peter, and Sergey A. Nefedov. 2009. *Secular Cycles*. Princeton, NJ: Princeton University Press.

United Nations Population Division. 2012. *World Population Prospects: The 2010 Revision*. http://esa.un.org/unpd/wpp/Excel-Data/fertility.htm.

———. 2015. *World Population Prospects: The 2015 Revision, Key Findings and Advance Tables*. Working Paper No. ESA/P/WP.241.

Vallin, Jacques. 1995. *La population mondiale*. Paris: La decouverte.

van de Kaa, Dirk J. 1987. "Europe's Second Demographic Transition." *Population Bulletin* 42, no. 1, Washington, DC: Population Reference Bureau.

van der Meer, Annine. 2013. *The Language of Ma, the Primal Mother: The Evolution of the Female Image in 40,000 Years of Global Venus Art*. Amsterdam: Pansophia Press.

Viel, Benjamín. 1976. *The Demographic Explosion: The Latin American Experience*. New York: Irvington.

Vittori, Ottavio. 1989. *Clima e storia*. Roma: Editori riuniti.

von Werlhof, Claudia. 1984. "The Proletarian is Dead; Long Live the Housewife?." In *Households and the World Economy*, edited by Joan Smith, Immanuel Wallestein and Hans-Dieter Evers, 131–47. Beverly Hills, CA: Sage.

———. 2012. "The Failure of the 'Modern World System' and the New Paradigm of the 'Critical Theory of Patriarchy.' The 'Civilization of Alchemists' as a 'System of War.'" In *Routledge Handbook of World-System Analysis*, edited by Salvatore J. Babones and Christopher Chase-Dunn, 172–80. London: Routledge.

Wagner, Marsden. 2001. "Fish Can't See Water: The need to humanize birth." *International Journal of Gynecology & Obstetrics* 75: 25–37.

Wallerstein, Immanuel, ed. 1996. *Open the Social Sciences: Report of the Gulbenkian Commission on the Restructuring of the Social Sciences*. Redwood, CA: Stanford University Press.

———. 1974. *The Modern World-System*. Vol. 1. New York: Academic Press.
———. 1978. "Civilizations and Modes of Production: Conflicts and Convergences." *Theory and Society* 5, no. 1: 1–10.
———. 1979. *The Capitalist World-Economy: Essays*. Cambridge: Cambridge University Press.
———. 1980. *The Modern World-System. Vol. 2: Mercantilism and the Consolidation of the European World-Economy, 1600-1750*. New York: Academic Press.
———. 1983. "The World-Economy, the Movements, and the Ideologies." In *Crises in the World-System*, edited by Albert Bergesen, 21–36. Beverly Hills, CA: Sage.
———. 1988. "Typology of Crises in the World-System." *Review* (Fernand Braudel Center) 11, no. 4: 581–98.
———. 1998. *Utopistics, or Historical Choices of the Twenty-First Century*. New York: New Press.
———. 1999a. "Ecology and Capitalist Costs of Production: No Exit." In *Ecology and the World-System*, edited by Walter L. Goldfrank, David Goodman and Andrew Szasz, 3–11. Westport: Greenwood Press.
———. 1999b. *Geopolitica e geocultura: saggi sull'evoluzione del sistema-mondo*. Trieste: Asterios.
———. 2000. *The Essential Wallerstein*. New York: New Press.
———. 2004. *World-Systems Analysis: An introduction*. Durham, NC: Duke University Press.
Ward, Kathryn B. 1983. "The Economic Status of Women in the World-System: A Hidden Crisis in Development." In *Crises in the World-System*, edited by Albert Bergesen 117–39. Beverly Hills, CA: Sage.
———. 1984. *Women in the World-System: Its Impact on Status and Fertility*. New York: Praeger.
———. 1985. "The Social Consequences of the World Economic System: The Economic Status of Women and Fertility." *Review* 8, no. 4: 561–94.
———, ed. 1990. *Women Workers and Global Restructuring*. Ithaca, NY: ILR Press, School of Industrial and Labor Relations, Cornell University.
Ware, Helen. 1988. "The Effects of Fertility, Family Organization, Sex Structure of the Labor Market, and Technology on the Position of Women." In *Women's Position and Demographic Change*, edited by Nora Federici, Karen Oppenheim Mason, Solvi Sogner, 259–84. Oxford: Clarendon Press; New York: Oxford University Press.
Waring, Marilyn. 1988. *If Women Counted: A New Feminist Economics*. San Francisco, CA: HarperCollins.
Wasserstrom, Robert. 1978. "Population Growth and Economic Development in Chiapas, 1524–1975." *Human Ecology* 6, no. 2: 127–44.
Watkins, Susan Cotts, and Angela D. Danzi. 1995. "Women's Gossip and Social Change: Childbirth and Fertility Control among Italian and Jewish Women in the United States, 1920–1940." *Gender and Society* 9, no. 4: 469–90.
Weeks, John Robert. 2012. *An Introduction to Population*. [Belmont, CA?]: Wadsworth/ Cengage Learning.
Weil, Peter. 1986. "Agricultural Intensification and Fertility in the Gambia." In *Culture and Reproduction. An Anthropological Critique of Demographic Transition Theory*, edited by W. Penn Handwerker, 294–320. Boulder, CO: Westview Press.
White, Benjamin. 1973. "Demand for Labor and Population. Growth in Colonial Java." *Human Ecology* 1, no. 3: 217–36.
———. 1982. "Child Labour and Population Growth in Rural Asia." *Development and Change* 13, no. 4: 587–610.
Wilkinson, David. 2000. "Civilizations, World Systems and Hegemonies." In *World System History: The Social Science of Long-Term Change*, edited by Robert A. Denemark, Jonathan Friedman, Barry K. Gills and George Modelski, 54–84. London: Routledge.

Wilkinson, Richard G. 1973. *Poverty and Progress: An Ecological Model of Economic Development.* London: Methuen.

Wilson, Chris, and Pauline Airey. 1999. "How Can a Homeostatic Perspective Enhance Demographic Transition Theory?." *Population Studies* 53, no. 2: 117–28.

Wood, James W. 1998. "A Theory of Preindustrial Population Dynamics Demography, Economy, and Well-Being in Malthusian Systems". *Current Anthropology* 39, no. 1: 99–135.

Woodburn, James. 1968. "An Introduction to Hadza Ecology." In *Man the Hunter*, edited by Richard B. Lee and Irven De Vore, 49–55. Chicago: Aldine.

Wrigley, Edward Anthony. 1961. *Industrial Growth and Population Change: A Regional Study of the Coalfield Areas of North-West Europe in the Later Nineteenth Century.* 2nd ed. Cambridge: Cambridge University Press.

———. 1969. *Demografia e storia.* Milano, Il saggiatore (original edition *Population and History*, 1969).

———. 2004. *Poverty, Progress, and Population.* Cambridge: Cambridge University Press.

Wrigley, Edward Anthony, and Schofield, Roger. 1981. *The Population History of England 1541-1871.* London: Arnold.

Wynne-Edwards, Vero Copner. 1962. *Animal Dispersion in Relation to Social Behaviour.* Edinburgh: Oliver and Boyd.

York, Richard, and Christina Ergas. 2011. "Women's Status and World-System Position: An Exploratory Analysis." *Journal of World-Systems Research* 17, no. 1: 147–64. http://jwsr.ucr.edu/archive/vol17/York_Ergas-vol17n1.pdf.

Zimmerer, Jürgen. 2001. *Deutsche Herrschaft über Afrikaner Staatlicher Machtanspruch und Wirklichkeit im kolonialen Namibia.* Münster: LIT Verlag.

Zucca, Michela. 2010. *Storia delle donne: da Eva a domani.* Napoli: Esselibri-Simone.

———. 2015. *I tatuaggi della dea.* Roma: Venexia.

## Datasets:

Human Fertility Project http://www.humanfertility.org/.

Human Mortality Project http://www.mortality.org/.

The Maddison Project: https://www.rug.nl/ggdc/historicaldevelopment/maddison/?lang=en.

UN datasets on fertility rates at the national level from 1950 to 2010 http://esa.un.org/unpd/wpp/Excel-Data/fertility.htm.

University of Minnesota: IPUMS (Integrated Public Use Microdata Series) https://international.ipums.org/international/.

World Bank: World Development Indicators (http://data.worldbank.org/.)

World Fertility Survey http://opr.princeton.edu/archive/wfs/ (su 42 paesi in via di sviluppo)

World Handbook of Political and Social Indicators Series: http://www.icpsr.umich.edu/icpsrweb/ICPSR/series/60.

# INDEX

Lightning Source UK Ltd.
Milton Keynes UK
UKHW011250280721
387870UK00001B/41